CRITICAL LIVES

The Life and Work of

Eleanor Roosevelt

CRITICAL LIVES

The Life and Work of

Eleanor Roosevelt

Sarah J. Purcell and L. Edward Purcell

ALPHA

A Pearson Education Company

International Standard Book Number: 0-02-864162-0
Library of Congress Catalog Card Number: 2001092306

04   03   02   8   7   6   5   4   3   2   1

Interpretation of the printing code: The rightmost number of the first series of numbers is the year of the book's printing; the rightmost number of the second series of numbers is the number of the book's printing. For example, a printing code of 02-1 shows that the first printing occurred in 2002.

Printed in the United States of America

Publisher:
Marie Butler-Knight
Product Manager:
Phil Kitchel
Managing Editor:
Jennifer Chisholm
Senior Acquisitions Editor:
Randy Ladenheim-Gil
Development Editor:
Tom Stevens
Senior Production Editor:
Christy Wagner
Copy Editor:
Rachel Lopez

Cover Designer:
Ann Jones
Book Designer:
Sandra Schroeder
Production:
Michelle Mitchell
Liz Patterson

CRITICAL LIVES

Eleanor Roosevelt

Introduction

Between the time of Eleanor Roosevelt's birth in the late nineteenth century and her death in the latter half of the twentieth, the place of women in American society changed dramatically. During her youth and early adulthood it was uncommon for women—especially women of her social status and family background—to venture into public life. By the end of Eleanor's career, American women were beginning to charge with irresistible momentum toward assuming full roles in almost every arena of life, from the highest government offices to corporate executive suites.

By any measure, Eleanor Roosevelt was one of the major forces bringing about this revolution in the status of women in our society. She did not live to see the fundamental changes we now take for granted, but she had advocated a full and responsible role for women ever since first moving into politics during the 1920s. She would very likely have been pleased to see the widespread power that women exercised by the turn of the new century. She herself was not one to labor quietly in the background while there was work to be done at center stage.

Given the limitations imposed by the social and political environment in which she functioned, Eleanor Roosevelt was a towering figure in recent American history. Her activities and accomplishments (as well as her foibles and failures) must be understood by anyone who wishes to understand what happened in the United States between the 1920s and the 1960s. Thus, it seems clear that her life deserves all the attention it has received from biographers.

Soon after her death, and in some cases before, biographers began the task of recording and interpreting her life and work. Because she was such a controversial figure and the target of almost constant criticism from some parts of society, many of the earliest biographical works sought to blacken her image and relegate her accomplishments to the dust heap. Of course, there were also loving and adulatory books published about her soon after her death, and many more biographies have been written since, including two Pulitzer Prize winners.

The first notable biography (or rather, series of biographical books) was by Joseph Lash, who not only had firsthand knowledge of her life from the time he met her in 1939 until her death, but who also had access to many of her private documents and letters. His was an adulatory approach, which only lightly probed the most difficult parts of Eleanor's life. Lash's work was enriched during the 1980s by a new round of research and writing by feminist scholars who looked to Eleanor's life for examples of pioneering social and political behavior. In the 1990s, the task of understanding Eleanor took a great leap forward in sophistication with the efforts of Doris Kearns Goodwin, who studied the wartime activities of both Eleanor and Franklin Roosevelt, and Blanche Wiesen Cook, whose detailed, multi-volume study of Eleanor's life has so far reached the year 1938, with more volumes to come.

The concise biography you hold in your hand is a personal and political history of Eleanor Roosevelt. Her psychology has been studied by many others, whose insights we have drawn on freely. Her mental and emotional makeup had a great deal to do with how she lived her life, but we have viewed Eleanor primarily as an accomplished politician who had a great impact on the twentieth century. She was a fragile human being, as many great political figures are, and she was an outstanding example of what women could achieve once freed from the confines of their traditional roles; however, we believe she not so much transcended her femininity as she confirmed and developed it to make possible her high level of public achievement.

Acknowledgments

We gratefully acknowledge the helpful staff and the valuable resources of burling library at Grinnell College, the Stewart Public Library in Grinnell, the W.T. Young Library at the University of Kentucky, the Lexington Public Library, and the Franklin Delano Roosevelt Library at Hyde Park, New York. We are also grateful to Victoria Brown and Ellis Hawley, who taught us about the history of the United States in the twentieth century and the New Deal. As usual, we are grateful most of all for the love and support of Mary F. Purcell, mother and wife.

Chapter 1

An Enduring Legacy

There is so much to do, so many engrossing challenges, so many heartbreaking and pressing needs, so much in every day that is profoundly interesting.

—Eleanor Roosevelt,
The Autobiography

Eleanor Roosevelt had the most important public career of any American woman of the twentieth century. The list of her accomplishments encompasses a broad spectrum of historically important issues, ranging from her status as one of the nation's most popular and well-paid daily newspaper columnists to her influence over the programs of the New Deal to her achievements as an international diplomat. She was the first—and only—woman to serve more than two terms as First Lady, the first candidate's wife to address a national nominating convention, and the first president's wife to hold a public office.

Her activities sparked much of the emergence of women in American society, one of the signal developments of the century, and she assisted her husband, President Franklin Delano Roosevelt, in bringing about a peaceful revolution in the structure of American society and government. She contributed to the homefront efforts that enabled the United States and its allies to win World War II, and after the war, Eleanor almost single-handedly wrung agreement on a statement of basic universal human rights from bickering delegates in the United Nations.

And she is not forgotten. In March 2001 the star of an offbeat teen-oriented television show (appropriately titled *Jackass*) felt free to make an off-color joke about Eleanor while appearing on David Letterman's popular late-night talk show. His joke about Eleanor's sexuality was not very funny, and by any standard above juvenile toilet humor it was tasteless; however, from a historical perspective, the joke was an astounding testament to Eleanor's place in American culture. Nearly forty years after her death and almost seventy years after she first stepped into the national spotlight, Eleanor still commands enough recognition that a TV jokester can assume a nationwide audience will understand the reference.

On a more elevated level, evidence that Eleanor's memory and influence are still alive and powerful was provided when Hillary Rodham Clinton became First Lady in 1993. She had ambitions to assume a national role similar to Eleanor's, and she repeatedly evoked Eleanor's memory—going so far at one point as to claim to have mystically communicated with Eleanor's spirit, which she implied hovered somewhere over the White House.

> *In 2001 an ironic memory of one of Eleanor's greatest accomplishments surfaced in the news when the United States was ousted from the United Nation's Commission on Human Rights, bringing to an end (at least temporarily) the nation's membership in a commission of which Eleanor had been the moving spirit in the first heady days of the international body, when hopes for worldwide peace and justice still ran high.*

This variety of historical interest revolves around a woman whose life story was one of considerable drama. Her personal life was characterized by emotional hardship, family depravation, stultifying social conventions, and repeated betrayal. That she overcame these problems to achieve so much in the public realm points to the immense strength of her character and her will to carry on in the face of personal pain.

It is therefore tempting to perform historical psychoanalysis on Eleanor at almost every turn. Her biography, so complex and so rich with adversity, seems fertile ground for probing her innermost emotional and psychological life, especially because she left mountains of correspondence and writings that provide a personal running commentary on her experiences and relationships. Even if one subdues the impulse to probe and analyze too much, a great deal still must be said about Eleanor's personality to understand her public life and accomplishments.

Although the persona she showed the public usually was ebullient and almost always animated, Eleanor seemed during much of her life to live in a slough of despondency. From her earliest childhood she was somber; as she grew to adulthood, the somberness developed into a full-bore tendency to slip into long periods of depression—she called them her "Griselda moods"—which at many points in her life almost debilitated her. She would fall silent and withdraw into herself, effectively cutting off all those around her. Changes in her life—and she underwent many very significant changes—seemed to set off the worst periods of depression and withdrawal.

In a rare mood of relaxation, Eleanor posed in 1948 with her famous Scottish terrier Fala at her cottage at Val-Kill, her private home on the grounds of Hyde Park, New York.

(*Courtesy of the Franklin Delano Roosevelt Library*)

She also was afflicted throughout her life by a severe sense of her own inferiority, an insight that in the 1930s and 1940s would have astounded critics who saw her as overbearing, presumptuous, and full of herself. Privately, Eleanor often failed to see the true significance of her achievements or the power of her abilities. In some ways she acknowledged the importance of who she was and what she could do, especially if she saw a chance to make the world a better place. However, whenever it was time to sum things up, Eleanor consistently expressed doubt and downplayed her own role, often failing to take credit for her legitimate accomplishments. Her published autobiographical accounts of her life usually gloss over or even skip some of her most important moments, and her private letters often express a characteristic low sense of her own worth.

There was opaqueness about Eleanor's personality that no one has ever quite been able to penetrate, neither close family and associates during her lifetime nor biographers and historians since. Her public life is a matter of record and shows a woman of huge energy and talents who maneuvered herself into a position of power and influence, which she used brilliantly for what she believed was the betterment of all society. In private, however, she usually was tense and on guard, seldom able to relax or put her public agenda aside. Almost everyone with whom she came in contact, including her family, was all too familiar with her constant intensity and the blank wall of silence she could throw up in an instant—and which she used as a powerful weapon to fend off the world.

She was particularly ill-favored in her ability to establish close relationships. Her relationship with her father, the most important of her childhood, was mostly based on a fantasy in which he appeared as a truly wonderful father and not the undependable alcoholic he really was. The most important relationship of her life, of course, was with FDR, but when her early, unquestioning love for her husband was destroyed by the discovery of his infidelity, the nature of the marriage changed drastically. It eventually became a powerful and important relationship, but it was never again intimate or emotionally satisfying.

Off and on, Eleanor managed to establish good relations with her children, but her career as a mother probably is most accurately characterized as inconsistent at best. She did succeed, however, in establishing a series of extremely close relationships with a very few selected companions during her later adult life. Although none of these relationships was totally durable, most of them were intense at the beginning, and Eleanor appears to have taken selected people, one by one, into her most secret life and intimate confidence.

There has been much speculation in recent years, as biographers have dug deeper into her papers and the surviving papers of those close to her, about the nature and extent of Eleanor's sex life. Much of this speculation appears to have sprung from prurient interest, especially because there are considerable superficial indications that Eleanor might have been bisexual as a middle-aged adult. No one has been able to find definitive evidence; however, there is much basis for speculation, as she was closely associated with a string of women who were openly lesbian, and she had what clearly was a very intense relationship with one of them, Lorena Hickok. She also had relationships with several younger men that have raised questions about her sexual activity, although it appears no unassailable conclusions will ever be possible.

This fascination with Eleanor's sex life is perhaps as much a comment on the interests of the American public at the turn of the twenty-first century as it is a matter of serious concern, but it does reinforce our realization that Eleanor was a flesh-and-blood entity, not simply a symbolic figure. She needed and craved a life that included at least a few intimate relationships, which apparently she found. Moreover, her husband's sexual betrayal, which he probably continued until the conclusion of their forty-year marriage, perhaps was the most significant event of her life, and her reaction to it is of considerable importance.

Despite the fault lines that ran through her life, Eleanor was possessed of an extremely powerful personality, which she developed into a magnificent political tool. She had little education and was not especially intelligent; however, she had a force of will and a persistence that were nearly unmatched. Moreover, she learned how to use her powers of persuasion and pressure in a most effective manner.

Her technique was to bore in on her target—usually her husband after he became president—and to never relinquish her attacks until she got what she wanted. She told people about a problem; then she exhorted them to do something to make it better. She continued to tell them over and over again with great vigor and earnestness until either measures were taken to solve the problem or some higher power made her shut up. From 1933 on there was seldom any such higher power with the capacity to stifle her. Only FDR could manage it, and his power to do so was sporadic and relatively feeble. As he was fond of telling people, "I can't do anything about her!"

It is in no way surprising that Eleanor served as an inspiration to Hillary Rodham Clinton as Clinton had ambitions as a politician and power broker (which she might ultimately achieve as a U.S. Senator; Eleanor sternly discouraged all attempts to persuade her to run for elective office). Otherwise Eleanor has had little permanent effect on the role of First Lady. Of the eleven women who have moved into the White House since Eleanor left in 1945, only Clinton has shown the slightest resemblance. All the others have timidly accepted a subordinate place and made no attempts to exert or acquire genuine power or to transcend the confines of domesticity. The inescapable conclusion is that it was Eleanor's unique personality and background that impelled her career as a public figure.

Certainly one important factor was the social class from which she emerged. She was the product of the upper reaches of nineteenth-century American society, a place where talent, wealth, and beauty were much prized and where genuine accomplishment was relatively rare. It is important to ask how an upper-class girl such as Eleanor could grow to become such a powerful political figure. Women of her social stratum were schooled to be decorative and moderately useful—but never, ever to make themselves conspicuous outside the home and family. Eleanor, of course, threw off these shackles during the 1920s, much to the continuing dismay of her proper relatives, especially her mother-in-law.

On the positive side, Eleanor's background inculcated a strong sense of social obligation, which in her case developed far beyond the usual expectations. She transformed *noblesse oblige* into a passionate, all-consuming concern for the poor, the weak, the marginalized, and the helpless. As her personality grew, she acquired many new ideas and beliefs and, as her close friend and biographer Joseph Lash wrote of her, "... she did not permit herself to hold beliefs without accepting their consequences in action."

As a result, she made herself into a superb politician who had experience in the rough-and-tumble world of party in-fighting and knew how to influence decision-makers and public opinion. Her critics gave the impression that she must have just stumbled in a busybody fashion into the controversial causes she so vocally championed, but the truth is, Eleanor usually knew exactly what she was doing when she chose her issues—and she knew how to get action. Only seldom did this knowledge and instinct for political action fail her; one notable example was during wartime, when she was to a large degree out of her element.

Eleanor was one of the foremost and purest American liberals of the century. She was absolved during much of the New Deal from having to worry about some of the practical consequences of her liberalism, because she could rely on FDR to always be on the alert for political fallout. This frustrated her sometimes, but it also gave her the freedom to develop the classic liberal themes in a time when conservatism and reaction were the norms in American political life.

She had first nurtured her liberal beliefs through more than a decade of work with women's reform groups and within the women's wing of the Democratic Party. When FDR's election put her in a position to do so, she refined her ideas into a few basic propositions: Government should act and act forcefully; government should be concerned first with the marginal in society who could not help themselves; and government based on democracy was the highest possible form of political organization.

These beliefs alone would have been enough to bring criticism down on her head, but when she coupled them with her assumption of what many construed to be an unfeminine activist role, she became the focus of a constant stream of vituperation and hate. Conservatives who still believed that poverty resulted from lack of moral fiber hated her. Men who were threatened by a powerful, prominent woman hated her. And most of all, white racists, especially in the South, hated her because of her long campaign to recognize the dignity and rights of African Americans.

Throughout her public life, Eleanor was almost always able to shrug off criticism from those she disagreed with, and she was seldom deflected from her crusades just because a newspaper columnist or a conservative congressman expressed outrage or disapproval. She told her friends that she had developed a hide like a rhinoceros when it came to withstanding her critics.

By the end of her life, Eleanor acquired the warm, cuddly persona of "First Lady of the World," exuding a kind of grandmotherly charm that was almost completely at odds with the combatitive First Lady of the New Deal era. It may plausibly be argued that both images were accurate and only reflected the complexity of her character and her ability to grow and adapt to new circumstances.

Whatever Eleanor's true nature or how one regarded her politics and activities, she was impossible to ignore, either during her lifetime or today.

Chapter 2

The Difficult Early Years

*If people only realized what a war goes on in a child's
mind and heart ... I think they would try to explain more
than they do, but nobody told me anything.*
                                        —*Eleanor Roosevelt,*
                                        This Is My Story

Eleanor Roosevelt's mother and father were miserable failures as parents. Moreover, they both died when Eleanor was a young child, leaving her in the care of a difficult and distracted grandmother. By the time she reached her late teens, Eleanor was more or less responsible for herself and her younger brother. Much has been made of Eleanor's early life, the trials of which she escaped only when she married her distant cousin Franklin Delano Roosevelt at age twenty-one, and without question, her childhood experiences must have left deep scars, the traces of which could be seen in the adult woman. Yet in recent years, biographers have pointed out that these early experiences, terrible as they were, formed a series of tests that Eleanor managed to transcend, and from which she emerged as a mature, capable woman who eventually had a profound effect on the nation and world.

Her father's family arrived in America in 1640—in what then was New Amsterdam—and over the centuries flourished, growing large and rich. By the time of Eleanor's birth in 1884, the Roosevelt family had divided into two branches, named for their principal family homes. One branch was identified with Oyster

Bay near Hempstead, New York, and was the slightly more socially prominent and devoted to the Republican Party. The other side of the family was known as the Hyde Park branch, in reference to the family estate near Poughkeepsie, New York. Both branches had encouraged the intermarriage of cousins, and the respective family trees were a tangle of cross relationships.

Part of the Oyster Bay branch, Eleanor's grandfather, Theodore Roosevelt Sr., was a successful businessman who built on the fortune he inherited; he also was a renowned philanthropist and humanitarian. His wife, Martha, came from far outside New York society. She was the daughter of a southern slave-holding family whose loyalties during the Civil War were clearly with the Confederacy for which her two brothers fought (Theodore Sr. paid a substitute to take his place in the Union army). The couple had four children: Theodore Jr., Anna (known as "Bamie" or "Bye"), Corinne, and Elliott, who became Eleanor's father.

The antecedents of Eleanor's mother, Anna Hall, were even more prominent. She was a member of the New York Livingstons and Ludlows, and her forebears had been among the most important American revolutionaries, including a signer of the Declaration of Independence. By the late nineteenth century, the family had amassed huge wealth and had become part of the social upper crust of New York City, known as the Knickerbocker Society. Anna and her mother, May Livingston Ludlow Hall, were original members of the socially elite "400," so named for the number of people Mrs. Caroline Astor could fit into her ballroom.

Anna's father, Valentine, ran his family with an iron hand but died young, leaving his even younger widow, Eleanor's grandmother, to assume responsibility for her six children; the family's brownstone mansion in Manhattan; and a country estate, Oak Terrace near Tivoli, New York. Anna's younger brothers and sisters proved to be extremely difficult personalities, causing endless trouble for their mother, but teenaged Anna herself was a glittering social star. She was one of the renowned beauties of the age, and her life revolved around parties, balls, and dinners, although she received little education, and her knowledge of matters beyond her own family and the New York party circuit was slight. Above all, she valued good looks, good manners, and position in society. Elliott Roosevelt appeared to have these qualities in abundance. He was handsome and well mannered; excelled at the upper-class sports such as sailing, shooting, and polo; and seemed a perfect match for Anna. Elliott's superficial attributes, however, hid deep psychological and personal flaws. During his childhood and early adolescence he developed recurring symptoms of severe neurasthenia—mysterious attacks of weakness and "nerves" that left him debilitated and were the harbingers of even more severe problems to come. As he grew older, Elliott and his brother Theodore (Teddy), who had been close to Elliott as a child, began to diverge. Teddy shrugged off childhood illnesses to become a rugged, powerful personality who eventually moved into political and public life; on the other hand, Elliott seemed increasingly shallow in his interests and prey to his mounting weaknesses.

Elliott and his brother represented two sides of the nineteenth-century notion of masculinity. Elliott was never able to transcend the characteristics of the neurasthenic, enervated elite, but Teddy responded by embracing "the strenuous life" of vigorous manhood. Elliott's brief tenure at St. Paul's prep school in New Hampshire provided him with only a rudimentary education, and his family's wealth absolved him from the need for useful employment, so he grew into a young adult whose major interests and activities were purely amusing and self-indulgent: parties, games, and above all, excessive drinking.

Despite his faults, which might have been viewed by many in New York's high society as positive features, Elliott seemed to Anna Hall and her mother to be an acceptable suitor. He was elegant, well mannered, a member of a suitable family, wealthy, and above all, he was physically attractive—nearly a masculine match for Anna's beauty. She might have had a few doubts about his occasionally erratic behavior (he would disappear for days at a time into his locked study), but on the whole, marriage to Elliott must have appealed to Anna as a fulfillment of her social and personal ambitions.

Their society wedding in December 1883 might have been the high point of the entire marriage. Two months later, Elliott's family was stricken by the deaths during a single day of both his mother and Teddy's young wife, Alice. The double blow sent Elliott into an emotional spin, and he descended into a period of depression and heavy drinking. Anna, pregnant with Eleanor, apparently could give her new husband little solace, and the couple began a process of emotional and psychological separation that continued for the rest of their lives.

A Grim Childhood

Eleanor was born on October 11, 1884, and immediately won the most lavish attention from her father, who could be a wonderfully loving person when not in the grip of his mental and emotional disturbances. Throughout her life, Eleanor would remember—often with a much-distorted vision—her father's love and affection, which she felt deeply as a very small child. In her memoirs, Eleanor wrote that her father was "charming, good-looking, [and] loved by all who came in contact with him," and she proclaimed "with my father I was perfectly happy."

Eleanor's mother was another story. Anna found her new child sadly lacking in almost all the qualities she most cherished. Eleanor was not a pretty child, and she was withdrawn and serious in demeanor. Because Anna valued good looks and gaiety above all other virtues, there was little the mother found to admire in Eleanor. To be fair, Anna—still herself barely out of her adolescence and faced with an alcoholic husband who was completely undependable and the source of increasing pain—probably kept Eleanor at arm's length as a form of self-protection. One of Eleanor's recent biographers speculates that Eleanor's childish solemnity (her photographs show an extremely sad-eyed little person) was a constant reproach to her mother and a reminder of the overwhelming disappointment of her marriage and the contrast to her former life as a society belle.

Whatever the cause of Anna's attitude, Eleanor came to feel a sharp estrangement from her mother, and for the rest of her life Eleanor remembered her mother's disapproval and lack of affection.

She recalled vividly that her mother derided her somber nature by calling her "Granny" in front of relatives and visitors, and that the name was a terrible reminder of her mother's dislike. Eleanor later remembered that every time she heard the name she "wanted to sink through the floor in shame."

Most of Eleanor's biographers have seen Anna's treatment of Eleanor as loveless, cruel, and frivolous, which to a large degree it was, but Blanche Wiesen Cook's recent biography sees Anna's behavior at least in part a reaction to the insane behavior and selfish cruelty of Elliott toward his wife. At times Anna might have tried to shield Eleanor from Elliott, although Eleanor never was able to appreciate this circumstance, and later in life built an ideal picture of her father and condemned her mother. While Elliott toyed with business pursuits in the city and spent most of his time drinking or playing games with his cronies, Anna took Eleanor to the Hall family estate at Oak Terrace for extended stays, along with Grandmother Hall and Eleanor's five wild young aunts and uncles.

When Eleanor was two and a half, the family decided that a European tour might revive their relationships. They sailed on the *Britannica* along with Eleanor's nurse and her young aunt Elizabeth, but only one day out of port, the ship was rammed and everyone aboard had to abandon ship. Eleanor was terrified and clung so hard to the rail that a crewman had to pry her fingers loose before dropping her into the lifeboat where her family waited. The Roosevelt party was saved, but Eleanor was traumatized and for years refused to go near any significant body of water or even small boats. Her mother used the child's fears as an excuse for leaving her behind with relatives at Oyster Bay while Anna and Elliott sailed again for England. As with other childhood slights, Eleanor never forgot the abandonment.

On his return to the United States, Elliott purchased land on Long Island, near Hempstead and Oyster Bay, and began to build a new house. He made a pretense of working at his uncle James Gracie's bank, but his main occupations remained drinking and playing. His behavior had slipped into a pattern that he was unable to break for the rest of his life: He ignored his wife and family for long periods of carousal and debauchery, then returned with promises of reform and better behavior, only to disappoint before long with a new round of drunken irresponsibility.

Elliott's problems grew worse after he broke his leg while performing at a charity circus at a friend's estate in Westchester, New York. The leg healed badly and had to be broken again. During the ordeal, Elliott became dependent on painkillers, thereby adding drug addiction to his already virulent alcoholism. Anna, to her credit, shielded Eleanor from much of her father's worst actions, but Eleanor—even if she secretly understood how disappointed her mother was—forever viewed her father in only the most favorable light. Throughout her autobiographical writings, Eleanor portrayed her father as constantly loving and wonderful, with only minor faults caused by weakness or illness. "Somehow," she wrote, "It was always he and I."

In 1889 a son, whom they named Elliott Jr., was born; however, rather than bringing husband and wife closer together, the new responsibility seemed to push Elliott into a new downward cycle. He left his family at their Long Island house while he drank and partied in New York City, and at the end of the year, he fled to Bermuda rather than spend Christmas with them.

The following summer Elliott decided that another European tour would help him regain his equilibrium, so the family sailed for Germany. The trip was a total disaster. As they moved from Germany to Italy and back again to Germany, Elliott's behavior grew worse. He drank constantly, took drugs, and became erratic and abusive to all around him. A short stay in a sanitarium did nothing to help, and he resumed his ways when the family moved on to France, where it became known that Anna was pregnant again. His sister Bye, Eleanor's favorite aunt, came to help deal with Elliott's problems.

Issues grew even more intense when news arrived from New York that one of their former servants, a girl named Katy Mann, also claimed to be pregnant by Elliott and was demanding money from his family on the threat of causing a scandal. The housemaid eventually was paid off and withdrew her threats (in later life Eleanor tacitly acknowledged her half-brother, who was born to

Mann that fall). Elliott's elder brother Teddy, who was by now a prominent politician and officeholder, was outraged. The years of increasing bitterness over Elliott's behavior boiled over, and he attempted to have Elliott declared incompetent and confined to an asylum. As her family seemed to disintegrate around her, Eleanor was sent to a French convent for temporary care while her mother waited to give birth. Eleanor was intensely unhappy in the alien surroundings and faked swallowing a coin in order to be returned to her mother.

Four-year-old Eleanor and her father, Elliott Roosevelt, sat for a photographer in New York City in the spring of 1889. All Eleanor's childhood photographs show her looking this somber.

Elliott came to France to await the birth of the new child; however, he continued to drink heavily and took up relations with a mistress, an American women, Florence Bagley Sherman, with whom he consorted intermittently until his death. This horrible period—of which Eleanor in later life had only dreamlike memories—came to an end shortly after Anna gave birth to a boy, Gracie Hall, and she, her children, and Aunt Bye sailed for home, leaving Elliott in an asylum near Paris. Teddy's attempts to have Elliott committed failed when they became public knowledge and received widespread newspaper publicity, and the rest of the family pressured Teddy to give up his crusade.

On returning to New York, Anna and her children moved into a house in the city and attempted to find a new life. Elliott never again lived with them. He was persuaded by his family to attempt a cure, and following a brief spell in Illinois at a center for the treatment of alcoholism, he was exiled—at Teddy's insistence—to Virginia, where he worked on the estates of his brother-in-law, Douglas Robinson. He returned to the city on occasion, and Eleanor remembered these visits with utmost fondness, even though others must have viewed them as delusionary or destructive. On one visit, Elliott took Eleanor with him for a carriage ride, promising treats and a good time, but dropped her off at the door of his club in the care of the doorman while he proceeded to drink himself unconscious. Hours later, after Elliott had been carried off prostrate, Eleanor was sent home in a cab by the doorman. For the most part, Anna refused to see him and lived with her children, cut off from her husband.

In November 1892 Anna had surgery and thereafter contracted diphtheria. She fell into a near coma, and on December 7, she died at her home, nursed by her mother. Before she succumbed, she had asked her mother to keep Elliott away, and he was denied a chance to visit her deathbed. When her mother became ill, Eleanor was sent to stay with her cousin Susie Parrish. When Parish told her of her mother's death, the eight-year-old child could think only that she might then be able to see her beloved father.

After their mother's death, Eleanor and her brothers went to live with Grandmother Hall at the older woman's brownstone mansion in Manhattan. Based on the evidence of her memoirs, Eleanor constructed for herself a romantic version of a relationship with her father. She imagined that at some remarkable time in the future, they would live together as a family and she would provide a home for Elliott (her younger brothers seem to disappear in this scenario).

In fact, Anna's death put Elliott into a final downward spiral. His efforts to rehabilitate himself through a healthy rural life on the Virginia farm came to an end and he moved back to New York City and resumed drinking and womanizing, moving in with a new mistress and behaving erratically in public. Eleanor was not told that he was back in the city, but she saw him in a passing cab on the street one day and demanded to know why he was in New York and had not seen her. The family tragedy deepened in May 1893 when Elliott Jr., Eleanor's brother, died of scarlet fever and diphtheria. Eleanor and her father wrote to each other, but Elliott was prevented from seeing the children often, either in New York City or at the Hall estate at Tivoli. On August 14, 1894, Elliott Roosevelt died at age thirty-four, succumbing to the effects of his lifelong alcoholism.

Eleanor now was bereft of the father she so adored. Her response was, according to her own account, to withdraw into a dream world where there was no need to face the reality of her loss. She continued for some time to imagine her father was still alive or would be returning someday to claim her from her orphan circumstances, and she preferred to be alone with her own fugue-like musings rather than in the company of others.

Orphanhood and Allenswood

Grandmother Hall took full charge of Eleanor and her younger brother after the death of her son. The Hall New York brownstone was, according to Eleanor's later testimony, a dreary place, heavily furnished and curtained in the nineteenth-century manner, and presided over by Mrs. Hall, who was still relatively young but apparently driven to distraction by the wild actions and personalities of her own children, who seemed amenable to no controls whatsoever. Despite occasional visits from "Uncle Ted," as Eleanor called Teddy, the lively Oyster Bay branch of the Roosevelt clan mostly ignored Eleanor. Teddy's new wife, Edith Carow Roosevelt, was hesitant to have Eleanor around, apparently fearing she had inherited too much "bad blood" from her father (conveniently ignoring that her own children would have a similar inheritance).

Eleanor was attended by a procession of servants and tutors, the latter of which had been added to her routine when it was discovered she was still unable to read at the age of eight. She also was trained in the social graces, although her grandmother probably had few hopes the girl would ever come close to Anna's social success. Grandmother Hall insisted on a strict code of behavior that avoided all emotional displays or excesses—surely a reaction to Elliott's character and her own children's displays—which reinforced Eleanor's natural shyness. Although she was allowed to have other children as friends, they were few on number and carefully chosen. The grandmother also insisted on dressing Eleanor in an inappropriate and outmoded style that added to the young girl's discomfort. One of her cousins later called Eleanor's childhood the "grimmest" she could imagine.

"Uncle Ted" Roosevelt's meteoric public career formed a backdrop for Eleanor's early life.

Teddy Roosevelt was a member of the U.S. Civil Service Commission when he attempted to have Eleanor's father, Elliott, committed to an asylum. During her orphan years, Teddy was a police commissioner of New York City and then assistant secretary of the Navy. He became a war hero in 1898 as lieutenant colonel of the famous Rough Riders in Cuba during the Spanish-American War.

He was elected vice president of the United States on the Republican ticket in 1900. Eleanor was at school in England when Uncle Ted succeeded to the presidency in September 1901 after President William McKinley was assassinated. Teddy Roosevelt was elected president in his own right in 1904 and brought a presidential glamour to Eleanor's wedding the following year.

A leading Progressive reformer, Teddy ran unsuccessfully for president in 1912. He died seven years later.

However, there were bright spots in the years following the death of her parents. No matter how depressingly solemn and dreary Grandmother Hall's house was, the atmosphere was a great deal more stable and emotionally secure than any Eleanor had known previously. The erratic cycles of her father's behavior now were safely relegated to fuzzy memory, and her mother's cold reproaches were gone forever. Moreover, the discipline that Grandmother Hall insisted on might have provided a form of comfort despite being superficially confining. However oppressive daily life in New York might have seemed to Eleanor, it was clear that her grandmother loved her and was doing her best by her own lights to make a home for the two Roosevelt orphans.

Probably the best parts of the period following her parents' deaths were the frequent trips upstate to Tivoli, where Eleanor was relatively free to spend her days outdoors, which she loved, and to read and enjoy herself with fewer social restrictions. Her cousins often were annoying in their behavior, especially the male cousins, but they also included Eleanor in activities at Oak Terrace. They taught her to ride a pony, play tennis, shoot a rifle, row a boat, and generally enjoy games. Throughout the rest of her early life, Eleanor was active and skilled in sports and outdoor pursuits.

Eleanor's intellectual training was in the hands of Frederic Roser, a fashionable tutor to the children of the most prominent New York families. Roser conducted classes in the homes of his clients, and Eleanor attended group sessions for several years, learning the rudiments of literature and the other humanities. She also was tutored in French and German, both of which she mastered, and was given music lessons. Eleanor also was sent to a socially approved dance class, where she took ballet lessons—unusual for girls of her social level. Because she was tall and no beauty, those around her often made the offhand assumption that Eleanor was awkward or gawky. Nothing could have been further from the truth. She was graceful and coordinated and proved to be a good dancer, just as she was a good competitive athlete when the opportunity arose. (She later used her early dance training to great advantage when she undertook volunteer work in a New York settlement house.)

After five years with Grandmother Hall, Eleanor's life took a new turn. Her grandmother announced that, in keeping with Eleanor's mother's wishes, she was sending the fourteen-year-old girl to England to attend an all-girl's school at Allenswood, located near London. Eleanor later wrote in her book *You Learn by Living:* "What I have learned from my own experience is that the most important ingredients in a child's education are curiosity, interest, imagination, and a sense of the adventure in life." She was to find all of these and formal academic training at Allenswood.

Women's Education

Female education was expanding rapidly in the United States at the turn of the twentieth century, but Eleanor's social status and class dictated a limit to her education.

In 1900, many American girls still attended female academies that had been popular since the early nineteenth century, but they also had access to 6,005 public co-educational high schools. By 1910, forty percent of college students were women.

Middle-class girls could dream of college or perhaps even a career as a doctor or lawyer, but education for girls in the most elite American families was still restricted.

Girls like Eleanor from wealthy families were more likely to be tutored at home or sent to posh girls' schools that stressed social graces as much as intellectual development. During her adult life, Eleanor frequently lamented her lack of formal education.

A Frenchwoman, Marie Souvestre, who was approaching seventy at the time of Eleanor's enrollment, ran the school. Eleanor's strong-minded aunt Bye had attended Les Ruches, a similar school Souvestre had run with a partner in France, and was enthusiastic about having Eleanor come under Souvestre's care. Eleanor's grandmother believed, probably correctly, that the education available at Allenswood would be superior to the girls' schools in the United States (it would have been out of the question for Eleanor to enroll in one of the American colleges that were by this time admitting women for full academic training).

In 1899 Eleanor sailed for England in the company of her aunt Elizabeth (known as "Tizzie"), who was married to the immensely wealthy Stanley Mortimer and who lived in a lavish estate on Long Island. The Mortimers loved England and English society; thus they were often close by during Eleanor's years at the English school, and Tizzie often invited Eleanor to travel or stay with her. When she arrived at Allenswood, Eleanor was confronted with an environment completely different from any she had known previously. Souvestre's school was not a typical finishing school where girls were educated only to become wives and mothers. Allenswood was a serious educational institution with a curriculum that challenged the students to think, learn, and grow.

Souvestre herself was formidable. She was the daughter of the famous French philosopher Emile Souvestre; thus she had grown up in a stimulating atmosphere and was well regarded in European and English intellectual and literary circles. She was an outspoken atheist and feminist and—contrary to the prevailing opinion among many in the higher social circles in the United States who thought women should have only a smattering of knowledge and training lest they become unfit for their roles in life—Souvestre believed women should have the best and most challenging education possible. Her thinking verged on the radical, and she was a strong public voice for several unpopular causes, such as support for the Boers in their war against Great Britain; however, she was extremely successful in attracting students from the best families to her schools.

She had shut down her school in France when she quarreled with her female partner (who also was her lover) and had reestablished herself in England, although her school was still conducted entirely in French. Eleanor was, fortunately, fluent in the language as a result of her tutoring in New York, which gave her a great advantage over some of her classmates. Souvestre was by all accounts, including Eleanor's autobiography, a dynamic teacher and a forceful personality who impressed herself powerfully on her teenage charges. Eleanor later wrote that Souvestre was "the fine person who exerted the greatest influence, after my father, on this period of my life."

Eleanor became one of Souvestre's favorites almost immediately. The Frenchwoman brought Eleanor into her closest circle of students and lavished time and attention on her in a way Eleanor had never before in her life experienced. Eleanor blossomed, and perhaps for the first time began to see herself in a positive light. At Allenswood, she was exposed powerfully to a world far beyond the narrow confines of her childhood. Moreover, Souvestre's close attention and undeniable signs of favor—Eleanor was given a place at meal times next to the headmistress so she could share conversation—must have been a joyful liberation for the previously solemn child whose only unqualified love had come from her undependable father.

Souvestre insisted that Eleanor spend some of her allowance money on new clothes, urging her to cast off the unstylish wardrobe foisted on her by Grandmother Hall, and Eleanor's physical appearance improved significantly when she began to stand straight and take pride in her full six-foot height. Photographs taken during this period of Eleanor's middle and late teenage years show her at her absolute best: perhaps not a great beauty on the model of her mother but an extremely attractive, well-dressed and well-coiffed young woman with a distinctive bearing.

As one of Eleanor's recent biographers points out, at Allenswood, Eleanor for the first time experienced female authority as a freeing influence rather than a series of insults or dismal constraints. She began to discover her inner self, free from her mother's or grandmother's prescriptions, and she had the freedom under Souvestre's tutelage to express herself physically, emotionally, and intellectually. Not surprisingly, Eleanor later remembered these years at Allenswood as some of the best of her life.

Eleanor's transformation was perhaps best revealed by the position of leadership she assumed among her fellow students. The shy young girl who had lived much of her life avoiding other people suddenly was not only the center of attention, she clearly was the leader among her peers. She was extremely popular with the other students, many of whom favored Eleanor with gifts and bouquets of flowers, and she built a circle of intimate friends from among the most accomplished and attractive members of the school.

The classes she took at Allenswood provided the only formal education she enjoyed during her entire life (although it was certainly true that she was a voracious learner and acute observer as an adult). Her studies were relatively broad and varied, especially for a young woman of her social class, and she appears to have done reasonably well in most of the traditional subjects taught at the school. Her greatest efforts went into the classes taught by Souvestre herself, and she excelled in whatever the headmistress demanded of her. Souvestre commanded a quick and well-educated intelligence and demanded the same from her favorites. She gathered around her for sessions in her personal library a group (with Eleanor at its head) that received the full light of her challenging teaching methods. The benefits Eleanor received from her close relationship with Souvestre were not limited to Allenswood. Eleanor was selected to accompany Souvestre on holiday to Europe during school vacations, and they traveled together to France and Italy, visiting great cities such as Paris and Rome, and journeying along the Mediterranean coast. Eleanor even ventured out on her own on many occasions, although this came to a halt when neighbors from New York reported to Grandmother Hall that the young girl was seen browsing a Paris neighborhood unescorted. Nonetheless, Eleanor's view of the world must have been forever altered by these enchanting experiences that were so at odds with her life in America.

After two years at Allenswood, Eleanor was summoned home during the summer by her grandmother. It proved to be an extremely difficult, if not traumatic, time for Eleanor. Not only was she bereft at the possibility of leaving Allenswood for good, but her aunt Edith Hall (known as "Pussie"), one of Grandmother Hall's unruly children and a woman known for her series of disastrous love affairs, verbally assaulted Eleanor. She told Eleanor point-blank that she was an ugly duckling and would never have suitors. Worse, she detailed for Eleanor the last years of her father's life and his terrible behavior.

Stung by these revelations, Eleanor asked her grandmother and cousin Susie Parrish to dispel the stories—but of course they had to reluctantly confirm the truth that Eleanor had for so long ignored. Eleanor was so upset by these conversations that she ardently begged her grandmother to be allowed to return to Allenswood for a third year, and Mrs. Hall agreed. Eleanor resumed her place at the school for a final year and once again was a favorite among her classmates, including her cousin Corinne, who was a first-year student, and of course, Marie Souvestre, who took Eleanor on a long holiday to France, Belgium, and Germany during the school's Easter break in 1902.

Although Eleanor's biographers touch on the subject gingerly if at all (those who were her close associates and wrote about her soon after her death completely ignored it), it seems clear that during her time at Allenswood Eleanor was exposed to lesbian society. Souvestre herself had lived with her former partner in France, and the young girls of Allenswood exhibited behavior toward one another—and often toward Eleanor—that on the surface at least could been seen as tinged with homosexual overtones. It was normal and accepted for schoolgirls in Europe and America to develop romantic "crushes" on one another, but this was seen merely as a phase that preceded marriage.

Even though many of the girls might not have realized it fully, Souvestre was more frankly and openly lesbian than most adult women. Moreover, thirty years later, Dorothy Strachey Bussy, one of the prominent Allenswood teachers who also had previously been a student of Souvestre at Les Ruches, anonymously published *Olivia*, a best-selling novel based on her experiences at Allenswood, which depicted a lesbian romance between herself and the character of Souvestre. Eleanor's character in the book explicitly disavows romantic feelings for the headmistress, but the inference remains that the real-life Eleanor must have been aware of the situation at the school. This was the first, but certainly not the last, instance of Eleanor's close association with influential lesbian companions.

Coming Out

At the end of her third year at Allenswood, Eleanor returned for good to the United States, leaving behind the freedoms and stimulation of Souvestre's school to fulfill her responsibility as a

Roosevelt and a member of the upper reaches of New York society: She was expected as an eighteen-year-old to make her so-called debut, or "coming out" into society. In theory, young women of the upper classes were sheltered in their parents' homes until this grand moment, when they were launched into the social whirl, announcing thereby that they were eligible for marriage.

It was a specific sort of social ritual involving a series of public balls and private parties, which had immense weight among people such as Eleanor's mother's family. Eleanor herself was unhappy to face up to what she assumed would be a difficult trial for her. She could scarcely avoid renewed comparisons to her mother, who had been the belle of all social belles during her debut season, and she became once again something of the shy child she had been before her experiences in England.

Moreover, Eleanor's return to New York meant a sharp reminder of her orphan status. She still lived most of the time with her grandmother, but her cousins were increasingly causing trouble. Valentine, the eldest of the Hall cousins, was the most erratic and distressing of the clan, shooting at visitors from the windows of Oak Terrace and joining his sibling Eddie in wild, drunken sprees. Eleanor could not have helped but be reminded of the behavior of her own father. Things were so bad at the Hall estate at Tivoli that heavy locks had to be installed on Eleanor's bedroom door, presumably to protect her from possible assault by her cousins.

Also about this time, Eleanor assumed almost full responsibility for her younger brother Hall, who entered prep school at Groton in the fall of 1903. Although she herself was still a teenager, Eleanor took over from her now-failing grandmother the supervision of Hall's education. She also took charge of running the Hall mansion in New York City, as her grandmother had almost entirely retired to life at Oak Terrace. Life in the brownstone was dull and somewhat lonely for Eleanor, enlivened in an undesirable fashion by periodic visits from her cousins, who came to town for sprees—but even this existence came to an end when Grandmother Hall decided to shut down the mansion. Eleanor, lacking her own residence, moved into the townhouse of her cousin Susie Parrish.

Eleanor's formal "coming out" portrait from 1902 shows her during her late-adolescent period of most attractive looks.

(*Courtesy of the Franklin Delano Roosevelt Library*)

Eleanor's formal entrance into society as a debutante came in the fall of 1902. She attended the annual horse show at Madison Square Garden, sitting in the box of James Roosevelt, one of the Hyde Park branch of the family, along with several of her distant relatives, including Franklin Delano Roosevelt, James's half-brother. She then began the round of parties and dances that made up the "season." The most important was the Assembly Ball in early December, which Eleanor experienced as a painful reminder of how much less beautiful she was than her mother, and she left early. The coming out parties dwindled and died by December, and Eleanor then was free of the embarrassment.

During the months after her return from Allenswood, Eleanor had found diversion from the vicissitudes of her family and social life in an activity that would be seen in retrospect as entirely typical of her life to come. She became intensely interested in working among the youngsters of New York's abjectly poor immigrant population, and she took up volunteer activities with enthusiasm. The conduit for her work was the Junior League for the Promotion of Settlement Movements, an organization that had been founded in 1900 by several young women from upper-crust families in New York City. They had been genuinely moved by the terrible living and working conditions among the poor of the city, primarily the huge and rapidly growing immigrant groups who were pouring into New York at a record rate and who had completely overwhelmed the available low-cost housing and barely extant welfare system.

Although some of the young society women might have only dabbled in social work among the immigrant poor, many, including Eleanor, took it very seriously. She volunteered her time at the Rivington Street College Settlement House, an institution on the Lower East Side of New York in the heart of the immigrant section. Based on the famous model of Jane Addams's Hull House in Chicago and Toynbee Hall in London (which was founded in part by Mrs. Humphrey Ward, a close friend of Marie Souvestre), the Rivington Street home aimed to provide a place for children of poor families to find wholesome amusements and a safe environment for cultural and social enrichment. Many of Eleanor's former classmates from Frederick Roser's tutoring sessions were involved in the work of the settlement house, and they recruited her to help.

She began regular visits to the settlement house with her friend, Jean Reid (daughter of prominent New York editor Whitlaw Reid), who had been one of the founders of the Junior League. Eleanor taught dancing and calisthenics, while Reid played the piano. Their students were children of the neighborhood, many of whom had worked twelve-hour shifts to help support their families before coming to the settlement house classes. Eleanor's reaction to her settlement house work was to some degree typical of pampered young women who wished to help the less fortunate, but she took her work rather seriously. She later reflected that during this period she was "a curious mixture of extreme innocence and unworldliness with a great deal of knowledge of some of the less agreeable sides of life."

The Rivington Street College Settlement was one of about a hundred such institutions in the United States in 1900 when Eleanor became a volunteer.

The first settlement house—so called because college-age volunteers came to "settle" and live in low-income sections of cities—was founded in England in 1884, and the movement soon spread to the United States.

In 1889 Jane Addams and her friend Ellen Starr founded Hull House in Chicago. The College Settlement began in New York City only a few weeks later.

By the time Eleanor volunteered to teach dancing at Rivington Street, most settlements were staffed by women, many of whom, like Eleanor, found their settlement house experiences both inspirational and good training for later participation in a wide range of social reform causes.

Eleanor separated herself from many of the young women volunteers by insisting on taking public transportation to and from the settlement house (many of the others arrived in family carriages) and walking many blocks through the blighted Lower East Side neighborhoods. She thus received a direct and vivid education in the conditions from which her dance and exercise pupils came, and she observed firsthand what life was like for the poor and neglected, lessons that stayed with her throughout her life.

She also joined the Consumers' League, an organization formed by upper-class women to investigate and ameliorate working conditions for women in the city. The Consumers' League had a much more political orientation than the Junior League, and many of its principals advocated publicity and direct action to bring to light and improve the ghastly conditions in the sweat shops of the city. Although she admitted in later life that she was perhaps too naïve to really understand the significance of her social welfare contacts with the Junior League and the Consumer's League, these were formative experiences, and they marked her first involvement with the issues she came to champion.

Chapter 3

Cousin Franklin, Marriage, and Family Life

... I was thinking things out for myself and becoming an individual. Had I never done this, perhaps I might have saved some difficult experiences, but I have never regretted even my mistakes.

—Eleanor Roosevelt,
This Is My Story

Eleanor's commitment to social causes is understandable, as many women of her class felt a sense of *noblesse oblige* to serve those less fortunate. But the real work of a refined young woman at the turn of the century was to prepare herself for marriage, and Eleanor was no exception.

She was courted by several prominent young men in New York who found her to be vivacious and interesting. The most ardent suitor was Howard Cary, who appears to have pursued Eleanor diligently both in New York City and in Maine, when she visited her Aunt Corinne there. Eleanor slighted the memory of his attentions when she wrote of them later in life, claiming that his main interest in her was as a person with whom he could discuss books; however, the evidence suggests that Cary, as well as two or three other young men, pursued Eleanor with possible matrimony in mind.

Eleanor's romantic interests had turned elsewhere. Soon after her debut season she began spending time with Franklin Delano Roosevelt (FDR), her fifth cousin once removed and a member of the Hyde Park branch of the family. They had first met as children but had not seen each other since a Christmas party when Eleanor was only fourteen. They renewed their acquaintance in 1902 when they met by chance in a railway car headed up the Hudson Valley. They were relaxed and compatible with each other from the beginning of their new relationship, and before long, a romance bloomed.

Over the following year, they met often at family gatherings and society parties. During the summer of 1903, they were both guests at the same time at several country houses, and FDR invited Eleanor to spend a few days at his family home at Hyde Park, New York. They also exchanged letters. Eleanor later destroyed her courting letters from FDR, but he saved hers, and the picture they present is of a young woman eager for romance, excited by her prospects for the future, and dedicated to the man with whom she increasingly fell in love.

FDR was the son of James Roosevelt and his second wife Sara Delano. James Roosevelt had inherited the family estates on the banks of the Hudson River in Dutchess County, New York, near the village of Hyde Park. He also had purchased a nearby manor house called Springwood, establishing it as his family home. His branch of the Roosevelt family had split from their Oyster Bay cousins in the eighteenth century, although they were still on good terms in FDR's father's day. After the death of his first wife Rebecca (who was the mother of FDR's half-brother James Roosevelt Roosevelt—known as "Rosy") in 1876, the elder James married the much younger Sara Delano, a famous beauty whose father had amassed a fortune from the China trade. FDR was born at the family home at Hyde Park on January 30, 1882.

Sara doted on FDR as a young child, and they formed an extremely close bond. FDR grew to be tall, handsome, and vigorous but was regarded by both friends and family as possessing negligible intelligence. He was sent to Groton School at age fourteen but made little impression on his classmates or teachers. He then moved on to Harvard, where his greatest accomplishment was winning the editorship of the *Harvard Crimson* newspaper. To his dismay, he was turned down for membership by the elite student club, the Porcellian (to which Eleanor's uncle Theodore had belonged as a student). After James Roosevelt died during FDR's first year at Harvard, Sara took an apartment in Boston to be closer to her son and divided her time between there and Hyde Park. FDR almost never openly challenged what his mother saw as her right to control his life.

He had not been entirely without romantic interests before meeting Eleanor, however, and had actively courted at least one young woman on the sly, keeping his amorous activities a secret from his mother. FDR had even proposed to seventeen-year-old Alice Sohier when he was twenty. The young woman's parents were not thrilled by the prospect of FDR as a son-in-law, however, so they packed their daughter off on a tour of Europe and the Middle East. She later said that she lost interest in FDR when he told her he wanted to have at least six children.

Because of his mother's overbearing interest in every detail of his life and her obvious antagonism toward his prospective wives, FDR had to court Eleanor almost in secret. The couple did manage to spend a good deal of time together, and they especially delighted in each other's conversation, which both considered to be a cut above the social banter they so often encountered in others. Even at this tender stage of their relationship, at least part of Eleanor's effect on FDR was due to the liveliness of her mind and her interests.

She asked him, for example, to meet her at the Rivington Street Settlement after her sessions as a teacher. He became a regular visitor, and unlike other members of Eleanor's family, FDR did not disparage her activities or try to dissuade her from working at the settlement. It was FDR's first exposure to the conditions that existed among the poor and disenfranchised, and Eleanor believed that his attitudes in the long run were influenced by the experience.

The months of courtship were surely among the happiest of Eleanor's entire life. The plaguing conditions of her childhood and the uncertainties of her orphan status seemed to drop away, and she expressed over and over again in her letters a sort of pure joy in living and finding love that was never again duplicated. What had been her characteristic solemnity and reserve was gone when she was around FDR. Her letters to him were full of love and exuberance. As she wrote to him: "Oh! darling I miss you so and I long for the happy hours which we have together and I think of the many which we have had these last two weeks constantly—I am so happy. So *very* happy in your love dearest, that all the world has changed for me."

On November 22, 1903, after attending a Harvard football game together (properly chaperoned as all polite couples would have been), Eleanor and FDR went to visit her brother Hall at Groton. After a Sunday morning church service the couple took a walk together, during which FDR proposed and Eleanor accepted.

Over the Thanksgiving holiday, FDR sprang the news on his mother that he planned to marry Eleanor. Although the couple had been seeing a good deal of each other, FDR had not let on the full extent of their involvement to his mother, who was shocked that her twenty-one-year-old son was engaged to his nineteen-year-old cousin. Sara persuaded FDR and Eleanor to postpone the public announcement of their engagement for a year. She called the postponement a test of their love for one another, but it also most certainly was a ploy by Sara to hold on to her son as long as possible.

> *When Eleanor and FDR became engaged in 1903, marriage was still the most important institution governing a woman's life. Only since the mid-1870s had most states even allowed married women to hold property of their own. Married women were expected to take part in their husbands' families, and as in Eleanor's case, to keep their husbands' relatives happy.*
>
> *While marriage was of social importance to the entire family, at the beginning of the twentieth century a new ideal of "companionate marriage" was taking hold, even among elites. The marriage between Eleanor and FDR bonded the two branches of the prominent Roosevelt family closer together, but the young couple probably also expected to find in one another mutual fulfillment, love, and sexual compatibility.*

During the year that Eleanor and FDR kept their engagement secret they met frequently, although Sara kept them apart when she could by insisting that FDR not visit New York City too often and by demanding he go with her on a Caribbean cruise. When the engagement was at last announced to the public, Eleanor's side of the family was pleased. As news of the match reached the society columns, she began what would be many years of paying court to Sara, trying to meet her expectations and to reassure her that she would be a good wife to FDR. Eleanor was anxious to succeed at the new relationship, and she hoped at last to be part of a loving, close family—something that had eluded her in her life so far. Sara learned to accept Eleanor, who was a good personal companion for her son and his ideal social match, but her attention often was stifling and her sometimes undisguised disapproval was hard for Eleanor to bear.

Although Eleanor often was filled with self-doubt during the period leading up to her wedding, she also was full of domestic ambition. At Sara's insistence, she had given up her charity work, but in marriage Eleanor hoped to find her new calling. FDR also was ambitious. A first-year law student at Columbia University, he harbored hopes for a career in national politics, hopes that certainly would not be damaged by marrying cousin President Teddy Roosevelt's favorite niece. Eleanor focused her own ambition on succeeding as FDR's wife and on furthering his career. In late-Victorian America it was usual for women to subsume their own desires to their husbands and families, and Eleanor took to her new role as FDR's helpmate with enthusiasm, even as she continued to fight occasional moodiness and bouts of anxiety.

Eleanor thus accepted her future and tried to banish her cares when she married FDR on March 17, 1905, her mother's birthday. Her Uncle Ted was in New York to attend the annual St. Patrick's Day parade, and he became the main attraction at the wedding. The ceremony took place in the double parlor of the attached townhouses of Eleanor's cousin Susie Parrish and aunt Elizabeth Livingston Ludlow. Although his second wife Edith was not overly fond of his niece, Theodore Roosevelt insisted on giving the bride away, and he walked Eleanor down the aisle. Teddy had offered Eleanor the White House for her wedding, but she wanted a simpler affair and thought the New York townhouse would be better. Teddy's daughter Alice, whose relationship with Eleanor was strained and who would become her bitter rival later in life, served as a bridesmaid. Eleanor was not surprised that Teddy was the object of much attention from the wedding guests, who ignored the bride and groom and trailed after the president following the exchange of vows.

Eleanor's bridal portrait shows her resplendent in a dress decorated with flowers and European lace, formal jewelry, and her mother's wedding veil. Eleanor's relatives concurred that she was a beautiful bride, and several of them noted that on her wedding day she bore some resemblance to her mother, an observation that surely pleased her. Eleanor and FDR spent a week at Hyde Park following their wedding before returning to New York, where FDR took his law school examinations (two of which he failed). While FDR finished his semester, the couple lived in a hotel with Sara and Eleanor's brother Hall before finally setting off for an extended European honeymoon in June. Eleanor conquered her fear of the water to enjoy their steamship voyage, and she was a hearty traveler as they visited Britain, France, Italy, and Germany.

Eleanor's formal wedding photograph showed off her elaborate dress and accessories.

(Courtesy of the Franklin Delano Roosevelt Library)

Eleanor enjoyed visiting landmarks and time spent with family friends who were abroad. She and FDR shopped extravagantly for linens, books, clothing, and furs; stayed in luxurious hotel suites; and attended dances and parties. The couple visited Allenswood, a trip made bittersweet by the recent death of Marie Souvestre. Even as she was getting used to her husband, Eleanor did not neglect her new responsibilities as a daughter-in-law, and she wrote solicitous and colorful letters to Sara almost every day. Eleanor's most anxious moments came in Cortina, when FDR went mountain climbing with the dynamic, single New York businesswoman Kitty Gandy. Almost in spite of herself, Eleanor was jealous of Gandy, who flirted openly with the outgoing FDR. When FDR returned his attentions to his new wife, Eleanor was comforted, but it was not the last time that his attentions to another woman would cause her anxiety.

When after three months the honeymoon was over, and FDR and Eleanor returned to America, she was pregnant with her first child. Eleanor later wrote in her memoirs: "As young women go, I suppose I was fitting pretty well into the pattern of a conventional, quiet young society matron." Becoming a mother completed the upper-class woman's transformation into the perfect font of domesticity, and Eleanor hoped above all else to have a home of her own. Her annual income of seven thousand five hundred dollars, which came from a trust she had received from her father, when combined with FDR's annual five thousand dollars would have enabled the couple to finance comfortably luxurious surroundings as he finished his law degree. However, instead of allowing Eleanor to come into her own as a pregnant wife and new mother, Sara continued to exert strict control over the entire family.

Most of Eleanor's biographers conclude that she was seeking the love and approval she so craved by constantly giving in and pleasing Sara, and it was clear in any case that FDR would not stand up to his mother. Sara rented, furnished, and hired the servants for the house on East Thirty-Sixth Street where Eleanor spent her first pregnancy, while FDR finished law school and he and his mother kept up the family's social obligations. When in 1906 Eleanor delivered her first daughter, Anna Eleanor, Sara hired the first in a series of tyrannical British and French baby nurses who intimidated Eleanor for years. Eleanor solicited Sara's opinion on all important matters, and she even took classes recommended by her mother-in-law. Eleanor became adept at deferring to the older woman but found some aspects of Sara's control quite smothering.

> As members of the two branches of the socially prominent Roosevelt family, Eleanor and FDR took part in the elaborate social rituals and customs established among the American upper class.
>
> New York City was the capitol of high society, although regional social circuits existed up and down the east coast. Members of the major American families, many of whom were related by intermarriage, used social occasions to cement their ties and display their wealth.
>
> Strict rules of etiquette governed social visits, teas, and dinner parties. The social obligations also included yearly attendance at horse races and a whole new series of parties during the summer after the families had retired to their country houses.

FDR graduated from Columbia in 1907 and after passing the bar went to work for the prominent Wall Street firm of Carter, Ledyard, & Milburn. Eleanor's career as a mother moved apace, and she delivered a son, James, at the end of the year. Still Sara seemed to be in charge of the family. She bought land on East Sixty-Fifth Street and as a Christmas present announced she was building a set of connected houses for herself and the young Roosevelts—that way mother, son, and wife would never be apart, whether in the city or at Hyde Park. Sara designed the homes and picked out the furnishings, and although Eleanor began to show palpable irritation with her family's lack of independence, still FDR said nothing to his mother.

In 1908 Eleanor delivered her third child, a sickly baby boy named Franklin Jr. As was the tradition among families who could afford it in the first years of the twentieth century, nurses, governesses, and servants performed most of the direct care for Eleanor's infants. Eleanor loved her babies, but they often made her feel ill at ease, as might be expected of a woman who received so little affection as a child herself. She dutifully read manuals on child rearing and insisted on trying out various forms of advice, including refusing to pick up a crying baby and hanging Anna outside a window sill in a wire box so she could absorb fresh air while napping (an experiment that aroused the ire of the neighbors, who threatened to call the authorities). Some of the self-doubt from her late teens resurfaced, and Eleanor occasionally had to fight off melancholy—what she called her Griselda moods.

Matters were not helped by FDR's frequent absences from home. He spent even less time with the children than might be expected of an ambitious young lawyer of his class. Worse still, from Eleanor's viewpoint, Sara doted on the children and attempted to extend her control over the family to include all aspects of raising her grandchildren. In later years, when Sara continued to extravagantly spoil her grandchildren, she told them: "I was your real mother; Eleanor merely bore you." Eleanor had not entirely escaped the complicated family dynamics of her youth, and her own social isolation did not help her to gain any perspective on her mother-in-law's behavior. Eleanor maintained friends in society circles but lacked the close circle of acquaintances she had so loved while at school in England, and she was forced to spend an inordinate amount of time with her mother-in-law.

Eleanor received some measure of freedom in 1909 when Sara bought a summer cottage for her son and his family on the Canadian island of Campobello, just off the coast of Maine. FDR's family had vacationed on the island for years, and Eleanor enjoyed the rural seclusion during the first summer she spent there with the children and her favorite nurse, Blanche Spring, who became a good friend. The children, especially Anna, came to relish memories of time on the island with their mother.

The pleasures of the family's first summer at Campobello were quickly forgotten, however, when Franklin Jr. became ill on their return to New York. He and the other children had been left at Hyde Park under the care of a nurse while Eleanor and FDR went on to their townhouse in the city. When she learned of the baby's illness Eleanor rushed to be with him, bringing a New York City doctor, but the chronically weak boy's flu turned to pneumonia and he died. Eleanor was devastated and blamed herself for leaving the child's care to nurses. She withdrew for several months into one of the prolonged silences that characterized her reaction to pain. Her grief had not totally subsided when her next son, Elliott, was born a year later in September 1910. Although her family was growing and she looked forward to spending summers in the house at Campobello, where she could direct the servants and arrange the furniture as she wished, Eleanor's life in New York City was lonely and seemed unfulfilling.

First Residence in Washington

The Roosevelt family life changed drastically in 1910 when FDR entered politics. He dreamed of following Eleanor's uncle's path to the White House and now took the first steps, running for the New York state legislature as a Democratic candidate in the heavily Republican Dutchess County. His family name carried much weight in the region and when he impressed voters with his vigorous face-to-face campaigning and his enthusiasm, he was elected easily.

Eleanor moved her children to Albany and became a political wife. She was happy to help advance FDR's political ambitions and best of all, she finally got to run a home of her own outside of Sara's direct influence. She hired a wet nurse for Elliott, completed her household staff, and held a large open house for FDR's constituents. Eleanor seemed to come alive as she went to observe the legislature in session and made a wider circle of friends. She gained new confidence over the care of her children, with whom she took tea every day, and each night she hosted a houseful of FDR's political cronies.

Although Eleanor had previously shown little interest in formal politics, by all accounts she took to her new role as a supportive spouse with great relish. Eleanor was an effective fund-raiser, and her latest biographer stresses that she was able to use her personal charm to bridge the gap between FDR and several of his Tammany Hall Democratic Party enemies, including Al Smith. She used her domestic skills and refinement to good political effect as she entertained other political wives and helped build important networks of support for FDR. Eleanor was not impressed with Louis Howe, the "gnomelike" former newspaperman who came to run her husband's 1912 campaign, but she couldn't argue with his success at guiding FDR to reelection. Many biographers have stressed how Eleanor continued to plead ignorance about formal political issues in this period, but her actions increased her husband's political capital nonetheless.

Even though Eleanor clearly was a successful political wife, FDR was always the more outgoing of the pair. FDR loved parties and was a notorious flirt. Although Eleanor was no longer a wallflower, it became clear during their time in Albany that she was less a social being than her husband. The couple effectively balanced their varying appetites for socializing in Albany; however, the differences between them sowed the seeds of future discord.

Some biographers, exercising hindsight, have blamed Eleanor for not taking a stronger position in favor of the wide-ranging social and political reforms of the national Progressive movement during these years, especially because her Uncle Ted was one of the foremost reformers, but that criticism misses the fact that Eleanor did not yet see herself as an exceptional woman. She certainly had shown her interest in helping to improve social conditions during her late teens, but after her marriage her domestic duties diverted her from pursuing public issues. She might have modeled herself as a reformer on Florence Kelly, who was working hard for Consumers League reforms in New York, or on Jane Addams, who was at the zenith of her national influence and who campaigned for Uncle Ted's "Bull Moose" Progressive Party in the 1912 presidential election; instead Eleanor chose to focus her efforts on the domestic sphere.

That Eleanor was a more traditional political wife should not be surprising; she had always channeled her own ambitions through her husband. She was merely following the dominant historical theme in relationships between men and women when she let FDR take the lead. She began to support the women's suffrage campaign, for instance, only after FDR became an advocate in 1911, declaring: "If my husband was a suffragist I probably must be, too." Her lack of formal political interest might seem surprising given her later activism, but it was normal among society matrons, and

Eleanor was slowly building experiences and interests that would influence her later politics.

By the 1912 presidential campaign, FDR's political fortunes were on the rise. He was one of Woodrow Wilson's staunchest supporters in New York State, and in June the couple attended the Democratic national convention to support Wilson. Eleanor was put off by the frivolity of the event, and she returned to the summer house before it was over. Just as the campaign season was beginning in earnest, both Eleanor and FDR came down with typhoid fever. Although she recovered rather quickly, FDR was slow to regain his health and Louis Howe was left to run most of his reelection campaign. Both Wilson and FDR won in November, but FDR did not remain long in Albany. After Wilson's inauguration in March 1913, FDR was appointed Assistant Secretary of the Navy, the same office that had aimed Eleanor's uncle at the White House.

Eleanor's career as a political wife was raised to a new level when she moved her family to Washington, D.C., and began to embrace the fact that her husband now was on a path to the presidency. Both FDR and Eleanor assumed typical roles for politically active Roosevelts, although their Democratic allegiances continued to alienate many in the Republican Oyster Bay faction of the clan. Nevertheless, Eleanor had a network of relatives and family friends to consult about how to play her new role successfully. She especially looked to Anna Roosevelt Cowles, her Aunt Bye, who at the advanced age of forty had married Capt. William Sheffield Cowles, a naval officer and military attaché, and had become a Washington wife. Just as she had provided Eleanor comforting advice on how to be a good student at Allenswood, Aunt Bye now briefed Eleanor on the Washington social scene and counseled her not to be afraid of occasional criticism. Although Eleanor was overwhelmed by Aunt Bye's descriptions of the volume of formal visits required of political wives in Washington and the rigidity of the social codes that prescribed their behavior, for FDR's sake she committed herself to the capitol's social scene.

When Eleanor and FDR arrived in Washington, D.C., in the fall of 1913 they made a formidable political team, and set about making their mark. FDR dedicated himself to his work under Secretary of the Navy Josephus Daniels, a conservative who was very close to President Wilson. FDR negotiated contracts for ship stores and naval supplies and traveled frequently to inspect ships and crews. Louis Howe had come along to Washington to serve as FDR's assistant, and he spent as much time working to build Roosevelt's political reputation and connections as he did on naval matters. FDR quickly won a reputation as an active and responsible administrator.

Eleanor, too, played a very important role in the social politics of the nation's capitol and in furthering her husband's career. As had been the case for more than one hundred years since the founding of Washington, D.C., much of the real politics in town took place in society parlors and at parties. Washington wives created the social circuit where their husbands' deals and friendships were cemented, and established wide networks of social connections of their own. Eleanor was no stranger to a world of parties and social connections, but she saw that the social scene in Washington, D.C., could really make or break a political career in a way that the endless round of balls and events in New York City never could. In Washington Eleanor built upon her experience in Albany and became a consummate hostess and political wife whose job it was to further raise her husband's political fortunes. Eleanor also established connections of her own as she gained confidence and political knowledge.

Eleanor made the circuit of social visits required of every good political wife and opened her home on K Street, which she had rented from Aunt Bye, to frequent guests and social activities. Each weekday during the political season, Eleanor called on the wives of congressmen, Supreme Court justices, senators, diplomats, and other important officials. Eleanor's social calls consisted of stopping for short conversations or, if the lady of the house was occupied with other visitors, merely leaving a card to announce that she had come. Eleanor noted that in the midst of all this social activity, "my shyness was wearing off rapidly." Although she took to the required round of calls with gusto and an almost manic energy, Eleanor received a warning from Aunt Bye that she must beware of keeping her conversations and calls too brief—it seemed that Eleanor engaged herself in the *process* of social calling but was less interested in the *content* of polite conversation. Eleanor opened her own home to callers one day a week, and kept careful records of the social networks she built over time for herself and her husband.

Almost every evening the Roosevelts went out to cocktail parties, dinners, or formal balls that further enhanced their social and political position, or they entertained in their home. Now free of Sara's direct day-to-day control, Eleanor managed a large household staff and gave frequent dinner parties of her own. Guests thought her graceful and elegant, though quiet, and she complemented FDR's frisky personality and abundant charm. The couple entertained both Democrats and Republicans, and they openly used their family connections to cement friendly ties with English and French diplomats, and with such major figures as the crusty old man-about-town Henry Adams, grandson and great-grandson of two former presidents. Eleanor also presided over Sunday evening dinners with "The Club," a close network of friends and political allies that included Interior Secretary Franklin K. Lane, Lathrop Brown, and several Roosevelt and Astor cousins. Political business and sometimes military matters were discussed in Eleanor's dining room and parlor, where she encouraged a lively and convivial atmosphere at Sunday dinners.

Despite all of the time-consuming social activity, Eleanor later wrote of her early years in Washington that "the whole of my life remained centered around my family." She gave birth to her last two children in this period, a second Franklin Jr. in 1914 and John in 1916. Eleanor no longer brooked any bullying from her hired nurses and governesses, and she even dispensed with a wet nurse and breastfed Franklin Jr. herself, but hired staff still took responsibility for most of the day-to-day childcare. It is a mark of the Roosevelt's wealth and social standing that Eleanor found it worth mentioning in her memoirs that she devoted a whole hour to caring for her children before they went to bed each night. Motherhood was less socially isolating than it had been during Eleanor's younger years, and she continued her Washington, D.C., social schedule even while pregnant with Franklin Jr. and John—sometimes even receiving callers while sick in bed.

In 1914 Eleanor hired Lucy Mercer as a social secretary to help deal with her demanding schedule. Mercer was the daughter of a socially prominent but recently impoverished Catholic family, and her responsibility was to keep track of Eleanor's appointments and visits. Mercer soon became an important part of the Roosevelt family's life as well, and Eleanor appreciated how easily Mercer incorporated herself into the Washington, D.C., social scene. Because of her own background, Mercer was a suitable and convenient figure to fill out any social gathering that needed a single woman. By the summer of 1916, Lucy Mercer was spending increasing amounts of time alone in the company of FDR, even staying in Washington, D.C., with him when Eleanor went to Campobello during her final pregnancy. Mercer and FDR were seen out together frequently, and Eleanor's cousin Alice openly encouraged the relationship. For the time being, however, Eleanor's attentions were focused elsewhere. After remaining at Campobello and Hyde Park longer than usual into the fall of 1916 because of John's birth and an outbreak of polio in the capital, Eleanor returned to Washington, D.C., and moved her family into a larger house on R Street.

Betrayal

The entrance of the United States into World War I in April 1917 changed the atmosphere in the nation's capitol, and all the Roosevelts were affected. Eleanor's brother Hall Roosevelt and cousin Quentin, Teddy's son, enlisted in the military as pilots (Quentin was killed in France). Eleanor's grandmother was astounded that the men did not hire substitutes, as her husband had during the Civil War. FDR, who had run unsuccessfully in the Democratic primary for United States Senate in September 1916, focused on his responsibilities in the naval department once the war began.

Eleanor also wanted to do her part for the war effort, but her first public foray turned out to be embarrassing. When asked by a journalist to describe how wives in Washington could contribute to the war effort, she guilelessly told of how she instructed her staff of ten domestic servants to economize. When the article was published, she of course appeared to be ridiculously out of touch with real life in the nation, and even FDR could not refrain from pointing out how silly and privileged she sounded.

Eleanor eventually found genuine forms of service. The war curtailed much of the social scene in Washington, especially the formal calls required of political wives, and Eleanor turned the energy thus freed to new fields of action that the war opened for her. Regaining some of the social commitment and confidence of her youth (she aptly titled the section of her autobiography that covered the war years "Growing Independence"), she volunteered in a Red Cross canteen and worked for the Navy Department. By all accounts she took to her new occupations with great enthusiasm. Eleanor's chauffeur taught her how to drive—a skill she relished for the rest of her life—so that she could deliver supplies for the Red Cross. She also knitted for soldiers and sailors and held social meetings for the wives of visiting foreign dignitaries who had come to Washington to consult on war matters. Eleanor's talents as a successful fund-raiser for charitable causes gained admiration from those who had been used to seeing her in mere social settings around the capitol. Eleanor balanced her family, social, and patriotic duties as she bundled the children off to school, visited wounded men in Washington's naval hospitals all day, and then often returned home to give dinner parties.

Eleanor's volunteer work during the war gave her a new sense of mission and purpose in life and awakened in her a belief that she might be able to make her own contribution to society, separate from that of her husband. She claimed that through visiting the wounded she "became a more tolerant person ... more determined to try for certain ultimate objectives." Eleanor worked so hard she almost wore herself out, but continued on through painful headaches and fatigue. The work seemed worth it, though, and she later remembered: "I had gained some assurance about my ability to run things and the knowledge that there is joy in accomplishing a good job. I knew more about the human heart." All too soon, Eleanor found out how vulnerable her own "human heart" might be.

In July 1918 as Eleanor continued with her war work and the children were at Hyde Park, FDR sailed for Europe on the destroyer *Dyer* to inspect U.S. naval facilities. When he returned in September he, like the rest of the crew, was gravely ill with influenza. The flu soon turned into pneumonia, and FDR was confined to bed at Hyde Park. Eleanor had to nurse her husband, five sick children, and three servants who also had contracted the flu. While FDR was still bedridden, Eleanor came across a bundle of letters from Lucy Mercer in one of FDR's drawers. We do not know how many of the letters Eleanor read or exactly what they said, but their contents quickly made clear to her that Mercer and FDR had been having a passionate affair. Even though she had always been the more reserved of the couple and FDR was notorious for his flirtations, Eleanor apparently had never faced the possibility of real betrayal, and by all accounts she was crushed.

Eleanor knew that infidelity, among other of her father's peccadilloes, had destroyed her parents' marriage, and she was not anxious to travel down the same long and painful path to separation. Although in serious psychological and emotional pain, Eleanor showed signs of her increasing strength of character and growing independence in the way she dealt with the marital crisis. She confronted FDR, and in the midst of what must have been an emotionally charged atmosphere at Hyde Park, they negotiated over whether and how they could continue their lives together.

First, Eleanor offered her husband a divorce. Since the 1870s, liberalized divorce laws had made the permanent dissolution of marriage a more viable option, and several of Eleanor's relatives had been divorced. FDR seriously considered her offer. It was clear from his behavior over the ensuing decades that his deep attachment to Mercer was unbreakable and that he had transferred his affection from Eleanor to Lucy, but in 1918 there were strong factors arguing against divorce. To begin with, Sara wholeheartedly disapproved of this option when Eleanor and FDR revealed the problem to her. FDR's mother told him in no uncertain terms that divorce would ruin his family's reputation, and she threatened to cut off his inheritance if he left Eleanor. Lucy Mercer's Catholicism made it unlikely that she would marry a divorced man anyway, so

FDR would have faced a life with no wife even if he continued his connection with Mercer. Perhaps most important, FDR realized that a divorce would end his political career. (Two years later, Mercer married Winthrop Rutherford, a rich widower twice her age.) FDR decided to decline Eleanor's offer of divorce, but that still left the couple to figure out how they could continue to live together. Eleanor demanded that he promise never to see Mercer again, a promise he later broke many times over, but FDR made the promise to remain with his family and continue his public career.

When Eleanor offered FDR a divorce in 1918, she joined the increasing number of Americans who were beginning to accept that marriages might end, although the couple would have faced social stigma and his political career could not have continued.

Divorce laws had slowly been liberalized in the United States over the course of the nineteenth century, and by 1916 the divorce rate had soared to one in every nine marriages. Adultery was the most common reason for divorce to be granted, but many states began to recognize "mental cruelty" as grounds for divorce as well.

Some social activists argued that divorce could liberate women from oppressive marriages, but divorced women also faced a battle to support themselves and any children in their custody. Stricter divorce laws, some of them akin to the labor legislation designed to protect women that Eleanor supported, forced divorce rates down in the 1920s.

Eleanor was hurt to the core by FDR's betrayal. He had been the focus of her love and devotion, and her life since marrying him had been given over completely to creating a family for him and fostering his career and well-being. Her pain and humiliation intensified when it became clear that many people around Washington, D.C., had known that her husband and Mercer were lovers. One of the ways Eleanor sought solace in the wake of the revelations about FDR's infidelity was to drive herself often to Rock Creek Cemetery and there sit in front of the brooding statue by Augustus Saint-Gauden that was known as "Grief." It had been commissioned and set in a grove of holly trees by Henry Adams in memory of his wife, Marian Hooper Adams, who had committed suicide when she learned her husband had been unfaithful.

The Roosevelts presented a united image in this family portrait from mid-1919, despite the tensions between Eleanor and FDR. Standing: Anna, Elliott, and James. Seated: Franklin Jr., FDR, Eleanor, Sara Roosevelt, and John.

(Courtesy of the Franklin Delano Roosevelt Library)

Later in life Eleanor wrote: "There is a price to pay for love, for the more happiness we derive from the existence and companionship of other human beings, the more vulnerable we are when there is any cause for apprehension." In her own marital difficulties, Eleanor faced the consequences of what she called the "purifying fire" of devotion to another person.

The marriage was not soon repaired, although both tried to restore a degree of mutual respect and affection. Eleanor, however, never completely forgave FDR for the terrible pain he had inflicted on her. The intimacy disappeared from their relationship forever, and her sons later claimed that after the Mercer affair, Eleanor and FDR never had sex again. As the couple struggled to patch up their relationship, they sailed together on an official trip to Europe in January 1919, and although relatives reported that they seemed more in love than ever on the trip, Eleanor continued to suffer. Biographer Blanche Wiesen Cook suggests that Eleanor's mental pain from the revelations about FDR's extramarital affair might even have brought on an eating disorder, as for years after Eleanor appeared to show signs of anorexia, including an increasing malformation of her mouth and teeth.

Eleanor had chosen, as did the vast majority of women in the early twentieth century, to shape her life around her family, but to an even greater degree than most, she had invested a large amount of time and energy actively contributing to her husband's career. The fact that she and FDR brought Louis Howe into the discussions of the future of their marriage testifies to the link between their personal and professional lives. Most historians agree, with varying degrees of psychologizing, that Eleanor was changed by her husband's affair. She certainly continued to be a valuable social and political asset to FDR, but she built upon the independence that had begun during the war years and emerged as a distinct personality in her own right. How much of this was due directly to the marital crisis is difficult to say, but following the decision to stay together, the couple found it possible to move beyond the loss of intimacy and discover a new dynamic in their relationship.

Increasingly after 1918 Eleanor and FDR would act together *and* as individuals. Eleanor appears to have decided that she would no longer totally subsume her public self into her husband. Eleanor's private self is more elusive, as she wrote little about the Mercer affair, but she clearly emerged from the war years and from FDR's betrayal with a new resolve to live her life differently.

Failed Vice Presidential Bid

America was not a nation at ease in the months after the war. Racial tensions, heightened by great numbers of African Americans who were turned out of their wartime jobs to be replaced by returning white soldiers, broke out into riots in several cities around the country, including Washington. Eleanor evinced little open interest in racial equality at this stage; she did not consider the oppression of African Americans much of an issue in her daily life in 1919. At one point she fired her white household staff and replaced them with an entirely African-American workforce, but this probably was done in defiance of her mother-in-law's and cousins' beliefs that blacks could not be trusted. Beyond providing employment for individual staff members, Eleanor demonstrated none of what later became a commitment to challenging racism. Other signs of social unrest hit near home for the Roosevelts in 1919. Following the Russian Revolution and the rise to power of the Bolsheviks in the new Soviet Union, the United States attorney general, A. Mitchell Palmer, had launched a virulent domestic anti-communist campaign that turned into a hysterical Red Scare. Disregarding civil liberties, Palmer hunted down and jailed radicals whom he suspected of being disloyal citizens. In revenge, anarchists blew up his house on R Street, which was located directly across the street from the Roosevelts' residence. Eleanor returned home from a dinner party to find a pile of rubble in place of Palmer's house and the need to comfort her son James, who was home at the time of the explosion, which blew off part of their roof and broke all the windows on the first floor of the house.

Despite these disturbing developments in the immediate aftermath of World War I, Eleanor continued her public works. She spent time visiting the wounded at St. Elizabeth's Hospital in Washington, where conditions during the war had so horrified her that she entreated Interior Secretary Franklin K. Lane to investigate and improve the treatment of the physically and mentally ill veterans. She was invited to act as a translator at social events during the International Congress of Working Women, but even though her eyes were opening to human suffering and she enjoyed meeting the delegates, their labor politics still seemed quite remote from her elite world. Among the delegates were Rose Schneiderman and other labor organizers who later would become Eleanor's close friends and political allies, but at the time she "had no idea how much more I was going to see of them in the future." As the war work slowly came to an end, Eleanor continued her charitable fund-raising and also lavished more attention on her children.

Eleanor, who was thirty-five years old in 1919, also experienced a shifting of the generations among her clan that year. Her uncle Theodore died while she and FDR were touring Europe during the Paris Peace Conference, and Eleanor was unable to attend his funeral. Grandmother Hall, who had largely raised Eleanor after her mother's death and whom she counted as one of the greatest influences on her life, died after the couple returned to the United States in August. Eleanor's remarkable and beloved Aunt Pussie, Edith Livingston Ludlow Hall Morgan, perished just a few months later in an apartment fire in Greenwich Village. As Eleanor was assuming a position of more adult authority among her own relatives, she also started to redefine her relationship with her mother-in-law, who spoiled her grandchildren and still exerted a large measure of influence over FDR. Although Eleanor remained polite to Sara, she put her foot down more often.

Eleanor began to spend more time with Sara at Hyde Park after FDR resigned from his post as Assistant Secretary of the Navy and returned to the practice of law. FDR had argued with Josephus Daniels and with President Wilson over several issues, and the president had been none too pleased that the Roosevelts had entertained the English politician Sir Edward Grey and others who opposed Wilson's position on the League of Nations. FDR desired to leave his post before too much fallout ruined his future political chances, so he withdrew from public office in 1920. While FDR moved back into private life, contemplated a variety of money-making schemes, and pondered his future political moves with Louis Howe, Eleanor reestablished housekeeping in New York, then moved the children to Campobello for the summer.

While Eleanor settled into the summer house, FDR attended the 1920 Democratic Convention in San Francisco, where he was one of the most vocal supporters of the reform candidate Al Smith, his previous nemesis in the New York state legislature. After an extremely contentious convention, which ended up almost dead-locked, James M. Cox, the governor of Ohio, was nominated for president, and he unexpectedly chose FDR as his running mate. Although FDR had supported Smith, he was still seen as a strong Wilsonian, and Cox hoped FDR would help him draw on Wilson's postwar popularity. Eleanor was shocked at the news of FDR's nomination when she received a telegram from Josephus Daniels but immediately prepared to re-enter the political fray. Husband and wife rendezvoused at Hyde Park, where FDR delivered his acceptance speech outdoors to thousands of supporters and the press, who trampled on Sara's lawn and disrupted her privacy.

After finishing out the summer at Campobello and packing twelve-year-old James off to boarding school at Groton in September, Eleanor joined FDR on the campaign trail. The pair embarked on a month-long train tour across the country that took them as far west as Colorado. Along the way FDR spoke for hours at every stop and spent time plotting strategy and playing cards with inside advisors. Eleanor attended all of his speeches and played the role of supportive wife, but found herself ill at ease on the campaign trip and spent much of her time reading alone in her rail berth. Eleanor claimed to be particularly perplexed when it came to dealing with the press because she had never spoken directly with newspaper reporters before out of allegiance to her grandmother's instructions that "a woman's place was not in the public eye." Eleanor's discomfort was heightened by the fact that she was the only woman along on the trip.

Instead of withdrawing entirely, however, Eleanor found a new friend and political educator in her husband's longtime advisor, Louis Howe. Eleanor had treated Howe indifferently for years, put off by his disheveled appearance and his closeness to her husband, but in the forced proximity of the whistle-stop tour she now warmed to Howe as he cultivated a new relationship with her. She wrote in her memoirs that Howe "made an effort on this trip to get to know me. ... He knew that I was bewildered by some of the things expected of me as a candidate's wife." Howe visited Eleanor in her berth to discuss politics and the press, and as the trip proceeded their friendship grew. She found their wide-ranging conversations enlightening and forged a close relationship with Howe, the first of many she would form with political advisors and compatriots. Howe, who was trusted by both principals, became an important link between her and FDR. Although Eleanor was along to promote her husband's candidacy, as she saw more and more of the country, her own mind and heart were opening to the wider world as well.

Eleanor's new experiences were short-lived, however, and came to an end in November when Cox and FDR lost by a landslide to Warren G. Harding and Calvin Coolidge. One of the factors that contributed to Harding's victory was the number of votes cast for him by newly enfranchised Republican women, a fact that discouraged many Democrats and feminists, who believed that the ratification of the Nineteenth Amendment in September 1920 would usher in a new era of Progressive politics supported by female voters. Instead, women's votes seemed as divided as men's.

Eleanor had never been a great advocate of women's rights during the long fight for suffrage, but with her political awareness growing daily, she took a new interest in the political world created by voting women. Although she had paid little attention to the issue of voting rights as late as the spring of 1919 when Alice Wadsworth, a senator's wife, had tried to talk her into supporting the cause, by the following year Eleanor became what she called "a more ardent citizen and feminist than anyone about me in the intermediate years would have dreamed possible." Eleanor was increasingly interested in pursuing policies of social reform, and she realized that "you could get far more attention if you had a vote than if you lacked one."

Politics and Polio

When the Roosevelts moved back to New York City following the 1920 campaign, FDR returned to the practice of law in his new Wall Street firm Emmet, Marvin, & Roosevelt, but he soon became bored. To add variety to his professional life and to pump up the family income, FDR took a job as vice president and head of the New York office of the Fidelity & Trust Company of Maryland, a large surety bonding company. He received a salary of twenty-five thousand dollars a year for what was essentially part-time work, since he split his days between the bond company office and his law firm.

FDR's schedule was coordinated by an attractive new secretary who had joined his staff during the campaign, Marguerite "Missy"

LeHand, a woman he had come to rely on and who became a permanent part of FDR's entourage. Over the next few years, Missy was an increasingly important part of FDR's life. Eventually moving in with the family, she remained close to him—arranging his personal and social life and acting as an official hostess when Eleanor was absent—until her death in 1944. To many observers over the following years, LeHand seemed to be a second wife to FDR.

For her part, Eleanor found that she was bored by formal high-society charity work that allowed her little contact with the actual people who needed aid. Moreover, the vice-presidential campaign had whetted her appetite for politics, which she entered for the first time on her own terms when she got involved late in 1920 with the newly formed League of Women Voters. Carrie Chapman Catt and other leaders of the National American Woman Suffrage Association founded the League as a lobbying and educational institution for newly enfranchised women. Unlike Alice Paul and the more radical feminists who founded the National Women's Party to continue the political fight for women's equality, League members worked to make women into educated, individual citizens and assumed that larger issues of social equality would naturally work themselves out in the process.

The League focused on traditional concerns of the elite female reform community such as protective labor laws that granted women workers special legal protections, but which also kept them from being considered equal or earning wages equal to men. The League forced politicians to pay attention to women voters and issues that concerned them such as pure food; however, League women were not ready to give up the idea that femininity gave women a special status that sometimes set them apart from men. The League, for example, opposed the Equal Rights Amendment when it was proposed by the National Women's Party in 1923, because it might erase women's "special" status.

The clearly political, yet markedly feminine, nature of the League made it the ideal organization for Eleanor's emergence into public work. Although at first Eleanor was wary when Narcissa Vanderlip, the New York state chair of the League who was both a society lady and a social activist, asked her to join the state board of the organization and to coordinate national legislative reports, she agreed to take on the task. She professed little knowledge of legislation or of the process of law-making, but she was willing to adopt the attitude of "learn as you go" that would serve her well for years in public endeavors of all kinds.

FDR's mother was distressed that Eleanor was at home less than she had been in previous years and worried that her daughter-in-law was neglecting social engagements, but Eleanor ignored Sara's criticism and took to her new legislative tasks with eager interest. To help with her legislative reports, Narcissa Vanderlip connected Eleanor with Elizabeth Read, a fiercely intelligent lawyer who lived in Greenwich Village with her companion Esther Lape, an English professor. Eleanor later recounted that she felt inadequate when she first met the highly educated and articulate Read, but she quickly decided: "I liked her at once and she gave me a sense of confidence." Read marked copies of the Congressional Record with issues of interest to the League and passed them to Eleanor along with instruction about any issues that might confuse her. This enabled Eleanor to complete her legislative reports after spending one morning a week studying at Read's law office.

As she grew more interested and more confident, Eleanor spent increasing time with Read and Lape, who became close friends and helped to shape her public activism and political interests throughout the early 1920s. Read and Lape were part of a generation of female intellectuals who had forged independent lives for themselves, in part by rejecting marriage and embracing long-term female relationships. Although Eleanor never commented on the physical and romantic side of Read and Lape's lives together, she enjoyed their company and close relationship, much as she had Mademoiselle Souvestre's during her school days. Their intellectual and emotional kinship awakened in Eleanor a sense that she was "drifting far afield from the old influences" and although she did not entirely ignore her family responsibilities, she openly acknowledged that she "was thinking things out for myself and becoming an individual." Much as her growing friendship with

Louis Howe had opened Eleanor's eyes, her new relationships with Read and Lape provided her support as she moved even further into the public.

The League of Women Voters was not the most radical female political organization of the immediate post-suffrage era, but that did not mean it was timid or uncontroversial, and it took quite a bit of backbone for Eleanor to remain committed to the League. FDR was sometimes displeased with Eleanor's newfound devotion to the League and to outgoing women, but he also helped her with legislative reports and on occasion spent time discussing politics with his wife and Elizabeth Read. Eleanor attended the League's New York state convention in January 1921, only to hear the organization denounced by the state's governor.

When she went to the League's national meeting in April, she met an even wider array of political women, some of whom were of a lower social class and a more militant frame of mind than those with whom she regularly mixed, but Eleanor came away energized and more committed than ever to the political work sponsored by the League. She supported the League's work to establish a World Court and the League of Nations, and she continued to write reports and began giving speeches to small groups after returning to New York. Her work on legislative issues and her blossoming ties to Elizabeth Read and Esther Lape convinced Eleanor that she could effectively engage in activism on her own terms.

Although she was becoming a public woman by the day, Eleanor did not abandon her family role, and she spent the summer of 1921 at Campobello as usual. All the children, now teenagers, enjoyed their vacations from school, and the whole family spent time in vigorous outdoor activities and water sports. Louis Howe, along with his wife and son, spent an extended vacation at Campobello, and Eleanor enjoyed their companionship, especially because FDR stayed in the city for most of June and July.

After FDR joined the family at Campobello in August, he sailed and swam as usual but soon complained that he felt tired and out of sorts. One day, after emerging from a swim, FDR felt a chill and fearing a cold, took to his bed. The next day, he was running a high fever and felt no better, so Eleanor sent for the local doctor, who at first thought FDR had indeed contracted a cold. After another three days, his fever was joined by serious pain, and his legs began to show signs of paralysis. Eleanor sat watch by FDR's bedside, but he showed no improvement and the local doctors were not able to confirm a diagnosis. Finally, after three weeks, Eleanor sent for a prominent Newport physician and polio specialist who confirmed their worst fears—FDR was suffering from a full-blown case of polio.

FDR and Eleanor exit the water at Campobello in 1920.

(Courtesy of the Franklin Delano Roosevelt Library)

Polio, or "infantile paralysis" as it often was referred to in the 1920s, was a serious and life-threatening illness of epidemic proportions in the first half of the twentieth century. The potentially fatal viral infection was highly contagious, and Eleanor worried that her children would be infected because the disease appeared most often in young people. The whole family had often dealt with serious illness, as witnessed by their previous bouts with influenza, pneumonia, and typhoid fever, and FDR's polio represented another in the series of potentially devastating illnesses. With the exception of the death of baby Franklin in 1910, the Roosevelts had always been lucky to recover fully, but this time FDR's health was seriously compromised. The polio virus spread outward from his brain and spinal chord through his central nervous system, to cause permanent muscle weakness and partial paralysis in his legs.

The long-term consequences of FDR's illness were unclear when he first fell ill at Campobello, however, and the family struggled to deal with the immediate circumstances of his infirmity. Doctors advised that FDR could be treated more thoroughly in New York, so Eleanor and Louis Howe arranged to have FDR loaded on a stretcher and carried to a boat for a trip down the coast. FDR, in terrible pain, was worried that local residents would see him, and Howe was equally concerned to keep full details of his affliction out of the newspapers, so the whole operation was conducted as secretly as possible. An ambulance met their boat and carried FDR to the Presbyterian Hospital in New York, where he underwent treatment for two months. Even in the early stages of FDR's bout with polio, Howe seemed clear that the public must not know the full extent of his illness, lest his future political chances be damaged. Eleanor was more immediately interested in her husband regaining his health, and she hoped that treatment might take away some of his pain and restore his mobility.

When FDR was discharged from the hospital he was no better, and Eleanor's new independence and strength of character were put to the test. On one hand, she exhibited devotion to FDR and stayed by his side as his constant nurse and companion when the children went back to school. She spent a torturous winter helping hired nurses with FDR's medical care. Plaster casts were applied to his legs to help stretch his atrophied muscles, and Eleanor had to help lift her husband in and out of bed.

On the other hand, Eleanor also had to deal with larger issues of how FDR's illness was to be treated and whether he had any future as a public man. His mother was convinced that he had become a permanent invalid, and she insisted that he retire to Hyde Park, where he could live the rest of his days as lord of the manor and a pampered cripple. Eleanor and FDR were not convinced this was the best course, and he continued to hope for years that various treatments would improve his mobility, even long after it was clear that he had sustained permanent muscle damage.

Eleanor suffered terrible emotional strain during what she later called "the most trying winter of my entire life." Louis Howe moved into the Roosevelts' townhouse during the week and spent days at FDR's office trying to keep alive his chances for a future public career. Eleanor appreciated having his supportive presence so near, but her house was filled with people and turmoil as Howe came and went along with the children, Sara, and a procession of nurses. Eleanor kept a certain emotional distance from the children, particularly from Anna, who was unhappy in her new school and who felt the stress of FDR's illness as well. It was her inability to comfort the children in times of crisis such as this that would lead them for years to portray her as cold and unfeeling, even though she was lavishing every attention on FDR and his medical care.

The pressure got to her early in 1922, when she was no longer able to "shut up like a clam" and to put her own emotions aside. One evening while reading to her sons, Eleanor broke down crying and could not stop sobbing for hours. She retreated to a room in her mother-in-law's part of the house to pull herself together, but later she thought this was the closest she ever came to having a complete emotional breakdown. Eleanor had clearly been unhappy before, not the least when she found out about FDR's affair with Lucy Mercer and offered to divorce him, but that turmoil had been more or less settled, and she had struggled to put the upheaval behind her as she became involved more in politics and public affairs. FDR's polio showed her that her position was fragile.

Eleanor was still defined by her role as FDR's wife. On top of her worry for her husband's health, the whole family had to confront whether the course that FDR's career had defined for them could or would continue. It was not clear that FDR would ever be able to resume a public role again.

Soon after the dark days of the winter of 1921–22 Eleanor, FDR, and Louis Howe decided that they would do whatever it took to give FDR that chance. FDR retired to Hyde Park to work on strengthening his legs, Louis Howe continued to plan his reentry into politics, and Eleanor prepared to take her own career as a public woman to a new level. As FDR worked to overcome the effects of the virus that had afflicted him, Eleanor regained her emotional strength and faced the opportunity to act as a public stand-in for her husband. For the time being, Eleanor would become the most visible and the most political Roosevelt.

Chapter 4

Becoming a Political Wife and Social Activist

I used to laugh at Louis [Howe] and say one could not plan every move in this world, one had to accept circumstances as they developed.

—Eleanor Roosevelt,
This I Remember

By 1922, when FDR retired temporarily from the public scene, Eleanor was already well-fitted to pick up the responsibilities thrust on her. Once it became clear that FDR faced a lengthy convalescence, Eleanor was not reluctant to step into the spotlight. Her commitment to social causes and her knowledge of politics had grown exponentially since the days of her first volunteer work during World War I, and her involvement in the League of Women Voters and her friendships with Louis Howe, Elizabeth Read, and Esther Lape had given her confidence and a new impulse to political action. Howe and FDR encouraged her in the hope that her visibility would keep the public focused on Roosevelt accomplishments so that FDR could someday make a smooth re-entry into politics.

Meanwhile, FDR made gestures toward resuming his work as vice president of the Fidelity and Deposit Company of Maryland, which had continued to pay his salary during his illness, but he focused most of his efforts on physical recovery—FDR was convinced that with enough rest and exercise he would one day regain normal strength in his legs. It was years before he accepted the fact that he had a permanent disability. Howe, who was nominally employed by Fidelity and Deposit as FDR's assistant, strongly urged FDR to continue to plan for a further career in politics. As Eleanor recalled in her memoirs: "Mr. Howe felt that the one way to get my husband's interest aroused was to keep him as much as possible in contact with politics."

Eleanor moved into the role of FDR's political surrogate. For the first time (but far from the last) she acted as FDR's field operative, investigating issues and becoming an information conduit who introduced him to issues and new political personalities. But because her woman's viewpoint was different than FDR's, she nurtured political interests that were not identical to her husband's, and she pursued her own course through the political world. Eleanor became involved with a wide variety of organizations, particularly women's organizations, in the 1920s—many of which were more radical than any FDR would have belonged to. Eleanor's activities during the 1920s bridged her past career as a wife and her future career as a politician as she worked both for her husband and for herself.

Eleanor's first opportunity to carry on the Roosevelt involvement in party politics came in the spring of 1922 when she was invited to speak at a fund-raising luncheon by Nancy Cook, the assistant to the director of the newly created Women's Division of the New York Democratic State Committee. Although she had been involved at League of Women Voters conventions and she was used to speaking in small meetings, Eleanor was leery of larger-scale public speaking. Her first reaction was to turn down the invitation, but at Howe's urging she accepted. She later remembered of the speech: "I trembled so, that I did not know whether I could stand up."

Despite her fears, she gave a successful speech and the luncheon raised more than one thousand dollars—she had always been a highly successful charity fund-raiser—but at this stage of her life, speaking at public venues made her nervous, perhaps a relic of the shyness of her youth. Eleanor liked political activism, but it took a long time for her to become relaxed as a speaker. In later years, she was known for her easy fluency at a podium, but when she first began speaking to groups, her remarks (delivered in her peculiar high-pitched public speaking voice) often were punctuated with nervous giggles. What she said was impressive, however, and shortly after the luncheon Eleanor was appointed chair of the Finance Committee of the Women's Division. Her own career in partisan politics had begun.

The decade of the 1920s marked a turning point in women's activism and feminist politics. After women gained the right to vote when the Nineteenth Amendment was ratified in 1920, female activists turned their energy in several different directions. In 1923, Alice Paul, leader of the National Woman's Party, proposed the Equal Rights Amendment, but several women's groups, including the League of Women Voters, to which Eleanor belonged, opposed the amendment because they feared it would harm their other concerns.

Many elite women and labor activists continued to pursue legislation that would provide special protection for mothers and female workers, instead of granting them full equality. With record numbers of women entering higher education and employment outside the home, a significant number of young women scorned political activism altogether, convinced that the liberated "flapper" era had already loosed women from social constraints.

That same spring Eleanor also solidified her commitment to women's reform causes by joining the Women's Trade Union League (WTUL) after the social activist Mrs. James Lees Laidlaw invited Eleanor to a WTUL luncheon. The WTUL was the most prominent group in the country that encouraged labor organization by and among women workers. Founded in 1903 by the AFL activist Mary Kenney, the WTUL had forged ties between a generation of American working women and middle- and upper-class women such as Eleanor who were drawn to more elite settlement house and reform work. By 1922, the WTUL had a mixed membership ranging from poor and radical working women to extremely wealthy socialites who put their money to work for the cause of women's labor organization and reform.

The New York branch of the WTUL was directed by Russian-immigrant factory worker Rose Schneiderman, a fiery organizer and public speaker who had become involved with the WTUL through her membership in the Jewish socialist United Cloth Hat and Cap Maker's Union. Schneiderman and Eleanor had met years earlier when Eleanor volunteered as a translator at the International Congress for Working Women in Washington, D.C., but they really got to know one another for the first time through their respective involvement in WTUL. Eleanor invited Schneiderman and Maud Swartz, another organizer, to dinner at the Roosevelt New York townhouse and later to visit Campobello, although they were women whose backgrounds and political opinions horrified many in her social group, including her mother-in-law. Over time, Eleanor developed a true friendship with Schneiderman and Swartz based on a common commitment to labor reform.

Initially, Eleanor's activities in the WTUL touched only on safe and familiar ground—fund-raising and social organizing. She presided over WTUL Christmas parties for poor children, and she raised money to help purchase a permanent headquarters building for the League on Lexington Avenue in New York. But she also began to acquire the deep commitment to fair labor practices and fair wages that would mark much of her public stance during the New Deal. By 1926 the WTUL had given Eleanor her first sustained up-close look at the world of "real" working women, and she had become sufficiently radical to take to the streets in a march to support striking paper-box makers. Without a doubt, Eleanor's work in the WTUL and the friendships she established with working women and labor activists advanced her political education and opened her eyes to a wider world of reform work.

Eleanor also in 1922 formed an attachment to two new friends: politician Marion Dickerman and her companion Nancy Cook, who had invited Eleanor to speak to the Democratic women. Cook and Dickerman, who were a bonded couple, were veteran political activists and had been involved in the suffrage fight, war work, and formal politics for years. As she had only a few years earlier with Elizabeth Read and Esther Lape, Eleanor took an immediate liking to these vibrant, smart women and began spending time with them at political occasions and privately. She later wrote: "Miss Cook and Miss Dickerman and I had become friends in just the way that Miss Lape and Miss Read and I had been first drawn together through the work we were doing. This is one of the most satisfactory ways of making and keeping friends."

Dickerman and Cook became the most important of Eleanor's friends during the 1920s, both personally and professionally, and the threesome was inseparable for most of the next fifteen years. Dickerman and Cook lived together in a Greenwich Village apartment, where Eleanor became a frequent guest. Dickerman had been the first woman to run for the New York State legislature in 1919, in a campaign managed by Cook, and had made an impressive showing as a Republican candidate who attracted support from many women's and reform organizations and many Democrats. Both women were highly educated teachers, and their articulate involvement in politics (both had switched to the Democratic Party by 1922) helped set the pattern for Eleanor's own partisan activities. They both provided emotional kinship for Eleanor and helped guide her path in public activism.

Because Eleanor tended to form strong emotional attachments to people who became her closest political advisors—Howe, Read, Lape, and now Marion Dickerman and Nancy Cook—some of her biographers have speculated that as Eleanor moved out into the public sphere she sought emotional support to soothe the wounds inflicted by FDR's infidelity and his illness. Although the husband and wife certainly were redefining their relationship in the 1920s, Eleanor seemed to have room in her heart for FDR and for a series of other close associates. It was during this decade that Eleanor and FDR began to form the unique relationship that enabled them to thrive as a political couple in the 1930s. They were close allies who cared for one another and who worked well together, but they each looked to others for their immediate emotional needs.

Democratic Party Operative

The Roosevelts moved to Hyde Park in the summer of 1922, and Eleanor had her first full-fledged test of political organizing in the Dutchess County Democratic Party. As FDR spent his days trying out remedies that promised to restore his strength, Eleanor went to work organizing the women of the county in preparation for the state Democratic convention in September. FDR was learning to use crutches, and Eleanor remarked: "Each new thing he did took not only determination but great physical effort." Meanwhile, she got out and cultivated the upstate political networks. She cemented a connection with Elinor Morgenthau, who lived nearby with her husband Henry Morgenthau Jr., and eventually Elinor became involved in both local and state party organizing with Eleanor.

Although Eleanor had built up years of interest and study on national issues—particularly labor and women's causes—in the fall of 1922 she devoted herself to the hands-on tasks of the political party activist for the first time. FDR supported Al Smith as the Democratic candidate for governor against newspaper publisher William Randolph Hearst, and Eleanor took up the banner for Smith. She held parties for the prominent women of the county, gave speeches in local towns, and blasted the Republican opposition in the newspapers, which always took an interest in her day-to-day political activities.

Smith was nominated in September, and after Eleanor led the celebration at the convention, her commitment to practical organizing accelerated. Some things she observed in rural Dutchess County disturbed her: "It was rather sordid in spots ... I saw how people took money or its equivalent on election day for their votes and how much of the party machinery was geared to crooked business." But overall Eleanor was energized by the work and by the "fine people in unexpected places."

On election day Eleanor personally drove voters to the polls, and although Smith narrowly lost in Dutchess County, he won the statewide election by a landslide. Eleanor's work had been so great and so visible that many people expected Smith to offer her a paid position in his administration, but she was content to continue on her own political path. Rose Schneiderman, Marion Dickerman, and Nancy Cook all were guests at Hyde Park that fall. No doubt there was much discussion of how reform work and party work could go hand in hand.

At the same time her public career seemed off to a running start, Eleanor still had to attend to family matters. FDR was trying to get along without professional nursing care, and Eleanor assisted in caring for him while also providing frequent updates about the political situation to raise his spirits. She oversaw Elliott's departure for Groton and prepared for the older boys to leave for Harvard. She tried to stay involved with her children, nursing the boys' football injuries and bringing them to WTUL charity Christmas parties, but she later admitted that she was still unable to completely close the emotional distance between herself and her offspring.

Physical distance between the family members also became a factor when FDR moved to Florida to stay on a series of houseboats for the winters. Although the warm weather was thought to be good for FDR's health, Eleanor never enjoyed the tropical conditions and objected to the lavish, wild parties that FDR sometimes threw on the boats. While FDR spent his time swimming, fishing, and searching for new business ventures, Eleanor stayed mostly in New York and focused on political work. This was the beginning of a pattern the couple would follow for the rest of their lives: FDR and Eleanor frequently lived apart and seldom found the same people, places, or activities to be sources of relaxation or stimulation.

With her new circle of friends and political connections growing ever larger and more intense, Eleanor soon moved in ever more daring political directions. In 1923, she agreed to be one of the judges of the competition for the Bok Peace Award, a fifty thousand dollar prize offered by the former publisher of *Ladies Home Journal* to the author of the best plan for how the United States could contribute to world peace and how to end world wars. Esther Lape was in charge of coordinating the prize competition, which found Eleanor sharing the judging with some of the country's foremost diplomats, government officials, and academics, including Henry Stimson and Ellen Fitz Pendleton. FDR submitted as an entry a plan for a "Society of Nations," and in the contest both he and Eleanor showed their commitment to internationalism, which would become a great part of Eleanor's work with the United Nations in the 1940s.

When the prize panel recommended that the United States subscribe to the World Court, Eleanor, Lape, and the others came under Senate investigation for activities considered "Un-American" by isolationist conservatives. Although the controversy earned Eleanor her very own FBI file, which eventually would fill thousands of pages of material reporting on her "suspicious" activities over the years, she remained committed to the winning plan and worked to support the World Court when Congress contemplated membership in 1925. Not for the last time, Eleanor learned that courage in the face of very public criticism was necessary to build effective political coalitions. She also learned that sometimes ignoring your most radical critics was the best way to carry on with the work at hand.

Eleanor put all of her newly honed political courage and skills to work during the 1924 presidential campaign. By now a familiar face on the political scene, Eleanor delivered speeches, organized women voters, became a convention delegate, brought labor reform issues to the national party platform, and engaged in one of the most strident conflicts over the rights of women in the Democratic Party to date. By 1924 Eleanor was seen as one of the most prominent female Democrats in New York—maybe one of the most important Democrats of either sex. She edited and published a newsletter on political issues for Democratic women, working with Marion Dickerman to write the articles and single-handedly raising money to keep the publication going.

Nineteen twenty four marked a transition in Eleanor's political career: She integrated her commitment to women's rights and reform causes with her political party activism as she sought a new level of recognition for women within the Democratic Party. At the state party convention in Syracuse in April 1924, Eleanor worked closely with Caroline O'Day, the head of the party's Women's Division, and joined Dutchess County's other delegate, Henry Morgenthau Jr., to support Al Smith for president. Smith was the firm choice of the convention, but Eleanor was unhappy with how the male state party leaders were going about choosing Smith's delegates to the national convention that would be held in June. She gave a strident speech to the convention (reported on by *The New York Times* in a front page article) and demanded that women be allowed to choose female delegates, who should make up one half of the New York delegation. Tammany Hall boss Charles Murphy refused to recognize her nominations from the floor, but Eleanor achieved success anyway when she headed a committee of women who negotiated control over the selection of Al Smith's female delegates.

Looking every inch like the purposeful social reformers and political activists they were, Ester Lape and Eleanor strode toward the entrance to a government building in Washington, D.C., in 1924.

(Courtesy of the Franklin Delano Roosevelt Library)

National Democratic Party leaders took note of Eleanor's leadership in New York, and she was appointed to head a women's platform committee that was slated to incorporate female concerns into the national platform. Eleanor assembled a formidable group of female political activists who recommended planks on child labor, a living wage, equal pay for equal work, and membership in the League of Nations to the national party after studying the matters for three months. The women's platform presented a list of a wide-ranging reform and political issues that had been championed by women over the previous decades, including several highly controversial matters as the enforcement of Prohibition, a thinly veiled denouncement of the Ku Klux Klan, and support for the Shepard-Towner Act, which provided health care for poor mothers and their infants.

The 1924 Democratic national convention was incredibly rancorous, and Eleanor did not escape unscathed. Al Smith, who had FDR give his nominating speech, was engaged in a tough bout with William McAdoo for the presidential nomination, and conflicts broke out over the party's approach to Prohibition and southern race relations. Even more disappointing to Eleanor was that the official platform committee ignored her women's committee planks and would not even allow her or other women into their meetings. She led groups of women who planted themselves outside the doors of back-room meetings, but she was never able to break in and have her say. While on the convention floor, Eleanor tried to look calm as she sat quietly knitting, but she silently seethed at being ignored. Eleanor later wrote that the 1924 convention allowed her to see "for the first time where women stood" in politics, and she was not happy with second-class status.

Eleanor's best moment at the convention came not as an active politician in her own right, but as a political wife. Standing at the podium with his legs in heavy braces and propped up by sixteen-year-old James, FDR gave a stirring speech, which most in attendance thought marked the high point of a dismal convention. The convention would be remembered more for FDR's speech than for the ugly political battle that culminated in a deadlocked vote after

106 rounds of ballots. In the end, neither McAdoo nor Smith was nominated, and John W. Davis, a Wall Street lawyer who became the party's last-minute nominee, proved a very weak opponent to Calvin Coolidge, who was elected for another term. Eleanor's involvement in Democratic politics in 1924 showed how far she had come from the timid wife who left the 1912 convention because she felt overwhelmed by the tumult. However, she and the women she supported still had a long way to go to be taken seriously on their own terms.

Val-Kill

Following the 1924 convention FDR returned to his convalescence. Louis Howe was pleased at his reception from the convention crowd and at the public accolades Eleanor had been drawing for her work, despite her snubbing by the platform committee, but FDR was not quite ready to completely resume his place on the public stage. FDR remained active by serving on the boards of public organizations such as the New York branch of the Boy Scouts, duties he could accomplish from behind the scenes but which still brought him public attention.

He spent much of his time in Florida, where he enjoyed the warm temperatures and the easy proximity of the ocean and fishing, but in the summer of 1924, he was introduced by financier George Peabody to the place that would became his second home. Peabody owned a ramshackle resort at Warm Springs, Georgia, where the main attraction was a large swimming pool of eighty-eight degree water, fed naturally year round by a remarkable underground spring. Peabody claimed that a local youth who had been paralyzed by polio had recovered the use of his legs by swimming in the pool.

When Eleanor and FDR visited Warm Springs in October, she was not impressed. The hotel on the property was run down and in need of major repairs, and the guest cottages were even worse. The resort was set among red-clay Georgia hills that to her eyes were not inviting. Worse, from Eleanor's point of view, the resort was strictly segregated, as could only be expected in the heart of rural Georgia. Her adamant inquiries about local racial relations caused an immediate reaction against her among the local white people who ran the resort.

FDR, however, was completely enchanted by Warm Springs as soon as he was lowered into the pool. The warmth of the water and its natural mineral buoyancy allowed him to swim and exercise as he had not been able to since polio struck him. When this experience was coupled with the promise that long-term exercise and therapy in the warm waters might return to him the use of his legs, FDR was convinced that Warm Springs was the place he needed. Even though Eleanor could barely stand to spend a night at Warm Springs, FDR embraced it completely. After two years of visits to the resort and promoting it as a therapeutic center for the treatment of polio victims, FDR bought the resort from Peabody, paying nearly two hundred thousand dollars, even though the purchase put him and his family at considerable financial risk.

Literally until the end of his life, FDR cherished Warm Springs and spent as much time there as possible. While at Warm Springs, where he built a cottage for himself (a more elaborate house, which came to be known as the "Little White House," was constructed in 1932), he was usually attended to by a network of friends and by his secretary, Missy LeHand. FDR spent endless hours in the natural spring waters, swimming and exercising, and then he would repair to his cottage for work on his correspondence or the cocktail parties he so loved.

Eleanor did not enjoy Georgia any more than she had Florida and spent even less time with her husband as her schedule grew increasingly busy. She was unenthusiastic when FDR bought the spa property at Warm Springs, investing a large share of his personal capital at a time when his expenses were outrunning his income, and she was distressed when he invested in rebuilding the spa as his own therapeutic center devoted to the rehabilitation of polio victims. And she hated the harsh racial climate of Georgia and could not make herself comfortable among the local whites, who came to see her as a meddling threat to their comfortable way of life.

FDR could barely afford his indulgence in buying Warm Springs, since he lost money during the 1920s in a series of speculative businesses that included a slot machine enterprise and a plan to build zeppelins for commercial travel. He also for a time acted as the figurehead for a Canadian firm that hoped to make money by speculating in the inflated German mark. Most of FDR's income came from a New York law partnership he had formed with Basil O'Connor in 1925. He still had his trust fund and his mother's frequent disbursements for support but found it hard to pay some bills on time during the 1920s. Eleanor achieved increasing financial independence through payments received for her frequent speaking engagements and for the occasional radio talks and articles she published in a wide variety of periodicals. Jointly, the Roosevelts were extremely wealthy by the standards of the day, but even in the financial realm, FDR and Eleanor were beginning to travel diverging paths.

By 1924, the pattern that would carry them through the next twenty-plus years of marriage seemed set. Eleanor and FDR were very attached to one another, and they provided vital political and personal support, but they each pursued their own interests and existed day by day in their own respective orbits. Eleanor was still defined in public by her status as FDR's wife, but she had taken on new importance in her own right—politically and intellectually. Most of all, she *felt* freer to do things she felt drawn to do and she expected FDR's support, as he expected hers. From a very traditional beginning, the Roosevelts had evolved a very modern marriage.

Perhaps the greatest symbol of their marriage's flexibility backed by fundamental commitment came in August 1924 when FDR agreed to pay for and construct a home for Eleanor on the grounds at Hyde Park. One day, while the family was on a picnic with Marion Dickerman and Nancy Cook by a stream on the estate, the idea was hatched that Eleanor ought to have her own residence, something of which she had dreamed since her marriage more than twenty years earlier. Having a permanent home near Hyde Park would allow Eleanor to establish a base from which to operate, even when Sara closed the main estate over the winter months.

Perhaps because he was pursuing his own interests in Warm Springs, FDR decided the time was right, and offered Eleanor and her two friends a life-interest in the piece of land. He hired architect Henry Toombs to design the Dutch Colonial stone cottage and took a personal interest in the drafting and construction process. By 1925 the new house, dubbed "Val-Kill," the Dutch name for the stream that ran nearby, was completed, and Eleanor was delighted to have her own space. Val-Kill became a symbol of Eleanor's independence and accomplishment; she later hosted many heads of state there, and the house currently is the only National Historic Site dedicated to a former first lady.

Val-Kill definitely was not planned as a family space (although its grounds did include a swimming pool for FDR and the children), but rather as a home for Eleanor. Nor did she go there to seek a life of solitude; instead she nurtured independent friendships and kinships with her female associates. Although Eleanor remained close to Louis Howe during these years, she pulled her women friends into a tight circle around her. When Eleanor occupied the house in April 1926, Marion Dickerman and Nancy Cook moved in with her. The three women created their own political and personal sphere that emphasized the bond between them, and they even had their intertwined initials embroidered on the new towels in the house. FDR didn't object; he was busy in Georgia with Missy LeHand, among others. Although other people eventually would take their places at the center of Eleanor's universe, Nancy and Marion were Eleanor's closest confidantes throughout the 1920s, and even after their relationship with Eleanor dissolved in the late 1930s, they continued to live at Val-Kill until 1947.

While Eleanor was building a new social life with Dickerman and Cook, she still struggled in her relationship with her children. Eleanor achieved a new confidence and vigor in the outdoors and took her younger sons on hikes and camping trips, but the older children were more of a concern. She bristled at the tales of drunken abandon in some of James' letters from his first year at Harvard, and she worried that he would end up with the "wrong" woman or with the socialite he met in England while bicycling. Anna graduated from high school in 1925, and after a disastrous season in Europe with her grandmother, Eleanor and FDR convinced her to try a short college course at Cornell University. Anna soon dropped out of school, married stockbroker Curtis Dall, moved into an expensive apartment given to her by Sara, and gave birth to Eleanor's first grandchild in March 1927. Eleanor still felt that she not only lacked a vital connection with Anna but that she exercised little influence over her still-immature children's decisions, a feeling (with some considerable justification) that would only grow worse with time.

In the meantime, Eleanor had plenty of work to distract her from family troubles and obligations. As soon as Eleanor had moved into Val-Kill in 1926 she began to plan a business venture with Dickerman and Cook. Cook was a talented craftsperson and woodworker and a devotee of the Arts and Crafts design movement and made most of the furniture for the house at Val-Kill—partly Arts and Crafts and partly reproductions of early American pieces. Building on that experience, the women decided to create a commercial furniture factory that would enable Cook to expand her production and to sell pieces for a profit.

The furniture factory established at Val-Kill in 1927 fit into the American tradition of Arts and Crafts design, which had been popular since the turn of the century. Although the design movement began in England, the American version took its own direction.

Prominent proponents of American Arts and Crafts, also known as mission style, such as Gustav Stickley, designed simple, native-wood furniture that matched similar architecture and landscaping. American colonial-style furniture was also popular in the 1920s, the same decade Colonial Williamsburg was planned. Nancy Cook designed both mission and colonial-revival furniture, and other designers mixed the two styles.

While English Arts and Crafts furniture and decorative objects were hand-made, and therefore extremely expensive, Americans mass-produced their goods in factories, designed to further improve the American workforce by providing training and jobs. Val-Kill was intended to provide jobs and to manufacture simple, beautiful, American furniture.

Eleanor, Dickerman, Cook, and their close Democratic Party associate Caroline O'Day put together money and incorporated

Val-Kill Industries. FDR strongly supported the venture, as he was interested in finding employment for rural craftsmen around Hyde Park to keep the sagging rural economy moving. Dutchess County had lost many young people who were looking to the city for employment, and as a traditional patron of the area, FDR wanted to reverse the trend. Eleanor's furniture venture provided the means for FDR's ends and creating work for the underprivileged in a model craft workshop fit in with the economic and labor agenda of the female Democrats as well. Eleanor also started a weaving class sponsored by the Hyde Park League of Women Voters, hoping that someday Val-Kill might also produce textiles. The idea to create jobs for underemployed wageworkers also prefigured some of the labor programs championed by the Roosevelts during the New Deal.

The partners erected a workshop building behind the house at Val-Kill, and the furniture factory opened in 1927. Contrary to their original plans, however, Nancy Cook, who directly supervised the furniture production, found that the local farm workers did not have sufficient woodworking skills to follow her designs. In the end Val-Kill industries hired mostly immigrant men from Norway and Italy who were already trained in the craft of furniture-making. Although Eleanor reported that FDR was disappointed in their failure to provide local employment, she noted that: "He always accepted things as they were and set such experiences aside as something to remember and perhaps use in the future."

The Val-Kill furniture factory produced beautiful work, and both Eleanor and FDR purchased a good deal of the product—he furnished the spa at Warm Springs with Cook's productions. Eleanor invited important clients to view the furniture in her New York house and at Hyde Park. Although Eleanor never made much profit from the enterprise, her participation showed the flexibility and ingenuity inspired by her new, expanded partnerships with her husband and her female friends.

Soon the threesome of Eleanor, Dickerman, and Cook (and probably Caroline O'Day) expanded their interest to Todhunter

School, a girl's preparatory academy in Manhattan. Dickerman was the vice principal of the school, which had been founded by the Oxford-educated Winifred Todhunter to offer high-society girls a polite but rigorous education. When Todhunter decided to return to England in 1926, the Val-Kill partners saw their opportunity to make a real mark on society and purchased the school outright, using mostly Eleanor's money. Dickerman continued to run the school, but Eleanor joined the staff as a teacher in 1927, adding a regular slate of classes to her schedule.

Eleanor viewed her teaching assignment as completing a circle that had begun with her own school days with Marie Souvestre, and she approached the task with great enthusiasm and vigor. Eleanor taught the high-school-aged girls American history, drama, and literature, and encouraged them to research and discuss current events. Although they were educating young female members of conservative upper-crust New York society, Eleanor and Dickerman adopted very progressive attitudes about education, and Eleanor's students, some of whom were the daughters of her political associates, adored her. Eleanor found teaching very satisfying, and although she was (as ever) modest about her accomplishments, she knew that her classes "were more practical than ... many of the courses given to sixteen- and seventeen-year-old girls." She was still apt to defer to Dickerman on policy matters because of her lack of college education, but Eleanor was blossoming intellectually and thrived on the attention from her pupils.

Eleanor, Cook, and Dickerman each took the lead in separate aspects of their enterprises. Eleanor edited the *Women's Democratic News*, a newsletter they published and distributed widely throughout New York, and she taught at Todhunter. Cook was in charge of the Val-Kill furniture production. Dickerman was principal of the Todhunter School. The fourth partner, Caroline O'Day, did not play a definite, day-to-day role as the others did, but she was immensely wealthy and probably provided funds for all the projects when needed.

By the late 1920s Eleanor was extremely busy, constantly on the run between Todhunter in New York City, Val-Kill, and a slew of public engagements and political events. She spoke on the radio to promote the educational efforts of the Women's City Club of New York, of which she was an officer. She went flying with Amelia Earhart and longed to take flying lessons herself. At Hyde Park she hosted Carrie Chapman Catt and four hundred other women who were meeting to support the Kellogg-Briand Treaty and to denounce warfare in the fall of 1927. She personally wrote much of the copy for *Women's Democratic News,* raised the operating funds for the Women's Division of the state party, and continued to keep up political contacts. Eleanor gave ever more frequent speeches and championed labor reform in front of the state legislature in Albany. She began to publish articles in national magazines such as *Redbook, McCall's,* and *Success Magazine,* for which she found she could earn impressive sums of money.

Back to Albany

FDR had intentionally stayed out of the political limelight for the most part since 1922, desperately trying to rehabilitate his body and slowly building his network of supporters. Louis Howe and the Roosevelts had calculated that FDR should, except for a few occasions such as his 1924 nominating speech for Al Smith, continue to lay low until 1932, when the time would be ripe for FDR to re-emerge fully into public life and run for governor of New York State. Accordingly, FDR declined a chance to run for the U.S. Senate in 1926. However, their plan was disrupted in 1928, when both FDR and Eleanor were thrust onto the center stage of American politics by the presidential candidacy of four-term governor Al Smith.

Both Eleanor and FDR supported Smith, a Roman Catholic from New York City, although in private they doubted that he could overcome the widespread Midwestern and Southern prejudice against Catholics or that his personality and New Yorkese accent would translate well to the national scene, despite his great popularity in New York State. Nonetheless, they threw themselves into the campaign to win the Democratic Party nomination for

Smith. Eleanor attended the New York State Democratic Party convention in April and seconded Smith's nomination as the state party's choice as a presidential candidate. When Smith's aide Belle Moskowitz asked Eleanor to head the Women's Division of Smith's national campaign office, she consented and gathered a team of her friends and political operatives to work for the candidate.

She did not go to the Democratic national convention in Houston (Blanche Wiesen Cook claims her absence was because of a relapse of her occasional depression), but Elinor Morgenthau, Caroline O'Day, and Marion Dickerman attended as either delegates or alternates and FDR acted as one of Smith's floor managers. FDR gave a powerful nominating speech, which Eleanor listened to on the radio, and the convention nominated Smith easily, avoiding the extreme rancor of the 1924 Democratic convention.

Eleanor was convinced that Smith's progressive social policies would be good for the country but worried about Smith's lack of support for protective labor legislation for women and children and for Prohibition. Nonetheless, she threw all of her energies behind his candidacy. As she would so often later do with FDR, she tried to change Smith's mind on several issues by constantly expressing her opinion to him and arranging meetings with people who she hoped would be able to influence the candidate. For example, she attempted to broaden Smith's view on labor reform by introducing him to Florence Kelley. However, Smith resisted her efforts and eventually she was willing to accept his "practical knowledge of how to achieve political results."

The major surprise of the fall was FDR's reluctant decision to run for governor as Smith's replacement. FDR retreated to Warm Springs in September after he tired of being ignored by Al Smith's advisors. However, as the national campaign went on, it appeared that Smith was in danger of losing in New York State. Smith decided that if FDR ran for governor, it would boost his own chances to capture the state's electoral votes, so he began a high-pressure campaign to get FDR to agree. For weeks, FDR resisted Smith's pressure to allow nomination by the Democrats of New

York State but finally, on October 1, despite Louis Howe's protests that the time was not yet right, FDR agreed to stand as the Democratic candidate for governor.

Eleanor did not want to return to Albany as wife of a governor, but she had reluctantly come to believe that nothing more could be gained by keeping FDR out of the political arena. Although FDR had not regained the use of his legs, Eleanor "wondered how much more could be achieved" by more months of attempted rehabilitation. She personally penetrated FDR's defenses and called him when he was hiding out at Warm Springs, putting New York party officials on the line to ask him whether he was willing to run. Faced with a genuine draft movement, FDR accepted the nomination and became the Democratic Party candidate for the governor's office.

As soon as FDR decided he would forsake his rehabilitation and make his return to active politics as an office seeker, he threw himself with great vigor into the campaign against the strong Republican candidate, Albert Ottinger, the popular state attorney general. Although he was well-known among the state's potential voters, FDR had to counter the Republicans' sly accusations that as a cripple he was not up to the physical challenge of the governorship. FDR told the press he would campaign in every part of the state in order to demonstrate that his disability was not a bar to serving as governor. As he told a press conference: "A Governor does not have to be an acrobat. We do not elect him for his ability to do a double back flip or a handspring. The work of the Governorship is brainwork." FDR campaigned during the first weeks by train, traveling to the conservative western New York counties where he spoke mainly on behalf of Smith and the national Democratic ticket. He then changed tactics and began to pound the Republicans on purely state issues, aided by Samuel Rosenman, a young lawyer assigned to the campaign as a speech writer (Rosenman became one of FDR's trusted and long-term aides). In what came to be recognized as the great Roosevelt speaking style, he used humor and ironic ridicule to make his points to the voter. For example, a speech attacking the Republican policy on turning hydroelectric power resources over to private business began: "This is a history and a sermon on the subject of water power, and I preach from the Old Testament. The text is 'Thou shalt not steal.'"

FDR campaigned during the final weeks by car, which allowed him more and closer contact with the voters. He traveled to small hamlets and villages where no train could go, and he spoke at a side range of venues, including the smallest rented public halls. During the last three weeks of the campaign, he traveled more than thirteen hundred miles and gave fifty speeches. He demonstrated conclusively that his physical strength was up to the demands of even the most rigorous campaigns, and he laid to rest any questions about his health.

Meanwhile, Eleanor had become co-chair of the National Women's Committee of the Democratic Party and practically lived at the national party headquarters, where she directed a staff that included her new and trusted secretary Malvina "Tommy" Thompson and Grace Tully, who would become one of FDR's staff members after the election. Eleanor wrote of their breakneck schedule: "In 1928 I was still fairly young and could put in prodigious hours of work, but I sometimes wonder how any of us, particularly Miss Thompson and Miss Tully, lived through that campaign. It proved that work is easier to carry if your heart is interested." Eleanor carefully executed plans to target the votes of defined Democratic female constituencies, and she approached her duties as any clever party boss would—with ruthless determination. She paused in September only long enough to get her youngest son John settled in as a boarder at Groton.

The Roosevelts' division of the political labor was notable, as Eleanor stayed focused on the national campaign even after her husband became the gubernatorial candidate. She seldom campaigned with him and joined him back in New York only for the final push for votes. FDR aimed to become governor, but the Roosevelt political team had their eyes firmly focused on the entirety of the Democratic Party and its national structure and agenda. Eleanor was gaining political know-how and experience that would become vital when it was FDR's turn to run for president.

In November, Smith was soundly drubbed by Herbert Hoover, amassing only a little over fifteen million votes to the Republican's more than twenty-one million. The early returns in New York State made it appear that FDR also was to be beaten, but after a fretful night the official results gave FDR the office of governor by a margin of slightly more than one-half of one percent. After a long absence, the Roosevelt family moved back to Albany, and FDR assumed an office that had historically been a stepping-stone to the presidential nomination.

Many biographers have stressed the reluctance Eleanor felt upon becoming first lady of New York State; however, it was not a reluctance born of political timidity. Eleanor did not resent the opportunity to become a public figure; she was more concerned that she might be unable to continue the public role she had fashioned for herself in the preceding years. Eleanor also appreciated the marriage that she and FDR had built, in which both of them worked as a united team but were free to find their daily companionship with others. Eleanor saw a transformation in her husband: "Once back in public affairs, Franklin's political interest and ambitions reawakened," and he was full of ambitious plans for reorganization and legislation in New York.

Eleanor balanced the demands on her time with extreme efficiency. Her campaign work for Smith had enhanced her national reputation and she was sought out by the press, which painted her as a typical supportive wife of the late 1920s who managed the household and attended to wifely duties. Although Eleanor did these things, she also preserved her own sphere of action as a separate individual. She commuted back and forth between Albany and New York City, where she continued to teach at the Todhunter School several days a week, and she kept up her end of the furniture factory partnership.

New York state trooper Earl Miller was assigned as Eleanor's chauffeur and bodyguard when she was first lady of New York State. He remained her close friend and confidant for the rest of her life.

(Courtesy of the Franklin Delano Roosevelt Library)

During her absences from Albany, Missy LeHand served as FDR's hostess in the governor's mansion, and Eleanor seemed unperturbed when rumors about the pair began to circulate. In the summer of 1929, she took her younger sons on a tour of Europe and left FDR alone with his secretary and the entourage of admirers who seemed to constantly surround him. For his part, FDR did not object to Eleanor's continued closeness to Dickerson and Cook. Whatever damage FDR's affair with Lucy Mercer had inflicted a decade before, the couple seemed by 1928 to have agreed to let one another seek their own happiness; even to tolerate what appeared to be open affairs on both sides.

A case in point was Eleanor's relationship with her new driver and bodyguard, New York state trooper Earl Miller. Soon after being assigned to guard Eleanor, the tall, handsome Miller was drawn into her inner circle and he formed a close bond with her, one that was doubtless romantic and might also have been sexual. Eleanor and Miller gave all those around them the impression of the closest shared intimacy by their behavior. Miller, who always referred to Eleanor as "Lady," was one of the few people in Eleanor's life who was allowed to treat her on completely informal, physical terms, touching and holding her while in the company of other friends—often to their amazement. Miller and Eleanor spent a great deal of time together, and he took her horseback riding and introduced her to outdoor sports. Miller accompanied Eleanor to social functions when FDR was away, and she kept a room nearby for him wherever she traveled. Dickerman and Cook especially were displeased with the lavish physical attentions Miller paid to Eleanor and his demonstrations of affection, choosing perhaps not to acknowledge that she returned his attentions.

After gossip about the connection began, FDR was unperturbed, even though he was well-acquainted with Miller's reputation as a renowned womanizer. Miller married the first of his several wives in 1932 in part to quiet public rumors that he and Eleanor were having an affair. Eleanor even encouraged him to publicly date Missy LeHand at one point, but through it all Eleanor and Miller never altered their close association. FDR rather pointedly refused to take Miller to Washington after the election of 1932, but Eleanor and Miller continued to meet, mostly in New York; often at Miller's upstate retreat at Lake Chazy.

Historians and biographers have drawn no final conclusions about Eleanor and Miller, because neither of them ever fully explained their relationship and almost no known letters between them survive. For his part, Miller resolutely refused all his life to discuss any personal details about Eleanor. However, it is certain that Eleanor's relationship with Earl Miller demonstrated her independence from FDR, the continued support they afforded one another, and their resolve to remain public and private allies.

FDR's and Eleanor's political alliance took on new potency once he was governor of New York. Eleanor later wrote: "Many people have suggested to me that when Governor Smith asked my husband to run for the governorship, while he himself was running for the Presidency, he had it in mind that he would still be able to direct the work of the governor," but that proved to be far from the truth. To banish the lingering influence of Al Smith, FDR quickly got rid of his advisors and cronies who had sought to extend their influence over the new governor. Eleanor particularly encouraged FDR to dismiss Belle Moskowitz, with whom she had worked on Smith's national campaign, because she knew Moskowitz's loyalties remained with Smith. If he kept Moskowitz, Eleanor told her husband, "It will always be one for you and two for Al."

Eleanor later wrote about the misconception that FDR would be Smith's puppet in the governor's mansion:

> In many ways Governor Smith did not know my husband. One of Franklin's main qualities was that he never assumed any responsibility that he did not intend to carry through. It never occurred to him that he was not going to be governor of New York with all the responsibility and work that position carried.

FDR set about assembling a set of close supporters, including Eleanor herself, who helped plan his policies. His New York gubernatorial advisors such as Sam Rosenman, James Farley, Henry Morgenthau Jr., Raymond Moley, Adolf Berle, and Rexford Tugwell later formed the backbone of his presidential cabinet and his famous "Brain Trust." Meanwhile, Louis Howe remained in New York City and concentrated on planning for a presidential run in 1932.

Eleanor exercised considerable influence on her husband's appointments and decisions, another pattern that followed them to the White House. For example, she introduced him to Molly Dewson, the civic secretary of the Women's City Club, who urged FDR to appoint Frances Perkins, formerly of the Consumers'

League and a state official under Al Smith, to the post of labor commissioner. Eleanor was always modest about her role in Perkins' appointment, but she had preached the merits of Perkins and other female appointees to her husband. Eleanor went along when FDR attended governor's conferences—and she certainly was the most politically accomplished state first lady in her own right. Although she proclaimed that she was "retired" from politics now that FDR was back as a real leader, the truth was that she really only shifted her influence, downplaying her activities in partisan organizations but pursuing every opportunity to advance any cause that was important to her.

Path to the White House

On the morning of October 24, 1929, the American stock market, which had soared throughout the 1920s, started to collapse. Prices declined sharply, and by the end of the day the stocks of many American companies went into free fall. Despite brief rallies over the next few days and attempts by major business players such as J. P. Morgan and John D. Rockefeller to shore up the market, the crash continued. Within weeks, stocks had lost forty percent of their pre-collapse value, and it became clear that the domestic post–World War I boom economy had crumbled and that the United States could look forward to the same severe conditions that had already racked many European countries. Confidence in the economy evaporated as rapidly as had stock prices, and as businesses cut back on investment and production, unemployment rose to astronomical levels and consumer spending sank to new lows.

Moreover, there was no safety net to catch people when their incomes disappeared. There were no nationwide welfare or relief systems, no unemployment insurance, no agencies for the homeless, no government healthcare. Except for underfunded state and local programs (which were quickly exhausted) and feeble private charities (symbolized by soup kitchens that offered a limited number of free meals), people had no place to turn for aid as the economic depression deepened during 1930.

Eleanor's occasional bouts of depression, what she referred to as her Griselda moods, were far from an uncommon experience for women at the turn of the century. Many women in the late nineteenth century, particularly of Eleanor's social class, were diagnosed with "nervous temperaments," and given to debilitating mood swings. While many women of Eleanor's generation silently bore their mental difficulties, depression increasingly came to be seen as a treatable medical condition following the turn of the century.

By the late 1950s and 1960s, feminists such as Betty Friedan began to argue that the stifling social restrictions forced upon many women caused some of their depression. Social activists in the 1970s made mental health a feminist issue, and more women changed their lives or sought treatment. Even with a rise in the medical interpretation of mental illness today, women are more likely than men to be diagnosed with depression.

Herbert Hoover, who had ridden roughshod over Al Smith on his way to the presidency, was an intelligent and humane man, famed for his work in aiding starving war refugees in Europe, but he was caught in an intellectual trap that limited his ability to respond to the massive economic and social crises. For many months he simply acted as a cheerleader, asserting that the economy would correct itself and that the mounting depression was only a downturn in the natural economic cycle. He also genuinely feared that if the federal government interfered by making attempts to correct the economy—or worse, sapped the character of Americans by offering governmental welfare to the unemployed—the very foundations of the nation would be threatened. As with many conservatives at the time, his mindset could not encompass what was happening to the nation.

As a result, Hoover and his Republican administration failed to deal with the realities of American life after 1929, leaving the way open for someone like FDR, who owed little to any philosophical position, and whose mind and will were flexible enough to embrace new approaches to solving the human catastrophe of the Great Depression. As governor of New York during the first three years after the crash, FDR demonstrated his flexibility and willingness to act; for example, he pushed through the state legislature relief measures far beyond anything previously imagined and set up a state agency to deal specifically with the social emergency.

Almost all of the major issues that had engaged Eleanor during the 1920s were intensified by the effects of the Great Depression. Her response was to continue her work with groups such as the Women's Trade Union League to promote employment for women, even in a time of massive unemployment. She slowly came to recognize that direct relief was required in the face of mounting human suffering, and she began work with new organizations; for example, finding housing for unemployed women. She also increased her support of union organization by women. Moreover, she intensified the pitch of her lobbying with FDR, reinforcing his inclination toward government activism. Some of his new advisors deeply resented her access to FDR and the constant din of her opinions, but as also would be the case after FDR was elected president, they could do nothing to silence her or prevent FDR from listening when it suited him.

Perhaps the most important development to emerge from these first years of the national crisis was that both Eleanor and FDR came to believe firmly that it was the duty of government at all levels—including the federal—to alleviate distress and promote the general economic and social welfare of its citizens. That they arrived at this position, given their starting point as members of an elite and privileged segment of society, was remarkable. Throughout the rest of their lives these beliefs separated them from traditionalists who could not shake off the dead hand of the past— as the Roosevelts had done successfully—when times called for new thinking and new action.

As was subsequently made clear during the 1930s, Eleanor was somewhat in advance of her husband and deepened her commitment to the concept of activist government as the years went on. FDR was much more cautious, and once he attained the White House, he tempered his actions in response to political necessity. Although Eleanor was constantly vexed by his political pragmatism in the face of what she saw clearly as injustice or social needs, she nonetheless drew comfort from the fact that she always had

FDR's ear and that she shared with him a basic understanding of what should be done.

After FDR was reelected governor of New York in 1930 in an immense landslide—his margin of victory was three quarters of a million votes and he won areas of the state where no Democrat had ever prevailed before—it was clear that he was on a course to win the Democratic nomination for president in 1932. Although this might have seemed like a major opportunity for Eleanor to achieve a position to influence nation events, it was clear from her behavior and comments to her friends and associates that she felt strongly conflicting emotions. Although the Women's Division of the New York State Democratic Party had done much to aid FDR's victory in 1930, Eleanor had kept her own involvement at a low pitch, and she maintained a low profile throughout the subsequent run-up to the nominating convention in 1932. The thought of moving from her secure place as an independent politician and social activist to the role of First Lady of the nation carried much anxiety for Eleanor, and it effectively dampened her enthusiasm.

On the other hand, FDR and his advisors plunged into the fight to win the nomination. These were the days when party conventions still selected the nominees, and the conventions themselves were controlled by party bosses and power brokers who operated mostly behind the scenes to make and unmake deals. The Democratic Party convention in Chicago during the summer of 1932 was no different. FDR's campaign was managed by James Farley and Louis Howe, who skillfully manipulated state delegates and FDR's rivals, and—after striking deals with Speaker of the House John Nance Garner of Texas, who was put on the national slate as the vice-presidential candidate, and with press baron William Randolph Hearst, who demanded a pledge from FDR to maintain isolationist policies—FDR was nominated as the party candidate.

Breaking with the long tradition of candidates waiting weeks to receive the official news, FDR decided on a bold stroke and loaded Eleanor and two of their sons, along with secretaries, bodyguards, and aide Sam Rosenman, onto a plane and set out for Chicago to accept the nomination in person. Strong headwinds slowed down the flight, but the party arrived in Chicago after nine hours of travel to be greeted on the tarmac by the other Roosevelt children and a triumphant Farley.

Once at the convention, FDR made his way to the podium and, standing in his heavy leg braces, delivered a stirring speech— mostly drafted by Rosenman and Raymond Moley but incorporating fragments from Louis Howe—in which he ended with a ringing peroration pledging a "new deal for the American people" and asking the Democrats in the audience to "constitute ourselves prophets of a new order of competence and courage." Newspapers picked up the phrase "New Deal," and it became permanently attached to FDR's programs and proposals.

Eleanor, on the far left, along with daughter Anna, Newton D. Baker, FDR, son James, and campaign chairman James Farley appeared on the rear platform of the candidate's train on a campaign stop in Galion, Ohio, in August 1932.

(Courtesy of the Franklin Delano Roosevelt Library)

FDR's vigorous manner of speaking, which belied his physical disability, and a strong national party organization boded well for his election in the fall. Even more important was a political coalition that formed behind his candidacy. A mix of voters that included members of organized unions and African Americans joined millions of Americans who were suffering from the Depression to support FDR. Moreover, President Herbert Hoover, who had been renominated by the Republicans, failed to counter his image as an ineffectual officeholder who had done little to remedy or mitigate the effects of the economic disaster that had overtaken the nation.

Eleanor took little part in the presidential campaign and was out of sight for most of the summer and fall. She joined the candidate's entourage for a few campaign swings, but for the most part her voice was muted and she seemed to withdraw into herself. She was sharply distressed when FDR repudiated the League of Nations during the campaign, as he had bargained he would with Hearst in order to assure the nomination, and for weeks she gave him the silent treatment that all those around her—family and friends included—recognized as a signal of her intense disapproval.

In the nearly seven decades since, historians have volleyed back and forth about the philosophical consistency of Herbert Hoover and the seeming vacillations and inconsistencies of FDR. At the time, however, during the summer and fall of 1932, there was almost no doubt at all: Hoover stood for the wealthy and the property owners of America who blamed the Depression and unemployment on everything and everyone except themselves; FDR stood for a vigorous movement toward experimentation and change that would try any reasonable tactic so long as it brought relief.

On Election Day, after voting at Hyde Park, the Roosevelts went to New York City to await the returns at party headquarters and at a suite at the Baltimore Hotel. As the reports rolled in from across the nation, it soon became clear that FDR had won a landslide victory. Hoover carried only six states, and FDR tallied 22,800,000 votes to Hoover's 15,750,000, which would mean a 472 to 59 victory in the Electoral College. The Roosevelts were going to Washington once again, but this time to the White House. Reflecting on the victory later, Eleanor wrote: "I was happy for my husband, because I knew that in many ways it would make up for the blow that fate had dealt him when he was stricken with infantile paralysis; and I had implicit confidence in his ability to help the country in a crisis." Then she added: "But for myself I was deeply troubled. As I saw it, this meant the end of any personal life of my own."

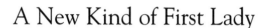

Chapter 5

A New Kind of First Lady

But if I didn't do what I think is the right thing to do, I
wouldn't be satisfied with myself. Everyone must live their
life in their own way and not according to anybody else's
ideas.

> —*Eleanor Roosevelt,*
> *White House press*
> *conference,*
> *May 15, 1933*

The period between FDR's election in November 1932 and his inauguration in March 1933 was one of the most crucial in American history. The economic chaos gripping the country deepened, and a nationwide panic took hold. It was no exaggeration to say the very fabric of society seemed threatened by collapse and dissolution, and many feared a revolution was not far away. Democracy and capitalism, the twin pillars of American civilization, faced powerful tests with no assurance of the result.

Although her political activities during the decade leading up to FDR's election had demonstrated her formidable attributes, it would have been difficult to predict in November 1932 that Eleanor would emerge as the most important and powerful woman in the country, a revolutionary figure who transformed the role of First Lady during her twelve years in the White House (the most of any president's wife) and dominated much of public life during the New Deal. Her image, thrust into the spotlight by her unrelenting activity and advocacy for her social and political agendas, became one of the most familiar of the 1930s and 1940s.

Moreover, FDR—a man who had been such a lightweight in his youth as to have earned the nickname "feather duster"—became one of the two or three greatest presidents in history. He moved to meet the immense challenges facing his new administration with a zeal and confidence that quelled panic and buoyed the spirits of the nation, even though he could find no solution to the systemic weakness of the economy. His political talents and zest for leadership were exactly the characteristics needed to see the nation through the dark times of depression and war. In their personal relationship the Roosevelts were at a nearly complete impasse; however, in public they forged an even stronger working alliance that was almost irresistible, although the subject of vehement criticism.

They came to national leadership in the fall of 1932 in an America still in the hard grasp of powerful conservative traditions that included sanctioned, violent racism and the restriction of women to a repressive homebound sphere. Even though at the turn of the century the reformist Progressives, led by Eleanor's uncle Teddy, had eroded its power to some degree, a traditional philosophy of unfettered capitalism still held sway among most American businessmen and politicians. Challenges to these traditions, such as those posed by the Roosevelts during the New Deal, were met with fear and loathing, which often was expressed in extreme rhetoric, and the dislocations of the Depression seemed to intensify the need for conservatives in America to strike out at perceived threats.

Eleanor, driven by an immense empathy for the marginal and the impoverished in society, stepped into the crisis in 1933 and unleashed an astounding burst of activity in the service of changing conditions for the better. As biographer Blanche Wiesen Cook asserts, Eleanor was convinced that women's energy, if freed from the bonds of tradition, could overcome economic need and social injustice.

Nonetheless, after the election in November 1932 Eleanor had been smitten with a good share of anxiety about what lay ahead. Her memories of life in Washington, D.C., were not pleasant. She remembered the stultifying pre–World War I social atmosphere of the city that also was the scene of FDR's infidelity and betrayal of her marriage. Moreover, Eleanor was only too well aware of the deadly effects of the White House on her predecessors, several of whom she had known personally, including Uncle Ted's wife Edith. These women, almost without exception, had been shriveled by their experiences as First Ladies. If she acceded to the traditional confines of her new position, she would be forced to give up her role in political life and her social welfare activities.

Eleanor also found threatening the prospect that FDR's position would focus unbearable attention on the Roosevelt's rocky family life and that Eleanor herself would be restricted in her day-to-day movements. She insisted that the Secret Service leave her unescorted and unencumbered whenever possible. She also rebelled against attempts by the press to cover her every movement by gently but firmly insisting on her privacy. Happily for Eleanor, those were the days before television and twenty-four-hour news coverage, so initially she had to elude or convince only a handful of reporters.

In January 1933, after brooding for several weeks about the challenges of taking up residence there as the president's wife, Eleanor made her first visit to the White House, walking over with a friend from her suite at the Mayflower Hotel to meet briefly with President Hoover's wife Lou and to tour the building. She quickly made all the basic decisions about room assignments in the family living quarters and changes in the décor. Her matter-of-fact approach caused some shock to the White House staff, as she later recounted in her memoirs: "My first act was to insist on running the elevator myself without waiting for one of the doormen to run it for me. That just wasn't done by the President's wife." After investigating the building from the basement up, she emerged from the building in less than an hour.

Despite this show of brisk efficiency, there was still much to be worked out about her new position. Just how she could stabilize her relationship with FDR under their altered circumstances was still a mystery, and she thrashed about at times, seeking answers. At one stage Eleanor suggested that she take over supervision of FDR's mail, which she imagined would be huge, but he firmly rejected the offer, saying he did not want to offend Missy LeHand by seeming to let Eleanor intrude. Looking back only a few months later, this idea must have seemed absurd, as Eleanor's own mail rapidly grew to a daily landslide that she couldn't possibly cope with. Between March and December 1933, Eleanor herself received three hundred one thousand letters. Nevertheless, the episode highlighted the ongoing tension produced by any overture toward intimacy by Eleanor.

> *The White House was home to the Roosevelts for twelve years, longer than any other presidential family, and they put their stamp on the building.*
>
> *FDR had a swimming pool built to allow him to indulge in almost the only exercise his polio-ravaged legs would allow. Later presidents, particularly John F. Kennedy, enjoyed the pool, but during Richard Nixon's term it was covered over and became the White House pressroom.*
>
> *During Eleanor and FDR's residence, the White House also acquired a mechanized dishwasher and, during World War II, a bomb shelter.*
>
> *Throughout the Roosevelt years, many guests came and went. They included semi-permanent residents, such as Eleanor's close friend Lorena Hickok and FDR's sickly advisors Louis Howe and Henry Hopkins, and visiting heads of state such as Winston Churchill, who wandered the White House hallways in his bath robe, looking for a late-night nip of brandy.*

The four-month period between the election and the inauguration of a new president was a constitutional holdover from the days of travel by horseback and carriage and would be eliminated before FDR's second term rolled around. During the long wait for ascension to office, FDR could do little constructive, so he took a fishing trip off the coast of Florida in February. On the evening of the fifteenth he arrived back in Miami after his cruise and was sitting in his open car at a rally talking to Chicago Mayor Anton Cermak, a previously anti-Roosevelt Democrat who had come to make peace with the new president, when an out-of-work bricklayer fired five shots from a pistol at FDR. The bullets missed Roosevelt but struck Cermak, who later died from his wounds. For Eleanor and the rest of the family, the attack was a dramatic signal of their changed status, but Eleanor still insisted on maintaining her freedom, as far as possible, from protection or supervision.

A New Intimate Friend

FDR's inauguration on March 4 was one of the most dramatic in American history. After slowly making his way to the podium, supported by the powerful arm of his son James, FDR offered inspiration to a nation deep in gloom. His most famous sentence asserted his "firm belief that the only thing we have to fear is fear itself—nameless, unreasoning, unjustified terror which paralyzes needed efforts to convert retreat to advance." His words and the oddly effective cadence of his delivery were galvanizing, and the hundred thousand listeners on the cold capital lawn and the millions who heard him on radio were moved by his call for a renewed faith in America and her ability to defeat economic decline and social distress.

Eleanor for her part was still fighting off a sense of menace over what the glare of the White House might bring. Early on inauguration morning, she had slipped away by taxi to Rock Creek Cemetery to pay another visit to the Saint Gauden's statue of *Grief*, a ritual that had sustained her often during the trying days after the revelation of FDR's affair with Lucy Mercer.

She put the gloom behind her, however, and moved into the day's round of activities with great energy and dignity, compensating for FDR's limited mobility and reluctance to appear in public situations that might reveal the true extent of his physical disability. While FDR went to the White House, Eleanor attended the official inaugural ball in the company of her mother-in-law, her children, her brother, and several of her closest friends and associates, including Earl Miller, Nancy Cook, and Marion Dickerman. She danced to the music of Guy Lombardo and Rudy Vallee and appeared to have a splendid time as the center of attention.

It is unclear from the historical record whether Eleanor knew that while she was dancing at the party, her husband was entertaining Lucy Mercer Rutherford at the White House during his first hours as president. He had invited her to the inauguration and had sent a car for her convenience. The episode only underscored the ongoing complexities of the Roosevelt marriage: Despite his promises to the contrary, FDR continued to see his former lover, literally until the day he died; yet Eleanor had to maintain appearances in public and even in front of her children and friends.

By the time of the inauguration, however, Eleanor had someone to confide in and to turn to for solace. Months earlier, during the election campaign, she had met Lorena Hickok, a talented and highly regarded reporter for the Associated Press who had been assigned to cover FDR's 1932 whistle-stop campaign through the western states. The candidate's wife apparently was immediately taken with Hickok: A close relationship developed rapidly. By early 1933 Eleanor and Hickok were spending most of their free time together, and Hickok was firmly entrenched as a member of the new First Lady's entourage.

Hickok was an intriguing person. In a day when newspapers held an extremely important place in American life, she was at the top of her profession as one of the most energetic and talented journalists in the nation. Moreover, she had lifted herself from a dismal background, greatly removed from the rarified New York world of Eleanor's childhood. Hickok was born in Wisconsin but moved with her impoverished family to South Dakota when she was ten years old. Her mother died two years later, and Hickok fled from her abusive father to a hard life of menial work. She was on her own, moving from place to place and attending school whenever her labors won enough money to support an educational interlude. She finally escaped these drastic circumstances when taken in by a kindly aunt and sent to finish high school in Michigan, then on to college in Wisconsin. Hickok soon abandoned her college studies, however, and began a career as a reporter with the Battle Creek, Michigan, *Journal*. She climbed the ladder of journalistic success very rapidly, moving first to Milwaukee and then to the Minneapolis *Tribune*.

Hickok had no romantic interest in men. She had what she later termed a "long friendship" with the famous opera singer Ernestine Schumann-Heink while living in Milwaukee and, after moving to Minneapolis, formed an attachment to a young reporter at the *Tribune* named Ella Morse. The two lived together for eight years; however, eventually Morse left Hickok to marry a man and the reporter moved to New York. In 1928 Hickok took a job with the Associated Press and soon was receiving the same assignments, privileges, and salary as the best of her male colleagues.

Throughout the final months of 1932 and during most of 1933, Eleanor and Hickok were inseparable. Hickok had been with Eleanor when she visited Rock Creek Cemetery on inauguration day morning and had lunch with Eleanor privately before the official ceremonies. Soon after inauguration day Hickok was assigned a permanent guest room in the White House, where she stayed whenever she was in town, and she and Eleanor traveled together privately and often dined alone. Over the following year they frequently spent weekends together at secluded inns and hotels.

Although the most intense period of their relationship burned out quickly—lasting only until 1934—the two remained close for the rest of their lives. Hickok gave a heart-shaped sapphire and diamond ring (which she had received from Schumann-Heink) to Eleanor as a token of their relationship, and it was on Eleanor's finger at her death thirty years after her first meeting with Hickok.

Much is known of the relationship between Eleanor and Hickok because from the day of the inauguration onward the First Lady wrote long, ten- or fifteen-page letters to her friend every day. Hickok later burned many of these letters and censored the rest, but those that survive contain a wealth of detail. They not only chronicle Eleanor's daily activities—this aspect of the letters eventually was the inspiration for her syndicated "My Day" column— but they also reveal the emotionally intimate nature of the relationship, even after censorship. Virtually every letter professed Eleanor's love for Hickok and her longing to be alone together, but only a few vague references to physical manifestations of Eleanor's love survived Hickok's later editing.

Because for decades earlier biographers, and Eleanor's friends and family, glossed over her relationship with Hickok or insisted that Eleanor had no interest in any form of romance or sex, the revelations about Eleanor and Hickok by her most sophisticated biographer, Blanche Wiesen Cook, caused a considerable stir when first published in the 1990s. There has been much subsequent speculation about Eleanor's sexuality and her undeniably close relationship with an obvious lesbian—who was in fact only one more in a long line of lesbian women with whom Eleanor was closely associated, starting with Marie Souvestre. Although titillating, the real significance of this topic comes from the light it sheds on Eleanor's psychology and emotions during the first months of her tenure in the White House. She was estranged from FDR at the personal level, and her children usually were sources more of pain than comfort. She turned to Hickok to fill these spaces in her heart, and Hickok appears to have done so admirably, although at great cost to herself.

Eleanor biographer Doris Kearns Goodwin claims that Eleanor's relationship with Hickok came at a critical time in her life and provided "a mix of tenderness, loyalty, confidence, and courage that sustained her in her struggle to redefine her sense of self and her position in the world. For Eleanor, Hick's love was a positive force, allowing her to grow and take wing ...." Goodwin believes that the security Eleanor received from an intimate, loving relationship was the key to her ability to develop her own public image during the New Deal and thus become an object of "the love of millions."

Because she was an intimate companion of Eleanor during the first days and weeks of the new administration, Hickok was privy to a great deal of inside information about what transpired in the White House. Unfortunately, because of her privileged status, she could not report on what was happening nor could she pass the information on to her colleagues at the Associated Press. After several weeks of twisting and turning, Hickok came to the full realization that if she continued her relationship with the First Lady, she would have to give up her life's work as a hard-charging, high-level journalist. She subsequently resigned from the Associated Press three months after the inauguration and took a job that Eleanor arranged with the Federal Emergency Relief Administration (one of the many New Deal agencies created by FDR). Hickok never returned to journalism.

The New Deal

FDR's first three months in office, known later as the "Hundred Days," were a remarkable time in American history. Having soothed the nation's battered psyche with his "we have nothing to fear" inauguration speech, the president proceeded to push through Congress a blizzard of laws that created the basic structure of what came to be known as the New Deal and changed forever the relationship of American citizens to their government. Moreover, the legislation of the Hundred Days created the context in which Eleanor operated publicly for several years to come. She was deeply concerned about issues of relief for the millions who were suffering and in need of basic help, and she was particularly concerned that women should be included in the New Deal's outreach. Eleanor eventually came to believe that "poverty is like a giant infection that contaminates everything," and she wanted to help FDR cure the infection at its source.

FDR was impatient with grand theories of economics or social policy, especially in the context of the great and growing needs of a nation that had suffered through the Depression for more than three years before he took office. His goals were not concerned with lofty systems or philosophies, but rather they were direct and down to earth.

FDR's initial programs were aimed broadly at two goals: recovery for the economy and relief for Americans who were unemployed and on the brink of personal disaster. There was little philosophical consistency in the early proposals and laws, but there *was* a great deal of activity. As Eleanor wrote about him: "Through the whole of Franklin's career there never was any deviation from his original objective—to help make life better for the average man, woman and child." Eleanor, who knew him best, explained that "a thousand and one means were used, difficulties arose, changes took place, but this objective always was the motive for whatever had to be done."

Eleanor also provided insight into those aspects of FDR's personality that allowed him to calmly tackle the huge problems that faced the nation in 1933:

I have never known a man who gave one a greater sense of security. I never heard him say there was a problem that he thought it was impossible for human beings to solve. He recognized the difficulties and often said that, while he did not know the answer, he was completely confident that there was an answer and that one had to try until one either found it for himself or got it from someone else.

FDR's first major act as president was to declare a bank "holiday," temporarily closing all the nation's banks and thereby forestalling a collapse of the bank system, which had seemed imminent during the weeks just before the inauguration. When the banks reopened four days later, faith in the system had been sufficiently restored so as to avoid collapse. The president's Emergency Banking Act, which passed Congress instantly, created a system of federal supervision and regulation of local banks, and a subsequent law established the Federal Deposit Insurance Corporation to provide a limited guarantee by the federal government for individual deposits.

The president then moved to cut federal spending—a tactic more in synch with a conservative approach to economic recovery than his other New Deal programs. The Economy in Government Act lowered all federal employee salaries by fifteen percent, eliminated several government agencies, and fired all married women federal workers whose husbands also were employed by the government. That this law was almost completely at odds with most of the other parts of the New Deal seemed to trouble FDR not at all; at least not at this early stage of his efforts to restore the national economy.

FDR then turned to efforts at relief. There was still a very strong belief in the nation that most relief efforts should be undertaken at the local and state levels, even though this had proven a dismal failure during the last two years of the Hoover administration. FDR and his advisors took a more aggressive approach. His first important attempt at relief was the Civilian Conservation Corps, established in late March 1933. It created a quasi-military organization for unemployed young men, who were organized into camps and who undertook public works projects such as building roads, constructing dams, and planting trees. They were paid thirty dollars a month in addition to free room and board, and twenty-five dollars of that went home to their families—twenty-five dollars was almost a fortune to many impoverished families. Nearly a quarter-million young men enrolled in the CCC—but women were completely excluded.

By May 1933 FDR pushed through a more comprehensive relief bill that created the Federal Emergency Relief Administration. FERA's mandate was to offer direct relief to millions and millions of Americans who were in economic distress due to the Depression. Congress appropriated five hundred million dollars, which was to flow through FERA to state and local relief agencies. The president appointed Harry Hopkins, a Midwesterner who had directed relief efforts in New York, as the head of the FERA. Hopkins moved very quickly to implement direct relief efforts and also to establish the Civil Works Administration as an agency to create jobs. Within a few weeks the CWA had put four million Americans back to work. Hopkins's direct and energetic approach to solving problems appealed greatly to Eleanor, even though the FERA programs discriminated against women, and he became one of her closest allies in the following years.

The most damaged segment of the failed United States economy was agriculture. A full-scale depression had hit American farmers several years before the stock market crash of 1929, and both market conditions and disastrous weather since had driven most farmers to the brink of extinction. FDR's Emergency Farm Mortgage Act halted the wave of foreclosures that was sweeping across the farmlands, and allowed many farm owners to refinance their threatened mortgages.

However, the major farm program was the Agricultural Adjustment Act, passed in May 1933, which aimed at correcting the imbalance in agricultural supply and demand. Instead of direct relief for farmers, the AAA provided for mechanisms to control markets by imposing restrictions on agricultural production and paying farmers to refrain from growing crops or raising livestock. Although this perhaps was a farsighted approach to solving deeply imbedded problems in agriculture, it resulted in the widely publicized destruction of "surplus" farm products—killing baby pigs, burning cotton, dumping milk—that seemed indecently cruel to Eleanor when she was learning daily of Americans who were hungry and ill-clothed. She often clashed with FDR's secretary of agriculture, Henry Wallace, a former plant scientist and farm editor from Iowa.

Another of FDR's innovations—from a philosophical viewpoint one of the most radical—was the creation of the Tennessee Valley Authority, a huge public works project to build dams and power plants along the Tennessee River valley. The plan was attacked as socialistic because it involved spending very large amounts of money for the benefit of only a relatively small portion of the country. Eleanor loved the project, however, because it provided direct aid to people living in one of the poorest regions, and she backed her husband strongly against his critics. Eleanor wished that other utilities could be fashioned after the TVA because "such experiments, changing for the better the life of the people, would be a mighty bulwark against attacks on our democracy."

Perhaps the most ambitious of the New Deal programs put forward during the Hundred Days was FDR's grand attempt to bring about national economic recovery by instituting supervision and control of industry by the federal government. Nothing of the kind had ever been tried before outside of wartime. The National Industrial Recovery Act set up the National Recovery Administration, a powerful new agency symbolized by a picture of a blue eagle, which was to draft codes for the direction of every industry. The codes set standards industry by industry for wages and working hours and encouraged employers to enter into collective bargaining with labor unions. In addition, the NRA was empowered to fix prices for basic industrial goods, thereby creating a form of government-sponsored monopoly. Production levels also were controlled by the NRA, as was advertising. In short, the NRA had wide powers to induce an economic recovery by government planning.

A secondary section of the National Industrial Recovery Act (NIRA) set up the Public Works Administration, headed by Harold Ickes, as yet another program to create public jobs for the unemployed. The PWA was well funded, and Eleanor had hopes it would put massive numbers of Americans to work. But Ickes, unlike his counterpart Harry Hopkins at FERA, was an extremely cautious bureaucrat who could not shake loose with the money appropriated by Congress without weeks or months of study and analysis. He moved at such a slow pace that Eleanor soon became impatient with his approach and often clashed with him over PWA programs.

Redefining a Role

In the normal course of affairs, Eleanor's opinions of the New Deal programs and directors would have meant little, and she would have remained within the confines of the role of First Lady as it had traditionally been defined, serving as a hostess for the president and staying out of politics and public policy. Under those circumstances her ideas and activities would have been of little note and small interest to the American public. However, although it was true that she managed to carry out most of the purely social obligations of her position—between 1933 and 1945 she entertained thousands upon thousands of guests at the White House at teas, receptions, and formal dinners—she was in the public eye from the first weeks of FDR's administration.

To a large extent she brought this situation about herself. At Lorena Hickok's suggestion, Eleanor invited forty women newspaper correspondents to the White House for regular Monday press conferences, open only to women. This was a remarkable innovation in White House coverage and resulted in a great deal of favorable and controlled publicity for the First Lady. Other First Ladies had held an occasional press conference, but Eleanor seized on the device as a major part of her public life. Over the following twelve years, right up until the day FDR died, she held press conferences on a regular basis, totaling 348 altogether.

These press conferences helped to sharply distinguish Eleanor from her predecessors and served notice to the nation that something new and different was taking place in the White House in addition to FDR's activities. Nothing could have been further from the old-fashioned notion that wives stayed in the background than to have Eleanor speaking regularly to the press and fielding questions.

The ban on male correspondents emphasized Eleanor's interest in building up the role of professional women in American society, since what she said and did was by definition news and the ban forced newspapers and syndicates to provide women reporters. The United Press, for example, had to hire its first woman reporter just to cover Eleanor's press conferences, which the wire service could not afford to ignore. Eleanor did allow men reporters into her out-of-town press conferences or the press conferences she held in 1941 and 1942 as part of her official duties with the Office of Civilian Defense.

Because many of the women correspondents were hired only because of these conferences, they owed their jobs to Eleanor, and most of them felt a strong sense of gratitude and loyalty. In turn, Eleanor treated the women writers with respect and consideration. As Bess Furman, the reporter for the Associated Press remembered, the atmosphere of the conferences was like a schoolroom, with Eleanor at the front of the class, dispensing information. Eleanor also invited the women reporters to parties and special events at the White House, further co-opting them into her orbit.

The small number of reporters at the beginning in 1933 grew over the years. In 1939, radio reporters were added to the official list of approved correspondents and governmental publicity writers were allowed to attend. During the first years of the war, more than a hundred writers were admitted to the conferences. By the time Eleanor left the White House, the number had shrunk again to under forty.

During the first months of the administration Eleanor restricted questions to nonpolitical matters and refused to discuss policies or comment on FDR's New Deal activities. She reviewed topics ahead of time with Louis Howe and FDR's Press Secretary Stephen Early. As time went on, however, she opened the women-only conferences to almost all subjects.

One of the first major stories on Eleanor was her visit to the second Bonus Army that had descended on Washington during the spring of 1933. This was a gathering of World War I veterans who wanted early payment of a promised bonus for their wartime services. The terrible conditions of the Depression had driven many veterans to the edge and they hoped to find relief through the bonus. The first Bonus Army had gathered in Washington during the previous summer, but when the Senate rejected the early payment, President Hoover feared the veterans might set off a violent revolution, so he had them forcibly cleared from their campgrounds by Army troops and tanks, a particularly brutal move that damaged his image.

In May 1933 a new army of Bonus Marchers returned to Washington with the same requests. Nothing could have signaled more clearly to the nation the change of philosophy embodied by the Roosevelt administration than Eleanor's visit to the marchers' camp. Louis Howe brought it about by asking Eleanor to drive him to the camp and then insisting she get out and talk to the marchers. The men were startled to see a woman who some of them recognized as the president's wife wander into their midst.

During her hour-long visit she charmed them with her quiet demeanor and matter-of-fact way of talking. After making a brief speech to the assembled marchers, she left with a good impression of the men, which was quite at odds with Hoover's fears, and they believed that FDR must be taking them seriously, even though the bonus was never forthcoming. The real payoff for Eleanor came when she told the next women's-only press conference about her visit and got widespread coverage of her low-key estimation of the "dangers" of the Bonus Army.

The overall relationship between the Roosevelts and the press was good, and there were tacit agreements between them that from the vantage point of the twenty-first century seem quite impossible. For example, the press virtually ignored the relationship between Eleanor and Lorena Hickok, even though what was happening must have been obvious to many of Hickok's professional friends and former colleagues. The most striking example of press restraint, however, was self-imposed blanket prohibition of ever showing FDR as a cripple. Great care was taken to never publish or hardly ever even take a photograph of the president when he was in his wheelchair or being carried from one place to another by his personal aides. He usually was shown standing erect, and only the most observant might have noticed that he was rigidly braced with a cane in his right hand and supported by the arm of a companion on his left. Nor did reporters ever discuss the president's severe disability in print. As far as most of the public knew, FDR was a vigorous man with only a minor problem with his legs.

Eleanor's experience with the Bonus Army illustrated a truth she learned early in her tenure as First Lady: If she personally visited people and places they became news, and her mere presence focused a public spotlight on the situation that concerned her. She scarcely needed to speak about whatever issue was at hand—although she seldom restrained herself—because the newspaper reporters, photographers, and newsreel cameramen were on the spot, recording and publicizing the cause.

Because FDR had reinforced her own predilections by asking her to travel and visit places and people that his immobility prevented him from seeing personally, Eleanor was free to indulge her interests by incessant travel and inspection, almost all of which received wide publicity. The reverse of the coin, however, meant that within a very short time, Eleanor lost the ability to move about on her own or with Lorena Hickok without being recognized. Eleanor sometimes convinced the Secret Service to let her drive herself around and to sneak away "on rare occasions to old friends" whom she rarely got to see, but in general she acknowledged, "The President's wife does not go out informally."

The new President and First Lady are shown seated in the
White House shortly after FDR's inauguration in 1933.

(Courtesy of the Franklin Delano Roosevelt Library)

The White House was Eleanor's official residence and principal
headquarters when she was not on the road. Her personal quarters
were the Lincoln Bedroom suite, adjacent to FDR's suite. She slept
in a small alcove and used most of her space as an office, where she
worked with Tommy Thompson, her invaluable secretary, or with
Edith Benham Helm, her social secretary. When in Washington,
Lorena Hickok occupied a bedroom and study across the hall from
Eleanor's personal quarters. Louis Howe also had rooms in the
White House in the president's wing, near a series of guest rooms
that usually were occupied by visitors or the Roosevelt children
during FDR's administration. Missy LeHand had her quarters on
the third floor.

Eleanor converted what had been Lou Hoover's solarium into a
sunny conference area where she held most of her staff meetings.

She was attended personally by a black maid, Lizzie McDuffie, whose husband Irvin was FDR's personal valet. The domestic staff of the White House was made up of black servants, as it had been for generations, and Eleanor did nothing to change that arrangement.

One of Eleanor's greatest strengths during her adult life was her extremely high level of physical and mental energy. She worked at a feverish pace almost all the time, fitting in dictation while traveling and working late into the evenings without flagging. Just reading about her daily schedule is exhausting, and she must have put a severe strain on her staff and all those around her with her unrelenting activity. She began her day with physical exercises as soon as she got out of bed, followed whenever possible by a horseback ride through Rock Creek Park. She then took a cold shower—she had a predilection for cold baths and showers—and ate a sparse breakfast. She often visited FDR as he ate his breakfast in bed before turning to her day's work. Unless she had a luncheon appointment, she ate a light meal at midday and returned to her agenda: visiting in the Washington area, meeting people at the White House, or writing.

After working until late afternoon, Eleanor typically took a swim in the White House pool, which had been installed so FDR could exercise, and then usually ate with FDR and whatever guests were on hand. Unless there was an official White House dinner scheduled, most of the Roosevelts' meals were relaxed and informal, often served in the president's study. However, the quality of the food was a major point of contention. Eleanor was nominally in charge of domestic arrangements for the First Family, and she had hired an irascible and incompetent woman, Henrietta Nesbitt, as head housekeeper.

Nesbitt was a poor cook and meal planner, and she insisted on serving dull meals that skirted the edge of being inedible. Eleanor was relatively indifferent to most food, good or bad, but the poor meals infuriated FDR. Even though he was President of the United States, his protests and complaints were almost always ignored. Some writers have suggested that this was one way Eleanor managed to passively express her long-term irritation with her husband. Whatever the case, the food was bad at the White House during the Roosevelt administration—including formal meals and state dinners.

Eleanor and FDR usually spent some time together after dinner when she typically brought up policy issues or projects she wanted FDR to act on. This allowed Eleanor to exercise her influence on her husband and was a crucial part of her day. As soon as the serious discussions were over the couple usually parted, with FDR going to his private quarters to relax with cocktails and the company of some of his more convivial friends and staffers.

Missy LeHand typically arranged for FDR's evening relaxation; Eleanor was politely excluded—not that she wanted to participate in any occasions that involved excessive drinking. She abhorred even the mild abuse of liquor, which is not surprising given the painful alcoholism of her father. She wrote in her daily newspaper column that "the less strong liquor anyone consumed the better it was." Eleanor probably was most relaxed in the White House when entertaining friends for informal Sunday evening suppers for which she personally prepared scrambled eggs—her only known culinary skill.

Eleanor's day usually did not end until after she had spent an hour or two at her desk writing letters or finishing the day's paperwork. It also was not uncommon for her to steal into the president's bedroom to say goodnight after he had been put to bed by his bodyguard and personal assistant Gus Gennerich, a former New York state trooper, and his valet "Mac" McDuffie.

During many days each month, however, Eleanor was on the road, traveling to see New Deal projects of interest to her or making formal appearances and carrying out official duties on behalf of the immobile FDR. She also maintained during the first years of FDR's presidency an interest in the furniture factory and in Todhunter School, so she spent considerable time at Val-Kill and at the family's New York City home. In addition, Esther Lape and Elizabeth Read provided her with a third-floor hideaway apartment in their Greenwich Village building, which she used to escape the public glare and to write or to meet quietly with her New York friends.

> A friend of Amelia Earhardt, American's most famous woman pilot, Eleanor wanted to become a pilot herself.
>
> Earhardt was an international celebrity as the first woman to fly the Atlantic solo (and the first solo pilot of either gender to reproduce Lindbergh's feat) and as the holder of many flying records.
>
> Eleanor loved planes and flew often as a passenger, but her great ambition was to become a pilot. Earhardt gave her flying lessons, and Eleanor not only learned to fly but also passed the physical exam in preparation for getting her license. Unfortunately, FDR hated and feared flying, and he insisted Eleanor give it up.
>
> However, shortly after FDR's inauguration, Eleanor was reported to have joined Earhardt in a nighttime airborne joy ride over Washington, D.C., with Eleanor at the controls.
>
> Earhardt disappeared on a flight across the Pacific four years later.

Eleanor seldom sat quietly, and she had the habit of knitting almost constantly while she carried on conversations. (Will Rogers had teased Eleanor about her furious knitting at the Democratic national convention in 1924.) Many people commented on the extreme speed at which she walked, as usually she left companions gasping to keep up. When she traveled by train or car—she was an excellent driver who loved to motor on the open road—her secretary Tommy Thompson usually was at her side to go over papers or to take dictation for Eleanor's correspondence, speeches, and writing. Except for specified periods of holiday or vacation, Eleanor appeared to go to great lengths to fill up every hour and minute of her official day with work or study.

Her displays of constant activity became an essential part of her public image during the 1930s. Even her worst enemies never accused Eleanor of being lazy or sedentary; in fact, usually they tried to characterize her ceaseless activity as a negative, calling her a "busybody"; especially when she had attacked something her conservative enemies were attached to. The name-calling also evinced the traditional belief that women—especially women from Eleanor's social background—should never lead public lives.

Some of her biographers have concluded that Eleanor's relentless schedule and hyperactivity were defense mechanisms she employed to compensate for her failed marriage and FDR's indifference toward her as a wife. It seems more likely, however, that the sustained routine of travel, speaking, meeting, inspecting, and so forth simply was an expression of Eleanor's astounding personal energy. She apparently was one of those rare human beings who thrive on nearly ceaseless activity. She appeared to be happiest when using almost every spare moment of the day to cram in more reading or writing or discussions.

The relationship between Eleanor and FDR during the New Deal of course is a topic that has drawn much attention from historians and biographers. From the first months of the new administration, it was obvious that Eleanor would play a major role in the New Deal and in the success or failure of FDR's attempts to revive the economy and stave off human disaster. She exerted a huge influence on FDR and was as a consequence one of the most powerful people in the nation, although she had no official position and only briefly ever held an appointed office (she always expressed abhorrence at the suggestion that she run for elected office).

Her power came solely from the unbreakable alliance she had forged with her husband over the years. No matter how distressed or detached they were in their personal relationship as husband and wife, they were bonded tightly as partners to carry out the mission of the New Deal. There is little doubt that they both had learned to find emotional satisfaction elsewhere and in the company of others, yet they formed a potent political team.

Nonetheless, they found much to disagree about in policy and programs. Eleanor was a relentless advocate for her causes and whichever issue seemed most pressing at any one time, and FDR was just as relentless in assessing each of her enthusiasms in light of cold political reality. This resulted in a continuous series of conflicts between the two, as neither was much inclined to give up on any important point; however, almost never was the discussion cut off and seldom did FDR fail to give Eleanor an audience, even when he became bored or worn down by her repeated entreaties to consider this or that problem. Almost every day if she was at the White House, Eleanor would leave papers, memos, and clippings in a basket at the side of his bed for him to consider—and he apparently always gave these leavings his attention.

Because FDR had to deal with major political problems in dealing with a Congress that was dominated by conservative southerners, including the U.S. Senate where southerners could derail any of his programs at will by use of the filibuster, he frequently rejected Eleanor's pleas on behalf of good causes. For many of her admirers this casts FDR as a villain who brushed Eleanor's interests aside in the name of political expediency, but that view fails to give enough credit to FDR for the basic changes his New Deal brought about in the face of grave obstacles. He probably did not reject Eleanor out of malice or indifference to her political and social interests; rather he was exercising his finely tuned sense of politics, which during the first years of the New Deal seldom failed him. Additionally, there were many cases in which he backed Eleanor completely and pushed forward her ideas and causes. FDR in fact did seem to trust Eleanor and support her unless her agenda appeared to him to carry too much political danger.

Eleanor provided FDR with a set of keen eyes and ears to go places he could not. She often functioned as his personal envoy and reported on what was happening in the country and how specific New Deal programs were faring. For a president with his disabilities, it was a huge advantage to have a tireless and completely trusted advisor such as Eleanor. She wrote in her memoirs: "I became, as the years went by, a better reporter and a better observer … and I decided this was the only way I could help him, outside of running the house." Moreover, Eleanor acted as a lightning rod for public opinion, and FDR often gauged his policies or tested ideas by the reaction drawn by Eleanor. This sometimes placed her in awkward or even painful situations, but it was an extremely important part of the partnership.

They had an unusual mutual tolerance that allowed them to disagree in public—often in print—over many issues. It was not unusual for Eleanor to take an extremely public stand against something FDR supported, or vice versa. What would have been embarrassing to other public personalities, especially celebrity married couples, was accepted and passed over by the Roosevelts. It was a relationship that is difficult to completely encompass, with proprieties and boundaries that were of their own devising.

It is clear that by the time of FDR's election there was little genuine affection or intimacy left—FDR looked to Missy LeHand and an inner circle of cronies for that, and Eleanor had Lorena Hickok, Earl Miller, and others. They led nearly separate personal lives, despite constant contact and exchange, yet there was demonstrably a huge reservoir of mutual respect and confidence between them. FDR trusted Eleanor's insights and judgment, and she in turn relied on his power and position.

Women and the New Deal

The humanitarian side of the New Deal—the side that dealt with relief and aid to the millions suffering genuine need—and the elements of FDR's programs that aimed to reform injustices in American society seemed like extensions of the women's social improvement causes that Eleanor had been involved with for decades. It therefore was natural that she and her longtime women's movement colleagues wanted to exert influence on how the New Deal would be run. The most direct avenue was to get women appointed to important jobs. Eleanor spent a great deal of time and political capital in pushing women forward at the key moments when the New Deal bureaucracies were being set up.

The most prominent woman in FDR's government was Frances Perkins, the former activist for the Consumers' League and labor commissioner in New York State when FDR was governor. She was not a close associate of Eleanor as so many prominent women Democrats were, but it was still a triumph when FDR appointed Perkins as his secretary of labor, making her the first woman cabinet member in history. She wielded great power and influence in an important segment of the economy during her tenure in office.

Most of Eleanor's influence in placing women in FDR's administration was worked out through Molly Dewson, who as head of the Women's Division of the Democratic Party claimed the right to help dispense patronage after the election. James Farley, new chief of the party and FDR's postmaster general, agreed to share patronage appointments with Dewson and Eleanor, so they submitted a long list of names of qualified and deserving women who should be given government jobs. Eleanor and Farley had been close political allies, and the party boss trusted her judgments.

In addition to Perkins, one of the most prominent women in the administration was Mary Harriman Rumsey, who was appointed to head the Consumers' Advisory Board of the NRA. Rumsey was one of the founders of the Junior League and the Rivington Street Settlement House, and one of Eleanor's oldest associates in the women's movement, their relationship dating to before her marriage to FDR. Other important women in the administration included Ellen Woodward, who became head of the Women's Division of the FERA; Rose Schneiderman, who was appointed to the Labor Advisory Board of the NRA; Josephine Roche, an assistant secretary of the treasury; and Nellie Tayloe Ross, who became director of the U.S. Mint. Dozens of lower-ranking jobs also went to women, who claimed a vastly greater presence in FDR's administration than in any previous government.

The first efforts of the New Deal were less promising for ordinary women who were in need of jobs or welfare assistance. Eleanor was outraged when one of FDR's first moves was to use the Economy in Government Act to fire thousands of women federal employees. And to her horror, many of the so-called "alphabet agencies" intentionally left women out of their programs or actively discriminated against them. Behind these developments was a pervasive philosophy that men were the principal breadwinners in the nation and should be favored when creating jobs or expanding relief aid to the unemployed. Single women, homeless women, and widows were virtually ignored, and millions of unemployed women who wanted to work were discriminated against routinely.

As Eleanor became aware of these inequities she began a private campaign with FDR and a public campaign in the press to correct the situation. Her greatest successes were with Harry Hopkins, who at least appeared to understand what she was getting at. He and Ellen Woodward moved in 1933 to find jobs for women. Although they faced resistance from local politicians who insisted women either did not need jobs or were too fragile to work, within a few months the FERA had created several hundred thousand jobs for women. There were still grave problems—women often received only a fraction of the wages of men in similar federal programs and there was a reluctance to allow unskilled women to work at anything except domestic chores, such as sewing—the efforts were a step forward.

One of Eleanor's least favorite of FDR's lieutenants, Harold Ickes, almost completely ignored her campaign, and the PWA under his direction did little to end unemployment among the nation's women. He demonstrated a strong streak of traditional anti-feminism, and he particularly disliked Eleanor's public campaign when it was aimed at him. He considered her a meddler and a pest and appeared to do his best to frustrate her wishes.

Eleanor also was intensely frustrated by the refusal of officials to set up camps for women commensurate with the highly successful CCC camps for young men. The familiar objection was that women could not stand up to actual outdoor work and that it would be dangerous to have women living together in large groups (which apparently was the same veiled fear of lesbianism that would be repeated during attempts to establish women's military units during World War II). There were no camps planned for women until Eleanor enlisted the support of Labor Secretary Frances Perkins to set up a single camp in New York State. Even then, when Eleanor paid a personal visit to the camp (known derisively as the "She, She, She Camp"), she found that bureaucratic foot-dragging had held enrollment down to a handful of women and that the camp was poorly equipped. She immediately publicized the shortcomings through statements to the press. Within weeks the worst of the problems had been remedied, but she was unsuccessful in lobbying for more women's CCC camps in other states.

Eleanor had a wider impact when she worked with former dean of Bryn Mawr College Hilda Smith, who was head of a small section in Hopkins's FERA called the Emergency Education Program. After Eleanor highlighted the need for camps for unemployed women by calling a White House conference on the topic in 1934,

Smith was able to set up a series of educational camps that enrolled several thousand women over the next several years, but the effort was far short of the resources funneled into the CCC.

A Relationship Fades

By the end of 1933 the most intense period of Eleanor and Lorena Hickok's relationship appeared to be slowly winding down. Their surviving correspondence still was filled with terms of endearment and expressions of love and longing but in fact they were seldom together. Hickok usually was absent on long trips for FERA, during which she researched and compiled reports on relief programs and conditions around the country—a series of assignments that drew on her skills as an experienced journalist. Eleanor likewise was busy traveling or absorbed with her work in Washington. The opportunities for Eleanor and Hickok to be together became fewer and fewer as the First Lady increasingly gained standing in the public eye. Not only was Eleanor's time closely scheduled, but it was difficult by late 1933 for her to go anywhere without being recognized.

Eleanor continued her association with Nancy Cook and Marion Dickerman, the two women she had shared living quarters with at Val-Kill, but she had less time also to devote to keeping that relationship alive. She still visited Val-Kill and invited the couple to the White House when she could, but the old ties seemed to be loosening. Neither Cook or Dickerman approved of Hickok, whom they snobbishly considered too rough-hewn for Eleanor and lacking in education and social polish, and their criticism further complicated Eleanor's emotional life.

Her children also were sources of pain and irritation rather than comfort. Eleanor was closest to Anna; however, when Anna divorced her husband and began a well-publicized affair with journalist John Boettinger, it caused Eleanor considerable embarrassment. Anna and Boettinger eventually married and moved to Seattle to take over a newspaper, but their rather tempestuous union was a continuing source of stress. Worse was the behavior of Elliott Roosevelt, who in 1933 abandoned his wife and children to pursue and eventually marry another woman. Eleanor tried to provide motherly advice, but Elliott was not interested in his mother's counsel and showed the hostility toward her that was so common between Eleanor and her sons. Moreover, Grandmother Sara blamed Eleanor for what she considered to be Elliott's disgraceful behavior.

When Hickok came to Washington on her vacation and moved into her guest room at the White House in December 1933, she discovered that Eleanor's schedule kept them apart for days on end. Bored and feeling neglected, Hickok fled to New York City, leaving a widening breach in her relationship with Eleanor. Both Eleanor and Hickok made numerous attempts over the following months to repair some of the damage. Their letters repeat over and over again their declarations of love and good intent, and Eleanor made efforts throughout 1934 to keep Hickock in her orbit. In March Eleanor included Hickok as part of her official party that toured the American Virgin Islands and Puerto Rico (where she was both shocked and moved by the severe poverty and underdevelopment she saw in America's Caribbean possessions). In May they nearly had a falling out when Eleanor objected to the racist overtones of some of Hickok's FERA reports on the South.

One of the last great attempts to repair the closeness of their relationship came later in 1934, when Eleanor stage-managed an extended trip with Hickok to the western states. Eleanor hoped to make the trip in secret or at least without wide press coverage or revelations that she was vacationing with Hickok, but even though she flew to Sacramento under a false name, the reporters were waiting for her plane. Worse, carloads of journalists followed Hickok's car when the two women tried to sneak out of their hotel, and an almost comic chase ensued. Eleanor finally backed down the reporters by threatening to return to Washington and blame them for ruining her vacation.

Thereafter, Eleanor and Hickok did enjoy several days of relaxation with friends near Pyramid Lake and then on a camping trip to Yosemite Park. At Yosemite Eleanor went off on her own strenuous hiking and climbing excursions during the day, leaving Hickok, who was in poor physical condition, behind. Once crowds of tourists discovered Eleanor was in the park the couple's peace was shattered, and they fled to San Francisco. The vacation trip Eleanor had so desired ended on a series of sour notes when reporters besieged her hotel in San Francisco and then followed her everywhere she tried to go with Hickok. They finally drove on to Portland, Oregon, where Eleanor met FDR on his return from an extended cruise through the Caribbean and the Panama Canal and up the Pacific coast. Hickok left before FDR's party arrived.

The lasting result of this failed attempt to escape the public eye with Hickok was to finally convince Eleanor that she could no longer pretend to be just another private person whenever it suited her. The price of her position and influence was a definitive loss of privacy. The notion that somehow she and Hickok could steal away whenever their schedules allowed—an idea Eleanor had clung to—was dead.

Eleanor and Lorena Hickok (on her left) visit an impoverished slum during their trip to Puerto Rico in 1934.

Chapter 6

The Most Powerful Woman
in the Nation

*As time went by I found that people no longer considered
me a mouthpiece for my husband but realized that I had a
point of view of my own ....*
—Eleanor Roosevelt,
This I Remember

The New Deal had begun with such fanfare and promise that
many Americans felt renewed hope that the national economy would soon recover and that the millions of unemployed
workers and their families would be able to return to productive,
secure lives. Unfortunately, this was not the case. During his first
term, when Eleanor emerged into the public spotlight and became
one of the most recognizable figures in the nation, FDR's efforts to
bring basic relief to those in need were reasonably successful; however, the president and his advisors failed to make much headway
against what proved to be an intractably sick economy.

The first hopes for engineering a recovery lay in the National
Recovery Administration (created by the National Industrial
Relations Act during the Hundred Days), which appeared to have
the potential to redirect national resources so as to stimulate economic activity and resolve many of the inequities in the workplace. Eleanor initially supported the NRA by supplying a series of

publicity-rich demonstrations of her involvement. She ceremoniously affixed the blue eagle symbol of the NRA to a window at the Val-Kill furniture factory, encouraging the press to report on her cheerful compliance with program, and she and Anna publicly received the first clothes made by the garment industry under one of the NRA's codes.

It soon became evident, however, that the codes drawn up under the NRA to direct and control each industry were filled with problems. Industry and business groups managed to tilt the process in their favor in most cases and despite the section of the law that authorized and encouraged the formation of labor unions, this vital aspect of the NRA often was circumvented. In short, the owners and managers to a large extent co-opted the process and limited the gains that many workers had initially expected. Moreover, the institution of industry-wide codes failed to make much of a dent in what was by the mid-1930s a prolonged and bitter depression.

Eleanor became disenchanted with the NRA relatively soon after her first burst of enthusiasm had cooled, when she became aware that many of the industrial codes blatantly discriminated against women in setting wages and work conditions. In many of the codes, women specifically were to be paid less than men, thus perpetuating or even reinstating discriminatory practices that women activists such as Eleanor had been fighting against for decades. Women's wages often were set at half the level of men and there were other inequities such as classifying qualified professional women at the same wage rate as unskilled men workers. Although she was distressed by these issues, Eleanor refrained from anything more than mild public criticism, as she continued to harbor long-range hopes for a national recovery that would pull women along with it and eventually become more amenable to reform.

Several provisions of the NRA codes touched on a sore spot between Eleanor and some of the most vocal and politically active women in the country. Eleanor and many of her close friends had worked hard since the 1920s to bring about official recognition that women and children needed special protection in the workplace. On the other side were women reformers represented by the

National Women's Party, who believed that the only legitimate goal was full economic and social equality for women. This was a fundamental difference of philosophy that Eleanor found hard to reconcile. She had spoken and written for years of her belief that a woman's nature was basically different than a man's. She specifically believed public policy should give consideration to motherhood and the responsibility of society to protect those who would give birth to future generations (a fundamental fact of nature in her view). To Eleanor, women were given the physical responsibility for the future of the race and that fact alone should be enough to win women protection from harm in the workplace.

Eleanor's position meant she had to support special treatment of women—something her feminist opponents on this issue saw as coddling—and by extension special treatment in the world at large. By the middle of the 1930s, however, this position was painfully at odds with Eleanor's own experience. She had completely outgrown in her own life any need for special treatment, and she was the most prominent example of the ability of women to function fully in the world of work and politics. Nonetheless, she continued to oppose the efforts of the National Women's Party to push through an equal rights amendment to the U.S. Constitution that she feared would damage the hard-won legal protections for women.

Eleanor did, however, believe fervently and deeply that women should work outside the home. Unless women were given freedom from the bondage of traditional homebound roles, they would fail to realize their potential; therefore the nation and the world would be deprived of their great insight and energy. Although she thought women's specialness had to be protected to some degree, Eleanor also wanted that specialness freed to improve the state of the world. As the New Deal wore on, she increasingly emphasized this aspect of her beliefs.

Eleanor communicated her ideas and concerns to an extremely wide audience, especially through her exhausting writing and speaking. FDR usually is described as a master of political communication, especially for the way he used the new medium of radio to reach into millions of homes with his disarming "Fireside Chats," but Eleanor was not far behind him in her ability to court the public with her words. It seems almost astounding that her great outpouring of writing and speaking during the New Deal was accomplished entirely without the help of ghost writers or any assistance beyond the clerical skills of her secretary Tommy Thompson. Eleanor absolutely refused to have even the slightest bit of text published under her name unless she had written every word. She had proven herself as an extremely effective political writer and editor during the 1920s, but after she became First Lady her gifts for communication exploded. Her prose was charmingly simple and unadorned, and she had a knack for writing and speaking in a way that even those of little education or sophistication could understand what she was saying. In short, she was superbly talented at communicating, although she seldom has been so recognized.

In 1933 she published her first substantial book, *It's Up to the Women*, based largely on her earlier speeches and articles, in which she forcefully espoused meaningful work for women outside the home and pointed to women as the greatest hope for the improvement of humankind. She wrapped these messages in a comforting discussion of the joys of marriage and motherhood interspersed with household tidbits, but she wrote explicitly and at length about the responsibility of women to take control of their own lives and to reach beyond the domestic sphere to find ways to realize what Eleanor believed was nearly unlimited potential. The book stated clearly her hope that women would be able to energize a movement for peace in the world and her belief that only those with the "understanding heart of a woman" had the power to do so. She also tacked on a spirited defense and endorsement of the NRA—which was still new at that stage—as potentially one of the best vehicles for women to move into the workplace.

In the same year Eleanor signed a contract to write a monthly column for the popular magazine *Women's Home Companion* at a fee of one thousand dollars a month, which was a very large payment for the time. She turned the column into a forum for

Americans, who were encouraged to write in to her so she could reply in print. This proved to be an effective medium for Eleanor to illustrate many of her ideas, as she had a huge correspondence to draw from and could take up virtually any topic by culling the sacks of letters. She used the column skillfully to bring up issues she wanted addressed or problems she wanted solved.

In the spring of 1934 Eleanor was contacted by radio executives and offered a chance to make a six-minute weekly radio broadcast that would go out all over the nation. She would have a regular radio pulpit from which to espouse her ideas and social and political agendas, and she would make a great deal of money: three thousand dollars a week. The programs were to be sponsored by the Johns Manville Company, and the network agreed to pick up her broadcasts by phone from wherever she happened to be so the radio commitment put almost no damper on her travels.

She also had a commercial booking agent who negotiated paid speaking engagements for her throughout the year and arranged for lecture tours through various parts of the country, which not only made money, it allowed Eleanor good opportunities to observe conditions wherever she went to speak. As she explained:

These trips gave me a wonderful opportunity to visit all kinds of places and to see and get to know a good cross section of people. Always during my free time I visited as many government projects as possible, often managing to arrive without advance notice so they could not be polished up for my inspection. I began to see for myself some of the results of my husband's actions during the first hundred days of his administration .... Of course, I always reported to Franklin on my return ....

By the end of 1934 she was making more than seventy-five thousand dollars a year—an immense amount for the day and more than FDR made as president. Despite a great deal of criticism that she took money for her speaking and writing, Eleanor was eager to maximize her income from such sources, as she used much of it to pay for pet projects or to fund things that the government would not or could not. For example, the three thousand dollars a week for her radio broadcast went directly to the American Friends Service Committee for aid to the poor. (She also regularly supplemented the funds she donated from her professional work with money from her own trust fund income.)

In January 1936 Eleanor began the publication of what became her most famous and popular writing venue, a six-time-a-week syndicated newspaper column for United Features Syndicate called "My Day." The column had its genesis in the long letters she was accustomed to writing to Lorena Hickok. As the name implied, she wrote quite simply about her daily activities as First Lady. Much of the time the column was not much more than a mundane run-through of her schedule—she lowered the temperature of her social and political pleading for the most part.

Some critics found the column boring, many on the left thought she missed chances for propaganda, and conservatives thought she was drawing unseemly attention to herself, but millions of readers found the details of life at the White House or what the Roosevelt children were doing or where Eleanor was traveling that week to be fascinating. Within months, the column was one of the most popular and widely syndicated in the nation. At regular intervals for several years the columns were collected and published in book form.

Arthurdale

Although Eleanor was interested in a wide range of social issues and how the New Deal dealt with them, her imagination and deepest concern were captured by a project she began in West Virginia after visiting a horribly depressed mining camp near Morgantown. The miners of the settlement of Scott's Run had essentially been out of work for years following a series of vicious strikes, and they and their families lived literally on the edge of extinction in the most foul housing and conditions. They had little to eat and survived in housing that was only on the bare edge of being habitable. There was almost no medical care at all in the community, which also lacked basic necessities such as clean water and sanitation facilities. Worse, the mining community had virtually no hope for the future because the labor unrest and the

Depression had closed most of the local mines. When Eleanor saw these conditions, she set about to energize the resources of the government and her wealthy friends to improve the lives of the miners and their families.

The National Recovery Act included a provision for a Subsistence Homestead Division, which Eleanor thought could be turned to her purposes. Bypassing Harold Ickes, who had nominal oversight of the program, Eleanor began to slash through Washington red tape. With the aid of Louis Howe, she had the sympathetic Clarence Pickett appointed as head of the mining community section of the Homestead Division and easily convinced Pickett that the miners of Scott's Run and their families should become the model of community redevelopment.

Howe himself took charge of the first months of the project. He selected and purchased a new site, which was christened Arthurdale, for the new homesteads and began to plan for the construction of new houses and community buildings, such as a school. The center of the new town was to be a factory where the former miners would be employed in the future. In short, an entirely new planned community was to be created, rural in feeling and setting but centered on small-scale industry.

Eleanor involved herself in all aspects of the planning and building of Arthurdale. She often traveled to the site to check on progress and constantly spoke or wrote to government officials who worked on the project. Without question, the Arthurdale community captured her imagination and interest more than any other project during the New Deal years, and no matter what other urgent or important matters were on her schedule, Eleanor always had time and energy to deal with any question or arrangement for the West Virginia community.

Why this particular project so engrossed her is a matter of speculation. The creation of a model community for destitute miners in West Virginia seems on the face to be an unlikely obsession for a woman of Eleanor's background and position, but it illustrates the powerful attraction and empathy she felt for the most marginal members of American society. Time and again she demonstrated an overwhelming personal commitment to the down and out, the dispossessed, and the powerless. She usually appeared to care much, much more for such people than she did for anyone else she came in contact with, save her family and closest friends. This was at once a mark of her greatness as a public figure and a target for her many critics who usually failed to understand how Eleanor could "betray" her background and place in life.

Eleanor visited Arthurdale, West Virginia, in 1933. The town was the site of one of her most cherished social betterment projects.

(Courtesy of the Franklin Delano Roosevelt Library)

Unfortunately, the Arthurdale project provided her critics much ammunition. Billed by Eleanor as a model for development of similar planned communities in the future, Arthurdale actually absorbed huge amounts of public and private money and failed almost every test as a pilot project. The first difficulties came when plans for the new houses for the miners were altered after Eleanor's direct intervention. The original plans had called for small, un-insulated, prefabricated houses with few amenities. After the first ten were erected at the Arthurdale site, it appeared they were not much improvement on the tents the miners had been living in and that the houses were not only too small for the average family but would scarcely stand up to the frigid winters of that part of West Virginia.

When Eleanor took up the cause of Arthurdale, she participated in a widespread phenomenon: spreading social welfare work into the Appalachians, which had recently been discovered as a place for outsiders to do good works. She differed only in the power and extent of the resources she could bring to bear on her favorite project.

Most mountain projects were sponsored by religious groups or nonprofit organizations with limited money to spend, especially during the Depression. Some projects were undertaken by colleges or universities as extension programs.

The most typical mountain social welfare institution was a settlement school (in approach not unlike the Rivington Street Settlement of Eleanor's youth) where mountain children came boarding schools to study academic subjects as well as social skills. Other Appalachian proj-ects shared Eleanor's emphasis on improving housing and developing the local economies, especially if traditional folkways could be preserved.

Eleanor insisted on completely redesigning the houses and start-ing over. The new homes were to be substantial buildings with every amenity and modern convenience, from coal-fired central steam heat to indoor plumbing. The floors and finish woodwork were high quality, and each house was equipped with built-in bookcases and closets. Eleanor even insisted on providing each home with a refrigerator. In a day when most rural Americans still relied on cast-iron stoves, ice boxes, and outdoor privies, Eleanor's plans for the unemployed miners of Arthurdale seemed wildly extravagant to her critics.

The cost of all this, plus building a school and factory, were far beyond anything Congress had imagined when it had approved the original section of the NRA that included "subsistence" homesteads. There were howls of outrage from members of Congress when the expense figures emerged and Harold Ickes complained bitterly to FDR about the amounts being spent from his budget on just one project. Moreover, the most conservative of Eleanor's critics saw the creation of new government-subsidized homes and a new factory as communistic innovations that deprived former landlords of rent and threatened the profits of other factory owners with unfair competition.

Moreover, it was unacceptable to the critics that Arthurdale's formerly destitute miners and their families should be allowed to live in comparatively luxurious homes and be afforded subsidized employment. This destroyed the very foundations of the economic and social order in their view—the miners had failed and sunk to the bottom of the economic pond, so why should the government and do-gooders such as Eleanor (who in the view of conservative critics was taking undue advantage of her position as First Lady) lift them up?

Eleanor's view was, of course, just the opposite. She believed she was engineering no more than a simple experiment in providing worthy people with a minimum standard of decent housing and an opportunity to work productively. Moreover, she thought that there was acute political danger in allowing people such as the Arthurdale miners to sink into economic oblivion. As she later wrote about the project: "Conditions were so nearly the kind that breed revolution that the men and women needed to be made to feel their government's interest and concern."

Despite the carping of critics Eleanor pushed ahead, funding much of the resettlement program out of her own pocket from the proceeds of her speaking and writing. In 1934, for example, she turned over thirty-six thousand dollars to the project through the American Friends Service Committee. She also involved many of her wealthy acquaintances in helping to fund aspects of Arthurdale when government appropriations proved insufficient. The most prominent of these was Wall Street financier and presidential advisor Bernard Baruch, who Eleanor took on a visit to Arthurdale. He was charmed by the people and the broad vision of the project, and he thereafter contributed tens of thousands of dollars each year for many years, primarily to pay for the Arthurdale school and education programs. From this time forward, he and Eleanor had a close relationship. Eleanor also recruited several others, such as her childhood friend Dorothy Elmhirst, who donated funds for health care and involved associates such as Nancy Cook, who offered consulting on handicraft furniture-making.

One of the most difficult problems proved to be finding a manufacturer who would be willing to open a small factory at Arthurdale. Baruch got the General Electric company to start up a vacuum cleaner plant, but it proved to be unsuitable. A mountain handcrafts and furniture enterprise was more promising but relied on subsidies and became the focus of virulent criticism from members of Congress, several of whom made personal attacks on Eleanor. An attempt to set up a printing press ran afoul of bitter opposition from bureaucrats of the Resettlement Administration, and the prospective publisher grew weary of red tape and sniping from the government officials. Eleanor finally scored a modest success when with Baruch's help she persuaded the Phillips-Jones company to install a small plant to manufacture men's shirts.

In the end the Arthurdale community project fell short of the hopes Eleanor had for it at the beginning but it also was far from the failure the critics made it out to be. Historians often have labeled Arthurdale a wrong-headed attempt by Eleanor to overreach her position as First Lady, but in fact a new community was established in the place of the some of the most horrible social and physical conditions in the country and, although not a prototype that could be reproduced other places, Arthurdale endured for several generations, long after the criticism faded.

Challenges to the New Deal

By late 1934 FDR saw the need to move beyond his initial programs and put forward a series of proposals that became known as the "Second New Deal," most of them aimed at further improvement in social conditions. The worst edges had been taken off the distress of many Americans by the first New Deal programs, but there were still millions whose lives were as yet untouched and there were basic inequities in American life that had not been addressed. Moreover, the economy had made only modest gains despite FDR's best efforts to stimulate a recovery.

In part FDR was responding to people such as the First Lady who continually urged more government involvement to better the lives of the average citizen, but there also was a growing series of political threats. FDR had managed for the first year and a half of his administration to deal deftly with the U.S. Congress—even the economic conservatives and the traditionalist southerners. However, by mid-1934 he faced challenges from critics who operated outside the usual political structure, taking their messages directly to the American people.

The most colorful of FDR's populist critics was Governor Huey Long of Louisiana, known popularly as the "Kingfish" because he proclaimed that his goal was to make "every man a king." Long was full of southern charm and bombast, but he won many supporters by arguing that FDR and the New Deal had stopped too short. He advocated a program to give every American cheap food, cheap housing, and cheap education. Long proposed a "Share the Wealth" scheme, whereby money would be expropriated from the wealthy and redistributed to the poor, resulting in a guaranteed annual income of at least two thousand dollars for every American. This message had considerable appeal for those to whom the New Deal had not yet brought full relief, and Long might have presented a strong challenge to FDR's reelection had he not been assassinated on the steps of the Louisiana state capitol in 1935.

A second political threat to FDR came from an unlikely source, a retired California physician named Dr. Francis Townsend, who proposed a wide-ranging program of government subsidy for the nation's elderly. Townsend proposed to levy a new two percent tax on all income and to distribute the money in the form of monthly two hundred dollar pensions to anyone over the age of sixty and as payments to the blind, the disabled, and widows. His ideas stimulated the formation of thousands of "Townsend clubs," which claimed to have ten million members. FDR apparently read the portents surrounding Townsend's popularity; by 1935 the president—goaded by other voices of reform such as Eleanor and many of her associates—decided to co-opt the issue by introducing a national Social Security program.

Less easily defused was the most dangerous of the New Deal's critics, Father Charles Coughlin, a Roman Catholic priest in Michigan who had initially supported FDR but who turned to vehement criticism. Coughlin used a highly popular radio show to portray FDR as a betrayer of the American people and to proclaim a bigoted philosophy of hate. He wanted the government to take over all private and public enterprise, abolish the banks (which he said were run by devils), and directly provide jobs for everyone in the nation. Coughlin claimed his broadcasts were immensely popular and that his fan mail ran to the tens of thousands of letters each week.

FDR also faced strident criticism from the small but vocal Communist Party, which reflected the theories of Karl Marx as they had been modified by the successful Bolshevik revolutionaries of Russia during World War I. American communists hewed faithfully to the international Communist Party line by proclaiming that FDR and all conventional American politicians and officeholders were mere lackeys of a corrupt capitalist system. The presence of communists on the American political scene was not very significant in and of itself; however, it provided a foil and a straw man for FDR's critics on the right. Whenever the president or Eleanor said or did something the conservatives feared or hated, they could be relied on to accuse the Roosevelts of being (or at least abetting) communism. This clouded political discourse throughout the 1930s.

The flurry of new legislation that FDR proposed in the first months of 1935—the so-called Second New Deal—embraced several aspects of his revived social and economic program, but one of the most widespread in its effects was the creation of the Works

Progress Administration, or WPA, which aimed at finally wiping out unemployment though the mechanism of the federal government. The WPA was a large-scale extension of the original Public Works Administration, which FDR had introduced during the first months of the New Deal, and the new program went further and cut more deeply into the ranks of the millions who still had no jobs. Eleanor had considerable influence on how the new program was shaped, especially when Harry Hopkins was named by the president to head the WPA. At this stage of the New Deal Eleanor had a close working relationship with Hopkins.

Hopkins received authorization to create five million new jobs with government money by spending on a very broad variety of public projects, ranging from building airports to painting murals on the walls of local post offices. It was one of the most significant undertakings of the national government (outside of war) in the history of the nation, and the WPA eventually reached into nearly every community and locality. Much of the basic infrastructure of the nation was improved or repaired by WPA workers, who built bridges, laid new roads, and constructed public buildings.

Perhaps the most innovative aspect of the WPA was the attention paid to the arts and humanities. Hopkins created the Federal Writers Project to employ historians and writers who undertook to research and write basic local histories and guidebooks and to conduct what has since proved to be invaluable interview research on a wide variety of topics. There also was a Federal Arts Project that found employment for out-of-work actors and directors by renting theater spaces and producing plays. Painters and sculptors, who had virtually no hope of selling their work during the Depression, were put on the federal payroll by the WPA and put to work creating public art. Additionally, thousands of musicians were given work by the creation of WPA orchestras, which offered free concerts to the public.

Particularly pleasing from Eleanor's point of view were the WPA programs for hundreds of thousands of women including many, such as single women, who had been left out of the first New Deal relief programs. Ellen Woodward, who had been working with Hopkins since 1933, was given charge of the women's programs and set up a variety of projects ranging from sewing rooms for the most unskilled women to cultural projects specifically for women writers and artists. Although she was still annoyed by some of the conditions placed on women who tried to qualify for the WPA employment programs, on the whole Eleanor viewed the WPA as an advance over the first of FDR's employment projects, and she was able to see some of her private lobbying efforts come to fruition.

She also was closely concerned with one of the most significant pieces of legislation passed during the Second New Deal: the National Labor Relations Act, usually called the Wagner Act after its sponsor, New York Senator Robert Wagner. The act extended the rights of workers to organize and join labor unions and virtually banned company-sponsored unions, which had been used to control workers and shut out independent unions. It also banished a variety of unfair labor practices such as the blacklisting of workers who tried to organize unions. Under the Wagner Act workers were guaranteed the right to form unions that would have the exclusive right to bargain with the employer over wages and working conditions.

Although it did not overnight reverse decades of government support for business owners and employers, the Wagner Act completely changed the role of the federal government in labor relations—at least formally. Many of the issues that Eleanor had worked for as a member of the Women's Trade Union League, such as organization of women textile workers in the South, were addressed by the Wagner Act, although women were still excluded by some of its provisions. Despite reservations about its limitations, Eleanor supported the bill and showed up unannounced at Congressional hearings to indicate her support by sitting quietly and knitting while the legislators debated passage.

Without a doubt, the most important single piece of legislation to pass during 1935, and perhaps one of the most important in the twentieth century, was the Social Security Act, which fundamentally altered the relationship of most Americans to their government. For the first time, the act created a system of federally funded old-age pensions and employment and disability insurance. Until Social Security became a reality under FDR, the responsibility for old-age pensions or assistance fell to localities, which seldom could deal adequately with the problems of how to maintain the elderly.

Moreover, there had been virtually nothing like the Social Security Act's employment insurance provisions before 1935. Millions of Americans could qualify for the first of what have come to be known as "entitlement" programs that provide benefits to which all citizens are entitled. Eleanor had been an enthusiastic supporter of a Social Security program and had poked and prodded FDR for months before the bill's passage. She wanted it to be as broad as possible in its reach and to push the limits of the highest possible benefits; not a surprising stance, given her general approach to relief and welfare.

Unfortunately from her viewpoint, FDR allowed his Secretary of the Treasury Henry Morgenthau Jr. to gut some of the coverage of the proposed legislation. Agricultural workers, which meant most black farm workers in the South and migrant workers in the West, were to be excluded, as were government workers and some categories of women. Eleanor saw this as another of FDR's compromises with the southern and conservative legislators and fell into a temporary funk over the president's failure to push for a complete Social Security system. However, in the end she recognized the Social Security Act as a great step forward and vindication of many of the efforts of women reformers. She consoled herself that the coverage could eventually be extended.

At the same time as FDR won passage of these important programs, the New Deal also suffered a major setback, nearly the first of his administration, when the U.S. Supreme Court struck down the National Industrial Recovery Act as unconstitutional, taking with it the entire complicated apparatus of the National Recovery Administration and its system of industrial codes. Worse, the unanimous decision of the Court struck at the basic assumptions behind the New Deal—that the federal government had the constitutional power to take over social and economic functions that had previously been the province of state and local governments.

This cast considerable doubt on the future of many of FDR's programs, as other cases involving more New Deal agencies were on their way to hearing before the Court.

Eleanor was aghast at the ruling of the Court, although she was sufficiently disillusioned with the NRA that she did not much mourn its passing. Hardly anything could have been more at odds with her beliefs than the Court's position that the national government had no concern with the welfare of its citizens. There was little she could do specifically, however, other than continue to publicly support FDR and to privately keep up her campaigns for various causes.

A Second Term

During the first months of 1936 Eleanor was engaged in a typical round of speaking, writing, visiting, and lobbying but was deeply saddened in April with the death of Louis Howe, who had long suffered from acute asthma and other serious ailments. Howe had been an integral part of the Roosevelts' personal and public lives for more than twenty-five years and had played an especially crucial role for Eleanor after they became close friends during the election campaign of 1920. From that time on, Howe had been a link between Eleanor and FDR and virtually the only person who had the trust and confidence of both. Howe, along with Jim Farley, had been most responsible for engineering FDR's victory in 1932. Now on the eve of the new election he was gone. His death left Eleanor despondent. She wrote of him in her daily column: "He hated sham and cowardice, but he had a great pity for the weak and helpless in this world, and responded to any appeal with warmth and sympathy. His courage, loyalty, and devotion to his family and friends will be an inspiration to all of them as long as they live."

Moreover, Howe's passing meant the advancement of several of FDR's advisors who were openly hostile to Eleanor. Many of them thought she was a political liability and wanted to stifle her public activities, which they saw as dragging down FDR's image before the electorate. In short, many of the new advisors voiced the old, tired traditionalist line that Eleanor should begin to behave like a "proper" wife and lady and leave the serious work to the men, and they resented what they believed to be Eleanor's influence on the president. As Sam Rosenman stridently put it, he wanted to "get the pants off Eleanor and onto Franklin."

When she became a celebrity, Eleanor was an easy target for satire and caricature, both friendly and derisive.

Her physical appearance gave political cartoonists much to work with. She had been an attractive teenager, and during her mature years she regained a pleasing grandmotherly appearance. But during her years as First Lady her physical attributes were at low ebb. Her prominent teeth and tall, gangly appearance were targets for ridicule.

Her distinctive and easily imitated speaking voice afforded satirists another opportunity for cheap making fun of her. When she spoke quietly in ordinary conversation, her tone was well modulated, but when giving a speech or addressing a radio audience, her voice soared into a high-pitch range that, combined with her East-Coast upper-class accent, struck many American listeners as distinctive at best and silly at worst.

Although FDR certainly did not accept such advice completely, he was sufficiently nervous about the election that he tended to keep Eleanor at arm's length during much of the campaign. For example, the platform issues that Eleanor and her Democratic women colleagues had tried unsuccessfully to propose to the party in 1924 were given a better hearing in 1936, but ultimately excluded yet again. Additionally, Molly Dewson, Eleanor's closest colleague in the party, was denied an appointment as vice chairman of the Democratic National Committee.

Eleanor herself kept almost entirely off the campaign trail and intentionally toned down the political content of her widely published columns and articles. In September she contracted an undiagnosed illness and for the first time in memory was confined to bed for several weeks. FDR was startled by her sickness and was genuinely alarmed for her health—it seemed to pierce his occasional indifference to Eleanor—and he broke his campaign schedule to be with her. She recovered in time to join FDR on a few campaign trips but was uncharacteristically subdued.

FDR and his advisors feared his well-financed critics, many of whom—including FDR's one-time political mentor Al Smith—had banded together as the Liberty League to oppose FDR's re-election. However, the Republican nominee, Kansas governor Alf Landon, proved to be an uninspired opponent whose dull speeches failed to arouse much enthusiasm among the majority of voters. The conservatives who so hated FDR and Eleanor by this stage of the New Deal often were vicious in their attacks, but their appeal was proven to be extremely narrow when the election results came in. FDR won a monumental landslide victory over Landon, polling nearly eleven million more popular votes than his opponent and taking all but two states. In the Electoral College, FDR defeated Landon by an astonishing 523 to 11, one of the greatest margins in American history.

Personal Problems

Eleanor's spirits, which had fallen so low during the campaign, were lifted by the overwhelming approval of both FDR and herself that the election signaled. After returning from a post-election lecture tour of the Midwest, where she had been greeted warmly by large and enthusiastic audiences, Eleanor seemed ready to move forward with the reasonable hope that life for her and her family would settle into a period of stability. However, the two years following FDR's reelection proved to be full of difficulties for the Roosevelts on both the personal and political levels. The Roosevelt children became embroiled in situations that caused Eleanor much anxiety, and FDR went into an almost inexplicable funk, seeming to lose his previously certain grasp on politics.

The first of the difficulties arose over William Randolph Hearst, the powerful newspaper publisher, who had been one of the principal behind-the-scenes kingmakers at the 1932 Democratic convention and had delivered the crucial California delegation votes in exchange for FDR's promise to not support World Court and the League of Nations. However, in the midst of FDR's first term Hearst viciously turned on the president and Eleanor and allied himself and his publishing empire with some of the Roosevelts' harshest enemies, such as the Liberty League, during the 1936 campaign.

When FDR crushed his opposition at the polls in November Hearst flip-flopped and made a transparent attempt to curry favor with the president by hiring Elliott Roosevelt at a lucrative contract (far in advance of his experience or demonstrated ability) to manage several Hearst-owned radio stations in Texas. Hearst also offered a sweetheart deal to Anna Roosevelt and her newspaperman husband, John Boettinger. They were given complete control of the Hearst *Seattle Post-Intelligencer* with large salaries for each of them plus generous percentage bonuses if the paper turned a profit.

Eleanor was distressed by these arrangements. First of all, she detested Hearst on both political and personal grounds. As a strong supporter of the World Court and the League of Nations before FDR's election, she had been devastated when her husband abandoned internationalism in response to Hearst's pressure. Then, when Hearst conducted a savage publicity campaign on behalf of FDR's political enemies during the election, Eleanor was further outraged and believed Hearst had transgressed the normal bounds of partisan politics. However, perhaps just as distressing for Eleanor was the fact that her children cheerfully accepted what could uncharitably be described as bribes from Hearst.

At Thanksgiving, only weeks after the election, Franklin Jr. was stricken with a life-threatening illness. What seemed at first to be only a minor sinus irritation developed rapidly into a full-blown bacterial infection, which in the days before antibiotics often was fatal, and he was hospitalized in Boston. Because FDR was away on a post-election cruise to the Pacific and South America, Eleanor took full responsibility for seeing to Franklin Jr.'s treatment. She spent days at his bedside until he finally recovered after a near brush with death. The distressing episode was capped when even before regaining his health Franklin Jr. rather ungraciously announced his engagement to Ethel DuPont, whose parents had helped finance the anti-Roosevelt Liberty League during the election campaign (the couple were married a year later, to FDR's and Eleanor's chagrin).

*Eleanor loved to ride horseback for relaxation in Washington's
Rock Creek Park. She is shown here with her youngest son,
John.*

(*Courtesy of the Franklin Delano Roosevelt Library*)

Perhaps the most distressing family issue arose over Eleanor's
eldest son James. FDR's longtime personal aide and bodyguard Gus
Gennerich had died unexpectedly and, coupled with the death of
Louis Howe earlier in the year, FDR felt a strong need to replace
his lost companions with someone he could both trust and relax
with. To Eleanor's shock and surprise, FDR and James hatched a
plan whereby James would become his father's personal and political assistant, replacing both Gennerich and Howe as FDR's
constant companion and confidant. James, who had never demonstrated any outstanding political abilities, was eager to take on a
responsible role, and FDR apparently felt a strong desire to have
his eldest son at his side.

Eleanor was appalled at the plan, ostensibly because she feared
James's presence would create undue criticism of FDR and the
Roosevelt family. Her comments on the affair also might be read as

a lack of confidence in James's abilities to handle politically sensitive problems.

Despite Eleanor's objections, FDR went ahead with the scheme and appointed James as one of his principal secretaries with authority to coordinate and oversee many of the most important New Deal agencies. True to Eleanor's predictions, James was attacked in the press and had serious problems in trying to deal with Congress.

Nonetheless, father and son enjoyed the opportunity to work together and they effectively shut Eleanor out of the equation. For a time, James even impinged on Eleanor's usual political access to her husband. Moreover, when James's wife, Betsey, moved into the White House she proved to be a thorn in Eleanor's side. Betsey seemed determined to antagonize her mother-in-law at every turn. She interfered with the household arrangements—abruptly changing table settings and menus of the First Family—and openly demonstrated her dislike and disrespect for Eleanor. Betsey behaved exactly the opposite with FDR, joining the flirtatious and fun-loving coterie that provided him with relaxation and entertainment. The conflict between Eleanor and Betsey was never resolved; it diminished only when James was forced to give up his post as his father's secretary due to severe bleeding ulcers, thought at the time to have been caused by the tension of his job at the White House. In part, James blamed his mother for his failure, which added more tension to Eleanor's relationship with her children.

Perhaps due to the pressures of the campaign and her difficult family life, Eleanor attempted during 1936 and 1937 to refurbish her relationship with Lorena Hickok, who had been on the road much of the time since 1933 as an observer and inspector for Harry Hopkins's Federal Emergency Relief Administration. She had corresponded regularly with Eleanor, but they seldom found opportunities to be together. During the summer of 1936 Hickok began traveling with a new young woman companion and several times ignored Eleanor's requests to see her. Hickok was extremely unhappy during these months, however, and the full weight of losing her career in journalism because of her friendship with Eleanor seemed to descend on her. Moreover, she was tired and ground down from her job with the FERA.

Eleanor found a new position for Hickok as a publicist for the New York World's Fair, which allowed them to see each other when Eleanor was in New York City. After a short period of renewal, however, the relationship began to deteriorate again. Hickok refused to visit Eleanor at Val-Kill—she felt strongly the jealousy and disapproval of Cook and Dickerman—and even when she eventually took yet another job engineered by Eleanor as head of the Women's Committee of the Democratic Party (Molly Dewson's old position) in 1938, her contacts with Eleanor never again achieved the immediacy and constancy of the early 1930s.

Eleanor's long-term relationship with Nancy Cook and Marion Dickerman also faltered. Eleanor's rise to national prominence and the extreme publicity and controversy surrounding her might have been at the heart of the problem, although her biographers also refer to fits of acute jealousy that her friends seemed prone to, especially as she became increasingly famous. Although she still regarded Val-Kill as her home, Eleanor spent less and less time there as the 1930s wore on, and the interest and attention she had lavished on the threesome's joint enterprises diminished greatly. Whatever the roots of the difficulties, in 1936 the partners decided to close down the furniture factory at Val-Kill, and Eleanor announced plans to take over the vacated building and to re-fit it as a home for herself, the original cottage shared by all three having proven too small for the procession of her guests and new associates. This was a bitter decision for Nancy Cook, who was the one most concerned with the factory, and it signaled a serious deterioration in the relationship.

While Eleanor experienced this blizzard of unhappy personal situations, FDR's landslide reelection victory seemed almost to unhinge him. At the least, he appeared temporarily to have lost his grasp of political reality. When he was inaugurated in January 1937 (the official date had been moved forward two months from that of his 1933 inauguration as the result of a Constitutional amendment) he dramatically drew a picture of a country that had made progress toward recovery but in which he saw "one-third of a nation ill nourished, ill clad, and ill housed," but his call to renewed efforts to fight the effects of the Depression also contained a veiled threat against the justices of the U.S. Supreme Court, who had recently struck down several key provisions of the New Deal, including the National Industrial Recovery Act and the Agricultural Adjustment Act.

Without consulting Eleanor or his other advisors, FDR decided that a total "reform" (as he called it) of the judicial system and the Supreme Court was the only solution. Historians and biographers have argued for decades about just what motivated FDR to undertake his attempt to "pack the Court" (the term his critics used to describe FDR's crusade). Some have believed it was a gigantic bluff to intimidate the Court into changing its conservative attitude toward the New Deal; others have seen the Court-packing episode as a genuine attempt by FDR to change the basic structure of American government.

He proposed a bill that would have allowed him to appoint one new, additional justice for every sitting justice over the age of seventy who refused to step down. The total number of justices would expand to fifteen. The criticism FDR directed toward the aging justices who had frustrated him often was intemperate, and he brushed aside suggestions that he tone down the crusade. In the end he was unable to get his bill through Congress and the number of justices remained fixed at nine, but the Court got the message and began to uphold many of the new cases that it heard concerning New Deal programs. (Natural attrition also worked in FDR's favor, and by 1941 he had named five new justices simply because of retirements.)

The entire affair hurt FDR's popularity and seemed inexplicable to some of his closest supporters, especially in light of his caution in handling other delicate political questions. Eleanor was strongly opposed to the Court-packing scheme and thought the entire adventure pure political folly that could have been avoided with only a little patience from FDR. She received a lot of pressure from her women political allies on the issue. Elizabeth Read and Ester Lape were especially fervent in urging her to try to influence FDR against what they—and many others in the country—saw as a damaging attempt to alter the basic balance of the American system. Unfortunately, FDR had cut Eleanor out when deciding on his plan, an exclusion that was almost as damaging in Eleanor's eyes as the actual scheme.

Race Relations

Eleanor's most courageous and controversial cause during the New Deal probably was her interest in improving race relations and furthering the cause of racial justice in America. During the 1930s she became the most prominent figure in the nation to champion the improvement of social and economic conditions for black Americans, and although she won no really significant gains on a broad front, she did much to elevate the questions of justice and equality into wide public consciousness using the same methods as in her other causes: incessant insistence on a full public examination of the issues and lobbying with FDR for specific remedies.

She did not campaign for racial equality or for an end to segregation as it existed in America at the time. These goals were far beyond realistic dreams of achievement in the 1930s. Her most successful efforts were directed at simply raising the consciousness of white Americans about the status of blacks and focusing on showing that blacks shared the same basic humanity as the rest of the nation's citizens. In short, from her high-profile position in the White House, Eleanor showed herself to believe blacks should receive the same treatment as whites in any normal situation. Additionally, she fought a spirited, although ultimately unsuccessful battle against the great national shame of lynching.

From the vantage point of the twenty-first century, Americans understand how racism has been one of the most powerful forces in our history and how it has conditioned almost all of our national development. Nonetheless, for those too young to remember it is difficult to grasp the all-pervasive nature of institutional racism as it existed in Eleanor's time. In all of the South, for example, segregation was enforced as a matter of both law and social custom. Blacks were forced into a subservient status and reminded of it every minute of the day by both official and unofficial forces. Moreover, white southerners of Eleanor's day were adamant in their zeal to make certain that nowhere and under no circumstances were black people allowed the slightest sign of respect or power. Racial prejudice was virulent and operated publicly and legally, and it was taken for granted by almost all white Americans.

Eleanor's own native New York upper-class society was one that casually accepted the inferior role of blacks, and she had unconsciously absorbed such attitudes from her childhood onward. However, at some point she began to understand that black Americans were fully human and came to believe that they should be treated with respect and common kindness. She had not by the 1930s completely rid herself of some of the reflexive and thoughtless vestiges of her early attitudes—she famously was called to task by a black leader for using the term "darkie" in the first volume of her memoirs she claimed to have not fully grasped that it was a derogatory term—but she had come further than almost any other prominent figure of white America.

Much of her attitude was linked to her fundamental interest in correcting injustice and bringing help to the oppressed. When the reality of black lives in America, and especially the lives of the poorest black citizens, came fully into her consciousness, she began to react. For example, she campaigned vigorously to extend New Deal relief efforts to blacks, particularly in the South where white local and state officials deliberately cut them out of federal relief and work programs. Eleanor also used her great powers of generating publicity to bring the conditions of impoverished blacks to light by visiting black leaders and black communities and speaking to the press about the issues. She also lobbied directly and successfully for public funds to improve black slum housing in the District of Columbia.

Additionally, Eleanor vigorously worked to bring black leaders into contact with decision-makers in Washington, including FDR. In 1934 she invited a group of five black educational and business leaders to the White House for a private conference with the president, the first time such a thing had happened. She continued thereafter to work hard to assure people such as Walter White, head of the National Association for the Advancement of Colored People, were afforded routine access to FDR and the upper reaches of government policymakers.

She also championed the cause of Mary McLeod Bethune, one of the nation's most prominent and successful black educators. Eleanor had first met Bethune, who was the founder of Bethune-Cookman College in Florida, at a biracial dinner for national women leaders Eleanor hosted in New York City in 1927. The two women formed a friendship, and Bethune did much to educate Eleanor on the realities of the status of blacks in the nation, particularly in the deeply segregated South. With Eleanor's backing, Bethune was named as one of the assistant directors of the National Youth Administration, making her the highest-ranking black woman in the history of the federal government.

Eleanor's grandest crusade was her support for a federal anti-lynching law. For generations following the era of Reconstruction in the South it was a ghastly tradition for white mobs to publicly torture and murder black men. This usually involved the open connivance of local government and law enforcement officials and often was regarded—even advertised—as a form of public entertainment. Crowds including women and children gathered to witness the most horrific scenes of burning, mutilation, and death, usually excused by references to alleged biracial sexual threats or transgressions by the black victim.

The frequency of lynching increased during the Depression, finally calling forth an effort in Congress to pass a federal anti-lynching law, which seemed the only possible way to slow down or stop the torture and murders. New York Senator Robert Wagner and Colorado Senator Edward P. Costigan co-sponsored an anti-lynching bill in 1934, and Eleanor immediately threw her weight behind the effort to get it though a Congress that was dominated by southerners. She brought Walter White into the White House to meet FDR and strongly lobbied her husband to make the bill a priority of his administration. She also enlisted the help of Sara Delano, who supported the anti-lynching legislation and added her voice to the effort to convince FDR. Unfortunately, FDR was unwilling to put the full prestige of his administration on the line for the anti-lynching bill. It was clear that the southern faction in the Senate would always defeat any such legislation through the use of the filibuster (which before the reform of its rules allowed any member of the Senate to bring public business to a halt by speaking nonstop).

The 1934 bill was defeated, as was a second attempt in 1938, but Eleanor never faltered in her desire to improve the quality of life for black Americans and to demonstrate by her own actions and utterances that she believed there should be no formal distinctions in American society based on race alone. Not surprisingly, this was one of the positions that brought the most violent hatred and criticism down on her head. Something so simple as being photographed with a black child unleashed the rage and fears of her racist opponents, but in most instances, Eleanor continued to keep a high profile regarding racial issues.

Perhaps the most famous and best remembered of her public stands came in early 1939, when the black contralto Marian Anderson, who had established a huge critical reputation as a singer in Europe, was denied a booking for a concert at Constitution Hall by the Daughters of the American Revolution. Eleanor very publicly resigned from the organization (one of her ancestors on her mother's side was a signer of the Declaration of Independence) in protest of the group's racist policy. Moreover, Eleanor used her syndicated "My Day" column to explain her action, telling her huge nationwide audience of readers that she usually preferred to fight for change from the inside, but that seemed impossible in the case of the DAR. From behind the scenes Eleanor then engineered a new concert for Anderson from the steps of the Lincoln Memorial in Washington. The subsequent performance in front of an integrated audience of seventy-five thousand was widely publicized, and although Eleanor did not attend, the incident was regarded as one of the most powerful statements of the time against public racism.

Chapter 7

The Coming of War

*We are, of course, going through a type of revolution and
we are succeeding in bringing about a greater sense of
social responsibility in the people as a whole. Through the
recognition by our government of a responsibility for social
conditions much has been accomplished; but there is still
much more to be done before we are even prepared to
accept some of the fundamental facts which will make
it possible to fight as a unified nation against the new
philosophies arrayed in opposition to Democracy.*

—Eleanor Roosevelt,
The Moral Basis of
Democracy

Sometime during the presidential campaign of 1936, when she was low in spirits and health, Eleanor decided to write a memoir of her early life, which she called *This Is My Story*. She later gave credit for her inspiration to Louis Howe, who had relentlessly encouraged her writing during their long friendship, but the book was her own; written in her distinctive direct, simple style, and it was an immediate hit. *Ladies Home Journal* bought the serial rights for seventy-five thousand dollars, an immense sum, and published the manuscript chapter by chapter, which stimulated heavy sales of the book when it came out. Moreover, the reviewers and critics were generous in their praise of Eleanor's telling of the tale of her life up to 1924.

The popular and critical success of *This Is My Story* reflected the extraordinary status Eleanor had achieved by the late 1930s. She of course had vocal critics who hated the New Deal, detested her stands on social issues, and disliked her abandonment of the traditional woman's role, but in many ways the nature of her critics defined her great stature. There was indisputable evidence of her broad popularity among the American public. In a January 1939 Gallup Poll a strong majority of sixty-seven percent said they approved of the way "Mrs. Roosevelt has conducted herself as First Lady." FDR's approval rating in the same poll was only fifty-eight percent. In further affirmation of her importance, *Time* magazine ran her picture on the cover and featured a glowing article about her.

Not only was Eleanor the first modern woman to be thrust so vigorously into the public eye, but she was endowed with immense energy and bottomless resolve that perfectly suited her for the position in which she found herself by the late 1930s. She had a quick intelligence, which, if not exceedingly deep, was nonetheless sharp and able to absorb new information and circumstances quickly, penetrating to the heart of issues—and she was relentless in pursuing her goals.

Several of FDR's associates during those years vividly remembered scenes in which Eleanor would fix her husband's eye and introduce a topic with the words "Now, Franklin ..." They knew at that point that Eleanor had the president's attention and would not relinquish it until she had gotten her message across. When FDR characteristically tried to duck her by spinning stories and making jokes, Eleanor usually responded with even more pressure, coming back to her point over and over again. She of course did not always get her way and FDR was never hesitant to ignore her pleading if he had other plans or insight, but without question she was the most potent influence of FDR during the first six years of his administration. He often used her insatiable curiosity to find out things that he had no other way of understanding, and he was never shy of allowing her to test the limits of public or political tolerance on any social issue.

During these years several of Eleanor's personality tendencies seemed to harden; particularly the duality of her nature that made her cold and unbending at times with her family yet capable of intense friendships and the warmest relationships with those she anointed as her intimates. Her family, including FDR, justly feared the apparent blankness of emotion she sometimes wielded against them—the president hated it when he was on the receiving end of her silent treatment and would go far to avoid it—and almost all who surrounded her on a daily basis felt the sting of her cold reproach sooner or later. On the other hand, with people such as Lorena Hickok, Earl Miller, and a few others she was warm, loving, generous, outgoing, and all that one could wish for in a companion and friend. She obviously reveled in her position and power; yet she would frequently disclaim responsibility for her accomplishments and act like the shy young girl she had once been.

Whatever the mysteries of her innermost personality, it is clear that the arc of her life, at least her public life, reached a high point about the time of the election of 1936. During her remaining years as First Lady she ran into increasing frustration and loss of influence, sometimes through no fault of her own, as world and national events engulfed her. At nearly the same time her personal life went through a sometimes painful reordering. During the summer of 1938 Eleanor experienced a bitter breakup of her longtime relationship with Nancy Cook and Marion Dickerman, the two women with whom she had shared a home and several business and political enterprises for twenty-five years. The partnership had already pulled apart to a degree two years earlier, when they had closed down the furniture factory at Val-Kill and Eleanor had made plans to move out of their shared cottage and into the remodeled factory building nearby, but a terrible final rupture occurred between Eleanor and Cook in August.

Eleanor was aggravated when Cook and Dickerman fed drinks to Hall Roosevelt, Eleanor's alcoholic brother who at this stage of his life lived near Hyde Park, and then let him drive off in an intoxicated state—leading to an accident in which Hall's passenger was injured. Eleanor was furious with Cook and Dickerman for egging Hall on and playing on his weaknesses, and she spun out her anger into a major blowup. The deeper reason for the breakup probably was Eleanor's growing disenchantment with Cook's and Dickerman's snobbishness toward her newer friends and associates, and the suspicion that the two women were taking advantage of her new fame and position. The previous year, for example, Eleanor had refused to endorse a fund-raising brochure for Todhunter School. Even though she wanted to capitalize on Eleanor's fame, Dickerman, who was the principal, perversely complained that some of the more conservative parents of prospective students rejected the school because of Eleanor's notoriety.

The final breach between Eleanor and Cook occurred during the summer while Dickerman was in Europe as a member of a presidential commission to study labor relations. Neither Eleanor nor Cook ever gave exact details of their blowup, but it was clear that Eleanor had learned that the other two women were claiming to friends that they were somehow responsible for her success and attainments. Apparently, she confronted Cook on this issue and a bitter scene took place wherein they said things that neither could ever take back. Eleanor felt betrayed and completely ill-used by two people who had been her closest companions.

From the day of the scene with Cook onward, Eleanor cut both her and Dickerman out of her personal and emotional life. Their relations thereafter were characterized by her well-known glacier-like demeanor of disapproval and disdain. She insisted on withdrawing her financial interest from Todhunter, although Dickerman and Cook tried to claim her heavy contributions over the years could not be retrieved, and she eventually demanded a full settlement of all legal and financial matters. Cook and Dickerman continued to live in the original stone cottage at Val-Kill for many more years and they were even included in some of the formal social events at the main house at Hyde Park, but their relationship with Eleanor was stone-cold dead.

About the same time as Eleanor's breakup with Cook and Dickerman, FDR experienced political problems that had a major impact on Eleanor. After making gains throughout most of FDR's first term in office, the economy had taken a dip in 1937. When FDR proposed new measures to combat the downturn he was opposed by a group of conservative Democrats, mostly from the South, who allied themselves with Republicans to form an anti-Roosevelt, anti–New Deal coalition in Congress. Almost needless to say, this coalition also furnished some of the most virulent Eleanor haters. FDR was determined to purge these Democrats and campaigned against them in the mid-term elections of 1938. Unfortunately for the president, the conservative Democrats won in almost every case despite his loud opposition. The results of the elections, coming as they did on the heels of his defeat in attempting to pack the Supreme Court, were a severe blow to FDR's prestige and political power, as the new conservative coalition now controlled Congress.

When FDR suffered politically, so did Eleanor's ability to affect social welfare and reform programs, so she was just as unhappy as the president over the bungled campaign and believed (probably with good cause) that such a thing could never have happened had Louis Howe still been alive. The new conservative Congress began to cut funding for New Deal programs, which signaled the beginning of a long-term struggle between the Roosevelts and reactionary political forces. In fact, as hindsight would show, the steam had gone out of the New Deal. Moreover, FDR's control of his administration was permanently weakened, and he never regained the initiative on domestic programs.

The Roosevelt children also continued to be a source of stress and anxiety for Eleanor. Whatever their virtues, the Roosevelt offspring never managed to achieve anything resembling marital stability— among the five of them they recorded nineteen marriages—and with the exception of Anna, they were likewise unstable in their professional lives. Eleanor apparently felt a good measure of guilt about what she perceived as her failures as a parent, perceptions that her children often intentionally reinforced and that her mother-in-law continued to provoke. Memories of Eleanor's own childhood, which had provided such poor models of parenthood, and her early uncertainty as a young mother only fortified her feelings of inadequacy. She also was determined to avoid the overbearing appearance of Sara Delano; thus she often tried to appear nonjudgmental, which probably was not always the best course.

After the eldest son James recovered from his bout with severe bleeding ulcers and resigned as his father's aide, he broke up with his wife Betsey (who had caused Eleanor much distress while living in the White House) and moved to Hollywood where he became a film company executive. Elliott, who was the most openly hostile of all the children, continued to live in Texas where he managed radio stations for William Randolph Hearst. FDR Jr. was in law school at the University of Virginia during the late 1930s, and John, the youngest and the least public of the children, was married to a socialite and worked in Boston as a manager in a department store.

Eleanor was closest to her daughter Anna, the firstborn of the Roosevelt children, and she genuinely liked Anna's second husband, John Boettinger. Anna appeared during the late 1930s to be the most stable of all the children, despite an early marriage and divorce. She and Boettinger ran Hearst's newspaper in Seattle and Eleanor managed to visit them often, despite the long distance. Over the years, she and Anna developed a close relationship, which Eleanor felt was based on trust and an ability to share thoughts and feelings that was missing from her contact with her sons.

In 1937 FDR built a new "cottage" (actually a small house in the Dutch style) on the Hyde Park estate, situated high on a ridge with a view of the Hudson River below.

Top Cottage was close to Eleanor's Val-Kill cottage, and according to conversations FDR had with his wife, he intended the new cottage as a kind of counterpoint to her comfortable quarters. FDR apparently intended to use Top Cottage as a hideaway after he retired from the presidency.

FDR himself designed the basic appearance and features of the cottage with professional and technical help from architect Henry J. Toombs, who had designed Val-Kill. The design incorporated many unusual features to accommodate FDR's disabilities.

FDR seldom used the cottage, except as guest quarters. Son Elliott moved into the dwelling in the late 1940s when he was managing the Hyde Park farm for his mother. It is now in public hands.

Even though they still professed a love for one another that probably was genuine on some level, Eleanor and FDR appeared to be most comfortable when apart. Eleanor's residence was still ostensibly the White House, but she was more often somewhere else: on the road for inspection trips or lecture tours, at her apartment in Greenwich Village, or at her new home (the converted furniture factory) at Val-Kill. FDR of course traveled less often, due to the press of business in Washington and his disability, but when he did leave the White House other than to go to Hyde Park, it usually was to visit Warm Springs, where Eleanor seldom ventured, or to go on one of the cruises he so loved and she so detested.

Storm Clouds

The period from 1939 to 1945, which accounted for half of the Roosevelts' tenure in the White House, was dominated by world events and war, which to a large degree overshadowed the domestic matters that had been at the center of their political agendas when FDR had been elected in 1932. For both Eleanor and FDR, war and the threat of war meant huge changes in their lives and interests, and they were forced to respond long before the United States itself was drawn in the global conflict.

Following World War I the nation had an intense reaction to European warfare, and many Americans opposed any U.S. involvement in international affairs that were not within the country's immediate purview. President Woodrow Wilson's high-minded plans for a better postwar world were ground underfoot by the victorious British and French at the Versailles Peace Conference in 1919. Additionally, his attempts to bring the United States into the world arena by joining the League of Nations were frustrated by political rivals at home who tapped the broad base of support for isolationism. This isolationism grew stronger and more acute during the 1920s and early 1930s, so that when war again threatened to engulf Europe and the Japanese Empire began to aggressively attack its neighbors, there was a powerful element in the United States that believed the nation could remain aloof behind the protection of two large oceans. For example, Congress passed new and stronger Neutrality Acts, which made it illegal for a president to actively aid belligerents.

To a large extent, the isolationists were allied with political and social conservatives who expressed hate and fear of foreigners. In 1924, for example, Congress passed strict anti-immigration laws that instituted a highly prejudiced quota system, virtually eliminating immigration from Asia and severely limiting any potential influx from eastern or southern Europe. There also was a powerful element of anti-Semitism that went hand in hand with support for the anti-immigration legislation. These became important issues in FDR's and Eleanor's political lives by the late 1930s.

Eleanor herself during the 1920s was an active internationalist who supported American entry into the League of Nations and after the defeat of Wilson's proposal, she shifted to support United States participation in the World Court. She coupled her internationalism with the strong pacifism she had developed after touring the devastation in Europe following World War I when she had accompanied FDR to the Paris Peace Conference. She was an active member and leader in several of the most important women's peace organizations, including the Women's International League for Peace and Freedom, and Carrie Chapman Catt's National Conference on the Cause and Cure of War. After FDR's election Eleanor made the peace movement one of her important causes. She often spoke at peace conferences and on her lecture tours and frequently hosted meetings of peace advocates at the White House.

Having served as a member of Wilson's administration for seven years, FDR shared Eleanor's support of the League; thus initially he was in synch with Eleanor's beliefs, although his experiences as an assistant secretary of the Navy led him to be much less a pacifist than his wife. Nevertheless, both of them had entered the White House with a degree of faith in the efficacy of international cooperation. However, to Eleanor's dismay, FDR opposed support for the League of Nations—which was operating during the 1930s as a crippled and nearly irrelevant institution—because of political pressure and, even more upsetting for her, allowed Congress to shut the door on American participation in the World Court despite her vigorous campaign for it.

Adolf Hitler had come to power in Germany at almost the same time FDR had assumed the U.S. presidency, and the destinies of the two regimes seemed to draw closer and closer together during the 1930s, when Hitler not only re-armed Germany but began a policy of aggressive diplomatic and military moves against other European countries that by 1938 left no doubt that he was bent on taking over as much of the continent as possible. Across the Pacific, a militarist party had taken control of Japan and set it on a course of imperial expansion that included at first piecemeal incursions and by 1937 a full-blown invasion and seizure of China. In short, by the middle of FDR's second term, much of the world seemed on the brink of war.

Europe had already seen a rehearsal of what modern war might be like during the brief and bloody Spanish Civil War in 1936 and 1937, when Hitler and Italy's fascist dictator Benito Mussolini had provided arms and pilots for the rebellious Nationalist forces of Francisco Franco against the popularly elected Republican govern-ment, which included communist and other leftist elements and was supported by the Soviet Union. Eleanor was aghast when she learned of the fascist-aided bombing attacks on defenseless civil-ians, and she came out vocally and forcefully for U.S. aid to the refugees created by the war. However, when she spoke out, the Roman Catholic press and clergy in America attacked her imme-diately, as the worldwide church staunchly supported Franco against the anti-clerical Republicans, and her Catholic critics were joined by pacifist isolationists. Because FDR, no matter what he might have thought about the Spanish Civil War, believed he could not afford to lose votes from American Catholics or isolationists—he still saw the domestic problems facing America as his main agenda—he stayed mute on the issue and refused to advance Eleanor's unsuccessful crusade for aid to the Republicans.

Despite this defeat, Eleanor learned a great deal from the actions of Germany and Italy and viewed the growing ascendancy of fascism as the primary external threat to American democracy. It was clear in her mind by the late 1930s that the United States must do everything in its power, including accepting leftist ele-ments into the mainstream of American life, to defeat fascism. She faced a dilemma as an anti-fascist pacifist, who feared for the fundamental future of democracy in the face of Hitler (whom she recognized clearly as an uncontrollable madman), but at the same time she hated the idea of military violence, the aftermath of which she had seen in 1919.

Eventually, Eleanor began to mitigate her pacifist stance, which had never embraced the extremes of devotion to disarmament, as she had always recognized the need for nations to defend themselves. After the example of the Spanish Civil War, she understood that democracies could not withstand fascist militarism unless well-prepared. This shift in her viewpoint separated her from previous colleagues in the women's pacifist movement, and by 1938 it allied her with FDR, who had become an ardent anti-isolationist as Hitler annexed Austria and faced down the rest of Europe to absorb Czechoslovakia.

In 1938 Eleanor published a manifesto of her new beliefs in the form of *This Troubled World*, a small book in which she sounded an alarm for the American people and explained her fears for the future of democracy if fascism was allowed to proceed with its aggression unchecked. She pointed out that although isolationism might have served America well in the past, it was no longer feasible to believe that oceans were the unbreachable bulwarks they once had been. After seeing the power of German air warfare in Spain, no thinking person could believe in unilateral disarmament or oppose preparedness. As she wrote: "… if war comes to your own country, then even pacifists, it seems to me, must stand up and fight for their beliefs." Although the slim volume did not enjoy the best-seller status of *This Is My Story*, it nonetheless sold an impressive twenty thousand copies within eleven months and established Eleanor as a voice for reasoned but vigorous response to international fascism.

She was less vocal in public about the issue of the Hitler's treatment of German Jews between 1933 and 1938, and she appears to have stifled to some degree any inclinations she may have had to speak out in consideration of FDR's foreign policy. Historians have castigated Eleanor in recent years for this silence; however, in fact any utterance of hers could have had very little effect on the Nazis, and in the 1930s it was highly unusual for one sovereign nation to comment on the internal affairs of another. There was no such concept as international human rights in 1938 and there would be none for another decade, when Eleanor herself became responsible for drawing up and passing through the United Nations a declaration on the subject.

Eleanor biographer Blanche Wiesen Cook asserts that in retrospect Eleanor's prolonged silence seems to have been at least in part the result of political pressure from FDR. Cook reasons that so long as the United States countenanced racial segregation and allowed public torture and murder in the form of lynchings, there was no basis for criticizing Hitler's punitive laws against domestic German Jews, which before 1938 were less harsh than laws against blacks in the American South. By Cook's account, FDR was frightened that Hitler would turn criticism around and thereby cost FDR support among the Southerners in Congress, a point about which he was ever sensitive.

After the Nazis intensified their campaign against the Jews in November 1938, a change signalled by the so-called *Kristallnacht* attacks on Jewish business and synagogues all over Germany, many Jews attempted to emigrate, and for a period of several months German officials allowed them to do so, albeit stripping Jewish families of all assets. During this period Eleanor and others worked hard to clear the way for Jewish refugees to get visas to enter the United States for asylum. She was prominent in working with the Non-Sectarian Committee to gain passage of a bill that would have allowed twenty thousand German refugee children to come to America; however, anti-Semitic, anti-immigration forces in Congress defeated the legislation.

Even more distressing was the malevolence of a group of influential anti-Semitic State Department officials, headed by Assistant Secretary of State Breckinridge Long, who occupied key positions in U.S. consulates in Europe. They flatly refused to issue visas to Jewish families because they believed America should be kept free of what they believed to be the taint of Jews and immigrants. Even though Eleanor managed to get her husband to okay a special quota for Jewish refugees in 1939, when conditions were deteriorating rapidly for German Jews, Long and the others blocked the order, allowing thousands of Jews to be sent to their deaths in the Nazi gas chambers.

American Youth Congress

In no case were the complicating effects of the international situation during the late 1930s more evident than Eleanor's tangled relationship with the organized American youth movement. She had long been concerned with how the federal government and the New Deal could deal with youth. She feared the effects on young people of the Great Depression—especially prolonged unemployment and the inability to pursue education—might create serious long-term problems for the nation at large. She urged FDR to intensify efforts to deal with these issues, and in 1935 he created the National Youth Administration, headed by Charles Taussig and Aubrey Williams, to serve as the focus for New Deal programs for youth. The NYA instigated new educational programs and a series of grants to allow students to continue their educations. Many of the educational programs included training in practical job skills in addition to more traditional academic courses. Despite the predictable criticism from racist southerners when the NYA spent money on black students, which it did with remarkable equality, the agency was successful in ameliorating some of the feared consequences of the Depression.

Eleanor's most intense and intriguing relationship with young people during the late 1930s and early 1940s was with the American Youth Congress, which involved a series of twists and turns that led her deeply into a complicated political situation that she appears to have miscalculated. Eleanor feared that the broad majority of American young people might lose faith in democracy because of the Great Depression, and she desperately wanted to find avenues to reassure them about the strength of the American system. She saw correctly that many young people were turning to leftist philosophies such as socialism and communism, and she hoped that by cultivating the leadership of youth organizations represented by the umbrella AYC she could pull them back from radicalism. She thought that most of the AYC leaders were honestly searching for answers, which she thought she could supply.

In fact, a significant portion of the AYC leadership were committed communists who had already discarded belief in democracy and capitalism and who during the late 1930s were taking direct orders from the government of the Soviet Union. Had Eleanor understood this situation clearly she probably would have not entered into the prolonged relationship that she did, but her desire to reclaim the youth clouded her vision. She was one of the outstanding liberals of her age, which meant that during the 1930s, like other American liberals, she was constantly on the edge of dealing with communists. Many, many committed and intelligent American liberals misperceived the communists during the Great Depression, and they—like Eleanor—flirted with ideas and organizations that they would later reject.

The subsequent Cold War, which dominated world affairs for forty-five years following World War II, so conditioned viewpoints that it is difficult now to understand how well-meaning liberals of the 1930s could have been so naïve as to believe the communists. Eleanor herself later remarked that she was better equipped to deal with the Soviets and their post–World War II duplicities in the United Nations because of her experience with the communists of the AYC. In 1938 and 1939, however, she saw her interest in the AYC as simply an extension of her fundamental concern for all those on the margins of American society.

There were young people of several political persuasions in the AYC in addition to the communists, but the communists controlled most issues within the organization. The background of their involvement was complex, as it was the result of changing policies of the Soviet Union regarding the western democracies. During the mid-1930s the Soviet dictator Josef Stalin came to believe that the Nazi regime in Germany and the fascists of Italy and Spain represented greater threats to international communism than capitalism, so he directed communists in democratic countries to support liberal parties and governments, including the New Deal in the United States, under a policy known as the Popular Front. Thus, after initially opposing the New Deal for several years, the AYC changed positions about the time Eleanor began to culti-vate the leadership, and the organization began to express favor for FDR and his programs. This encouraged Eleanor to deepen her relationship with the AYC.

In August 1939, however, Hitler and Stalin surprised the world by signing a nonaggression pact, which allowed Hitler to invade Poland and precipitate a European war without fear of having to fight on two fronts. Within a matter of days the official interna-tional communist stance toward liberal democracy changed com-pletely. In direct response to its orders from Moscow, the AYC leadership dropped its support of the New Deal and began to crit-icize FDR and his programs. Eleanor was concerned by the flip-flop but was reluctant to conclude the worst about the AYC as its com-munist leaders had assured her repeatedly that they were not in fact communists.

In November the House Un-American Activities Committee, known as the Dies Committee after its chairman Rep. Martin Dies, began hearings on the loyalties of the AYC leaders. Eleanor stood by the young people called to testify by appearing in the hearing conference rooms, and although she made no attempt to speak, her presence appeared to restrain the questioning. During their testi-mony, most of the AYC members denied affiliation with the com-munists despite clear evidence to the contrary.

Eleanor found herself beginning to doubt, but maintained her loyalty for the group for the time being. During the hearings she had taken extra notice of Joseph Lash, the thirty-year-old head of the American Student Union (one of the constituent groups of the AYC). He was a professional youth leader who had flirted with the communists but was at that stage trying to pull away. Over the fol-lowing weeks, Eleanor and Lash established a close relationship that would intensify and continue for years and years to come. Lash became Eleanor's closest friend and dearest companion and even-tually also became her Pulitzer Prize–winning biographer. In late 1939, however, he was thrilled but slightly mystified by her per-sonal attention.

Things came to a head between the AYC and Eleanor the fol-lowing February. The AYC called for a protest in Washington to dispute the administration's foreign policy, which at that stage was growing more stridently anti-German each month and therefore at odds with Stalin's wishes. The communist youth leaders had been instructed to push as hard as possible for American neutrality and therefore help clear the way for the Soviet Union to grab part of Poland.

Eleanor was increasingly nervous about her connection to the AYC, but FDR was interested in keeping her communications open. She arranged for several hundred protesters to assemble on the South Lawn of the White House so FDR could address them as a group. The occasion turned out to be a disaster when the disrespectful young crowd booed FDR's defense of the New Deal and of his foreign policy. Even though she was unhappy that FDR seemed to have gone out of his way to provoke the crowd, Eleanor could not forgive their boorish behavior on the grounds of the White House. Worse, she herself was subject to boos and hissing the next day when she attended a meeting of the AYC leadership and reiterated the president's remarks.

Although she continued to contribute money to some of the AYC programs and to press individual AYC members about the superiority of liberal democracy versus collectivism and socialism, Eleanor's relationship with the youth movement was increasingly distant after the February confrontations. The final disillusionment came in June 1941, when Hitler turned on Stalin and invaded the Soviet Union. The communist line changed immediately to support an aggressive anti-Nazi policy, and the AYC leadership suddenly began to voice approval of FDR's administration, making offers of cooperation. The rank cynicism of the switch of the communist position was too much for Eleanor to tolerate at last, and she broke off relations once and for all.

Changing Relationships

Despite the bitterness of her experience with the AYC, Eleanor's new friendship with Joseph Lash proved to be enduring and important. Lash, the son of Russian Jewish immigrants, had grown up in New York City and attended City College and then Columbia, where he earned a graduate degree in English. While a student, Lash joined the Socialist Party and soon after became head of the radical American Student Union, one of the Popular Front organizations. He was intense in his political beliefs and well-grounded in political ideology and philosophy. He was, however, suspicious of the communists who had taken control of the AYC and their switch of policies in allegiance to the Soviet line in mid-1939. After testifying before the Dies Committee, Lash had a crisis of conscience and resigned his position in the American Student Union soon thereafter.

By mid-1940 Eleanor gathered Lash into her inner circle and entertained him at Val-Kill over the summer. While they relaxed together out of the political spotlight of Washington, D.C., Eleanor began to unburden herself to Lash and soon was confiding her emotions to him in a way that she could with few others. They forged a close bond and by the end of the summer Lash had taken a central place in Eleanor's personal life. She continued for many years to arrange to be with him whenever possible and to bask in his presence and concern for her.

Now in her mid-fifties, Eleanor seemed to have lost little of her famous energy and zest for travel and work. She still was in motion most of the time, moving from residence to residence and seldom turning down a chance to visit and observe conditions around the country. Her actress friend Helen Gahagan Douglas told of a visit they made in 1940 to a migrant worker camp in the San Joaquin Valley of California. Eleanor got out of the car and advanced across a muddy field to where several migrants were at work. They immediately recognized the First Lady and, according to Douglas, seemed unfazed by her appearance, acting as if they assumed it was natural that she would sooner or later pay them a visit. After seven years of Eleanor's high-profile activities as First Lady it was no longer a novelty when she turned up unannounced to inspect working conditions and substandard housing.

She also had come to rely increasingly on Tommy Thompson, her devoted and highly efficient secretary and aide. Thompson's marriage to a schoolteacher ended in a divorce in 1939, and from then on she lived in whatever residence Eleanor was occupying.

She had quarters in the White House and at the converted furniture factory at Val-Kill, which now was Eleanor's primary home. Thompson usually traveled with Eleanor to facilitate the column- and speech-writing Eleanor did at odd moments when on the road; additionally, she dealt with the huge volume of Eleanor's correspondence.

Although on the surface life seemed to proceed apace for Eleanor, in fact from 1938 until FDR's death seven years later, her role in national affairs and influence on her husband diminished to some degree. In part this was a natural consequence of the advent of World War II, but the trend had begun earlier with the death of Louis Howe. No one ever replaced Howe as a mutual confidant of both Roosevelts, and after his death, FDR had a procession of advisors, few of whom lasted long or were in tune with Eleanor. As she commented about them to Joseph Lash: "Each imagines he is indispensable to the president. All would be surprised at their dispensability. The president uses those who suit his purposes. He makes up his own mind and discards people when they no longer fulfill a purpose of his."

Two of FDR's most durable aides were Gen. Edwin "Pa" Watson, his appointments secretary, and Stephen Early, the press secretary, both of whom caused Eleanor difficulty at times. Watson was a Southerner whose political and social sympathies usually were at odds with Eleanor's, and because he controlled official access to the president, Watson not infrequently frustrated Eleanor by failing to find time for people she wanted FDR to see. Early also was a Southerner whose unabashed disdain for blacks was an ongoing point of conflict.

Surprisingly, Eleanor's greatest unhappiness resulted from the elevation of her longtime friend and supporter Harry Hopkins, who had served in New York as a social worker and then moved to Washington with FDR as head of the Federal Emergency Relief Administration, later becoming head of the Works Progress Administration. From the earliest days of the New Deal he had been one of Eleanor's closest allies and one of the administrators she turned to first when she needed something. Hopkins had lost his young wife to cancer and in 1939 himself fell ill with a stomach cancer. An operation saved his life but left him chronically sick and debilitated, often unable to work for long stretches at a time. After Hopkins's brush with death, FDR grew closer to him and in May 1940 incorporated him into the intimate life of the White House. FDR casually told Hopkins after a meeting one afternoon to stay for dinner with him since he was lonely. Hopkins ended up staying the night and in fact never returned home, moving into the Lincoln suite until he remarried.

Eleanor loved to dress in high style, and on public occasions, she usually appeared decked out in expensive clothes. The fox stole she wears in this photo was one of her trademarks.

(Courtesy of the Franklin Delano Roosevelt Library)

Eleanor viewed the developing relationship between FDR and Hopkins as a grave breach of their friendship. As Hopkins grew closer and more loyal to the president, he pulled away from the First Lady. He virtually abandoned his interests in social welfare, which Eleanor had supposed to be a permanent bond between them, and became concerned almost exclusively with foreign and military affairs, which were the two areas in which FDR most needed advice after 1939.

Eleanor became sharply jealous of this tug-of-war for Hopkins's affections and interests, and she was extremely upset when it occurred. Unlike Howe, Hopkins could not relate simultaneously to both husband and wife; when he chose FDR, Eleanor lost a good measure of influence and power. Not surprisingly, Hopkins's defection, which she viewed as another in a long line of betrayals, pushed her into one of the recurring periods of depression that seemed to accompany points of significant change in her life, and she took to her bed in a bout of unhappiness and grief.

Rising Tensions

As Eleanor became less important to FDR's administration and the range of his concern with domestic issues constricted, she had increasing difficulty in relaxing and turning off her compulsive hectoring. By all accounts, including her own, when she was in residence at the White House at the same time as FDR she took every opportunity to lobby him about one cause or another. When these opportunities grew less frequent, she seemed increasingly unable to stay away from serious social or political topics when in FDR's company. The White House became primarily a political arena where she played out a daily drama of asking, cajoling, and lecturing on whatever topic was foremost in her mind at the time.

Although FDR for the most part tolerated her sober conversation, as war and foreign policy came to take up ever-increasing amounts of his time (that is to say from 1938 on) and his health began to decline under the severe strain, he increasingly needed to relax whenever possible, and this Eleanor would seldom allow him to do. This conflict between FDR and Eleanor, which drew in Anna and Missy on FDR's side (Eleanor angered them when she refused to recognize the president needed rest), intensified as time went on.

Despite the difficulties Eleanor encountered from the middle of FDR's second term, she still maintained her ceremonial role as First Lady whenever she was in Washington. This involved an almost unimaginable amount of time discharging social duties. Eleanor reported that in 1939 alone she entertained 4,729 people for meals, 323 overnight guests, 9,211 tea guests, and "received" 14,046 others (meaning shook hands with them in a receiving line). Eleanor commented that at "the first few receptions of each season my arms ached, my shoulders ached, my back ached, and my knees and feet seemed to belong to someone else." In one year alone more than 1.3 million visitors came through the White House and although to some degree she begrudged the ceremonial time and effort required of her as First Lady (reminiscent of the social duties she had so hated during her first residence in Washington from 1912 to 1919), Eleanor recognized the powerful symbolic meaning of the president's official residence carried for many Americans.

The most famous guests at the White House during FDR's second term were King George VI and Queen Elizabeth of Great Britain, who paid a state visit in 1939 just as Hitler was pushing affairs in Europe to a crisis over Czechoslovakia. The visit was seen by FDR as an opportunity to show American solidarity with Britain, and Eleanor played her role quietly throughout the time the royal couple was thrown together with the Roosevelts. In that odd sort of way that Americans—who would otherwise seem to detest monarchy—love British royalty, the country responded enthusiastically to the king and queen, and FDR gained a significant public relations victory in his struggle with the isolationists. The only critical comments from the press came when it was revealed that Eleanor had entertained King George and Queen Elizabeth at an informal picnic at her cottage at Val-Kill and had been so bold as to serve them fire-roasted hot dogs.

From mid-1939 onward the world situation increasingly came to dominate FDR's time and attention. As Hitler revealed himself as a menace to the other nations in Europe, FDR became convinced—and Eleanor with him—that the United States had to do all within its power to bolster the democracies. After Germany touched off warfare in September by invading Poland, FDR began to push ever harder for the authority to aid France and Great Britain with munitions and war materiel. He still was faced with strong isolationist and pacifist opposition until May 1940, when after a long period of so-called "phony war," the Nazis swept across Europe and demolished all opposition. France collapsed and was occupied, and the British army escaped by the thinnest margin from Dunkirk, leaving most of its arms and equipment behind.

Thereafter, many Americans woke up to the threat posed by Hitler. FDR was successful through a variety of semi-legal tactics to begin the effort to re-supply Great Britain and finally to win Congressional approval for re-armament and buildup of American armed forces through the first peacetime draft. As American factories began to rev up for a massive military effort, jobs became plentiful for the first time since 1929, and the lingering effects of the Great Depression finally disappeared.

Convention Triumph

In the summer of 1940, as he approached the end of his second term, FDR embroiled Eleanor in a political situation that ultimately cemented her reputation as the most remarkable, precedent-breaking First Lady in American history. In retrospect, it seems ironic that just as it appeared that Eleanor's influence on FDR and her place in his life were to be diminished by worldwide concerns, developments in domestic presidential politics conspired to bring her to the highest moment of her political career.

FDR was faced in 1940 with a tricky prospect: He desperately wanted to remain at the nation's helm to continue preparing for the war he believed would soon be visited on the United States. However, to do so he would have to buck one of the strongest and most hallowed traditions of American political life. After George Washington stepped down from office after serving two terms as president, declaring that was enough for any man, no American president had seriously contemplated a third term. It seemed chiseled in stone that presidents would serve no longer than Washington had.

Eleanor had few discussions with her husband about whether he intended to run for a third term, and for many months she assumed he was preparing to retire gracefully to Hyde Park and take on the role of elder statesman. She spoke to her closest friends and associates of her eagerness to be out of the limelight and to have FDR put down the burdens of office. On the other hand, she realized that FDR had done almost nothing to anoint a replacement for himself as president, and she understood full well the grave situation any new president would face upon taking office.

For more than a hundred years the national party conventions were at the center of the presidential election process.

The primaries were great ritualized spectacles, enacted every four years. They were marked by rousing oratory and exuberant floor demonstrations by the delegates. While the demonstrations were often orchestrated, there was during Eleanor's and FDR's time still an element of spontaneity to the delegates' expressions of enthusiasm as well as the occasional surprise during the sonorous state-by-state roll call votes.

Party bosses and power brokers sought to control the conventions by making deals and trading policy commitments for delegate votes, but sometimes, such as in 1940, the conventions took on a life of their own.

The advent of television coverage, the growth of state primaries, and the reform of the delegate selection process conspired by the end of the century to turn party conventions into sterile media events.

Gradually, Eleanor became aware that FDR was manipulating affairs in his typical fashion by avoiding any form of direct conflict and sliding laterally toward nomination by the Democratic Party for a third term. He was careful to never announce his intention or desire to serve longer in the White House, but he cautiously let it be known to party insiders that he would not turn down a draft for a third term. In acting in such a coy manner he alienated his long-time political manager and head of the party James Farley, who had presidential ambitions of his own, and FDR managed to confuse the majority of the Democrats about his intentions.

As the July party convention approached it gradually became clear that FDR would not publicly seek a third nomination, as that might be seen by voters as too ambitious in light of the no-third-term tradition, but would look favorably on a draft. Because Farley now was in opposition, FDR sent Harry Hopkins to Chicago to set up a campaign operation. Eleanor discussed the situation with FDR and told him she did not wish to go to Chicago and did not want to be involved in the convention. They agreed that she should retreat to Val-Kill and that FDR would stay in Washington, awaiting developments. After some confusion and organizational disarray (Hopkins proved relatively inept as a political operative), the Democratic Convention nominated FDR for president and awaited his choice for a running mate.

Unfortunately, that very question turned the convention on its head. "Cactus Jack" Garner, the former Speaker of the House who had been FDR's vice president since 1933, had turned on the president during FDR's second term and become one of the most outspoken opponents of the New Deal, so he was out of the question and a new candidate had to be found. Confusing matters further, FDR declared that he wanted to throw open the vice-presidential nomination and allow the convention delegates to select their own candidate; however, he made it clear that he wanted Henry Wallace, his secretary of agriculture, to get the nomination and that Wallace's nomination would be the price of FDR's acceptance. However, a majority of the delegates disliked Wallace, who had few political skills although he was a sound administrator and an interesting thinker, and left to their own devices, it appeared they would reject Wallace. The convention went almost completely out of control because of FDR's lack of leadership.

At that point Farley and Frances Perkins put out a frantic call to Eleanor to come to Chicago and address the convention. They felt that short of the president himself, no one else could settle the agitated delegates and push through Wallace's place on the ticket. After conferring with FDR by phone, Eleanor boarded a plane and set out for Chicago.

Upon arrival she held an impromptu press conference at the airport, then proceeded directly to the convention hall where names were being placed in nomination for the vice-presidential slot on the ticket. Wallace was booed and jeered by the delegates on the floor when his name was entered. The atmosphere was loud, undisciplined, and edgy, with no one apparently in charge and a disaster in the making; moreover, the party was entering uncharted waters by inviting a First Lady to address the delegates, something that had never happened before in all of American political history.

As Eleanor took the podium the tumult ceased, and the delegates settled down to hear what she had to say. All of her many years of work with the Women's Division of the Democratic Party and her carefully cultivated abilities at public speaking came together at this moment. As was her style, Eleanor spoke briefly and directly without notes, using no great oratorical flourishes and couching her message in simple language.

This was, she told the delegates, "no ordinary time." The impending international crisis called for the delegates to put aside their usual concerns and to concentrate on doing what was best for the country. The president could not campaign in his usual fashion because he was absorbed night and day in his duties. Therefore if he accepted nomination for a third term, he must have the full support of a "a united people who love their country." Without mentioning Wallace or the contentiousness of the vice-presidential nomination process, Eleanor made it clear that it was the duty of the delegates to give FDR whomever he wanted if they were asking the president to carry the immense burdens of his office into a third term.

The delegates greeted her short speech with thunderous applause, and then proceeded to nominate Wallace as FDR's running mate. Satisfied that she had done her duty, Eleanor left the hall and flew home again to New York. In the days that followed, she received large numbers of letters and telegrams of congratulation on her speech, and newspapers nationwide lauded her performance. For Eleanor, the campaign in the fall was almost an anticlimax. The Republicans had nominated Wendell Wilkie, a highly intelligent and successful businessman with little political experience, and although he was an attractive candidate who many Americans admired, he could not out-poll FDR, who won the unprecedented third term in November with a little over fifty-seven percent of the popular vote.

Chapter 8

The Stress of War

*All human beings have failings, all human beings have needs
and temptations and stresses. Men and women who live
together through long years get to know one another's failings; but they also come to know what is worthy of respect
and admiration in those they live with and in themselves.*
—Eleanor Roosevelt,
This I Remember

It might not be entirely accurate to label the years from 1941
until 1945 as the lowest period of Eleanor's life—surely parts of
her childhood or the months following her discovery of FDR's infidelity must have been as bad or worse—but it is fair to call them
the most difficult of her mature adult life. The trends that developed in 1939 and 1940 continued as the United States approached
and then plunged into World War II. Many of the issues Eleanor
held most dear and for which she had fought so hard since the
1920s almost disappeared from the national agenda, and winning
the war became virtually the only cause.

The partnership she had formed with her husband following his
debilitation from polio two decades earlier frayed during the war
years and nearly disintegrated. Together they had done astounding
good for the nation, leading it back from the brink of social and
economic collapse and introducing a form of modern government
whereby the interests of the weak and powerless were taken into

consideration and the poor and unemployed were rescued from disaster. However, Eleanor seemed uncertain in 1941 that their achievements were permanent, and the stress of changed wartime circumstances seemed to bring out some of the least attractive aspects of her mature personality—or at least the revised context of wartime made her attributes into liabilities.

In short, Eleanor could not bring herself to give up her overriding concerns for a social agenda or to curb her single-minded attempts to influence the president to pay attention to social issues even though he was performing heroic feats of wartime leadership. There was still a need for a voice such as hers to remind Americans what they were fighting for, but in her relationship with FDR she lost perspective to the point that she seriously misjudged his waning strength and the seriousness of his degenerating health. None of this became completely apparent until FDR's death in 1945.

Meanwhile, the war confronted Eleanor with a serious intellectual and emotional dilemma. She understood full well the ultimate threat to all she held dear posed by Hitler and Imperial Japan, but her instincts and her memories of a shattered post–World War I Europe led her to regard war as the most terrible of all human follies. She seemed to flinch when presented with the need to support victory at all costs, and whenever possible she tried to deflect the debate to issues of how social justice could be fostered both at home and in the world at large.

When she later wrote about the war she revealed the essence of her conflict:

> I ... could not help feeling that it was the New Deal social objectives that had fostered the spirit that would make it possible for us to fight this war, and I believed it was vastly important to give people the feeling that in fighting the war we were fighting for these same objectives. It was obvious that if the world were ruled by Hitler, freedom and democracy would no longer exist. I felt it was necessary both to the prosecution of the war and to the period after the war that the fight for the rights of minorities should continue.

An additional bitterness for Eleanor came from her sense that no matter how important the social agenda continued to be despite the war, she and her crusades had been moved to the margin for the duration of the conflict. FDR and others in their quieter and less harassed moments might be brought to agreement with her, but FDR seldom had a quiet or unharassed moment from 1941 onward. As he told the nation, "Dr. New Deal" had been replaced by "Dr. Win-the-War," and he lacked the energy or opportunity to stop and listen to Eleanor with the sympathy of purpose and understanding he once had given her.

Although Eleanor's personal position of power and influence did not disappear completely, it certainly diminished. She could no longer turn to people such as Harry Hopkins, who had been her ally since 1933, for help because nearly all efforts and interests were now focused on defeating the Axis Powers. No one came to Eleanor and asked her how to convert auto plants into airplane manufacturing facilities, and no one sought her advice on when to open a second front in Europe or whether island-hopping was the best strategy in the Pacific. It was a telling point that FDR refused to take her along to any of the grand wartime conferences where he met with the leaders of the other allied nations.

As it turned out she still had a great deal of importance to say on matters of race relations and women in the workplace, which the war brought forward into American consciousness, but there was no question that Eleanor's role in American national life was diminished. Moreover, as critics found it very difficult to openly voice opposition to the president once he became the undisputed wartime leader of the nation, they focused on Eleanor as an even more convenient target. Whenever they wanted to poke at one of FDR's policies or to lash out against some of the societal changes brought on by the war, they turned viciously on Eleanor. She parried these criticisms and insults with her usual thick skin, as she had for many years, but it must have been increasingly difficult, as she perceived FDR as much less of an ally.

By 1941 the nation was well on its way to assuming a full-bore wartime footing. FDR had pushed long and hard to make the United States the "arsenal of democracy" as he termed it, and the nation's manufacturing sector was in the process of gearing up to produce fantastic amounts of military equipment and materiel, much of which was flowing to Great Britain to allow the Britons to maintain the fight against Hitler. The result was the stimulation of business to levels unseen since long before the stock market crash twelve years earlier. Unemployment, which had been the most crippling effect of the Great Depression, was diminishing rapidly, and the demand for workers was beginning to call forth what seemed like far-reaching changes. African Americans were moving in very large numbers from their homes in the agricultural south to the industrial cities of the north and finding the kinds of jobs most of them could never have won before the nation moved toward a wartime footing. The demand for workers also meant that some plant managers were beginning to cast longing eyes on the source of "manpower" represented by America's women homemakers. Eleanor found one of her most meaningful wartime roles in helping to deal with the opportunities and dislocations of these changes in the workforce.

The approach of war put strains on the relationship Eleanor and FDR had worked out so carefully during their years together in the White House, but on public occasions, such as this parade in early 1941, they appeared to be a happy couple.

(*Courtesy of the Franklin Delano Roosevelt Library*)

Domestic Changes

On a personal level 1941 brought many significant changes to the Roosevelts and the White House. In March Lorena Hickok moved back into guest quarters and appeared to be settled for a long stay. She and Eleanor had never rekindled the intensity of their previous relationship; in fact Hickok had fallen in love with a younger woman. Still, Eleanor and Hickok remained very close friends who shared much with each other, even though Eleanor no longer pretended that Hickok had a claim on her time. She did, however, still feel responsible for Hickok, and when the former newspaperwoman moved to Washington to take a job with the Women's Division of the Democratic National Committee (a position arranged by Eleanor) and pleaded an inability to pay the high rents demanded in the capital, Eleanor invited Hickok to move into the White House. Even though she was glad to accept free housing, which allowed her to maintain her home in New York, Hickok was embarrassed by the situation and hid the fact from her fellow workers in the Democratic Party by pretending she lived in the Mayflower Hotel and sneaking in and out of the White House.

Another frequent White House guest—one who scarcely could have offered more contrast to Hickok—was Crown Princess Martha of Norway, who had become a favorite of FDR after she had escaped the Nazis and washed up in the United States as a glamorous refugee. She was tall, beautiful, elegant, and an outrageous flirt who charmed the president the way many such women had during his lifetime. Her husband Crown Prince Olav had remained behind in Britain along with his father King Haakon. For several months Martha had lived in the White House with her children before finally taking a house in Maryland. Her presence enlivened FDR's famous cocktail hours, and he often visited her Maryland residence after she moved out of the White House. She also accompanied FDR on visits to Hyde Park, even after her husband joined her in the United States.

The greatest change for the Roosevelts came in June 1941, when Missy LeHand, the president's longtime secretary and aide, suffered a devastating stroke. She had a history of ill health, including at least one psychological breakdown and childhood rheumatic fever (which might have damaged her heart and circulatory system), but the stroke deprived her of speech and left her partially paralyzed. She had played a huge role in FDR's life as his closest and most constant companion. Living in the White House since FDR's inauguration, she carried a heavy load of official duties in dealing with his correspondence, meetings, and schedule and usually was in charge of arranging his off-hours relaxation.

There had been many stories and much gossip over the years about the exact nature of their relationship, but whatever the case, Missy had been indispensable to both Roosevelts. As an attractive and socially graceful assistant, for decades she had served FDR as an official hostess in Eleanor's frequent absences. Eleanor usually expressed only appreciation and friendship for Missy, and as a matter of routine showed her kindness and affection. As historian Doris Kearns Goodwin points out, Eleanor was liberated by Missy's presence to pursue a life of travel and independence, especially after FDR was elected president.

Missy's loss would prove very significant to both FDR and Eleanor. Never again in the years remaining before FDR's death was the household so settled and well-ordered. None of the new arrangements FDR made to satisfy both his official and social needs worked as well as when Missy was by his side. Grace Tully, who originally had come to the Roosevelt entourage as a secretary to Eleanor, moved forward and took over most of the burden of official business that Missy had carried and performed admirably; however, the spark that Missy had provided outside business hours when she paid court to the president while he relaxed with his friends and cocktails or worked on his beloved stamp collection was hard to replace. Princess Martha for a time became more important to FDR, and he gathered two of his unmarried cousins, Margaret Suckley and Laura Delano, more closely into his orbit, but none of them were able to fully replace Missy.

Moreover, the nature of Missy's debilitation was almost impossible for FDR to deal with. Despite his public compassion and his astounding abilities in dealing with the gravest national and international crisis, he could not stand constant exposure to unpleasantness or ill health. He found he could not bear to be in Missy's presence more than a few minutes at a time after her stroke. She could no longer communicate with him and without the verbal give and take he thrived on, there was no way the president could tolerate the pain of the meetings. He never again was able successfully to visit or comfort Missy, whose life was prolonged agony after the stroke (she apparently tried to commit suicide several times but was too crippled to succeed).

His behavior, although perhaps understandable in psychological terms, was nothing short of heartless and brutal. At the same time, in what seems like an irony, FDR showed his deep concern and affection for Missy by altering his personal will to give her a life interest in half of his estate, removing his children from his will to do so. FDR's generosity was never called on, as Missy died in June 1944 at age forty-six, less than a year before the president. Eleanor wrote in her syndicated column the next day that "I am sure that for her, after her long illness, death will be a release. But those who loved her ... will feel her loss deeply."

The personal losses for Eleanor and FDR in 1941 did not stop at Missy's illness. On September 7 Sara Delano Roosevelt died at Hyde Park with FDR at her bedside. She had been in declining health during the summer, and a blood clot in the lungs carried her away. It was another devastating blow for FDR, who had been extraordinarily close to his mother for his entire life. She had coddled and nurtured him from early childhood, transferring to FDR all of her care and attention after the early death of her husband, and had never ceased to lavish him with the love and unabashed adoration on which he thrived.

Eleanor of course had a different experience of the "grand dame," as she called her. Sara had opposed FDR's marriage and afterward had stifled Eleanor at almost every turn, refusing to let Eleanor acquire or run her own household (the cottage at Val-Kill was Eleanor's first independent residence) and usurping Eleanor's place with the Roosevelt children. The hurt and frustration of their relationship ran deep.

However in the latter years, as Eleanor gained status in the world despite Sara's belief that her daughter-in-law should stay at home, she learned to accept more tolerantly some of Sara's foibles.

In fact, the two women had been surprisingly allied on social issues on occasion and had unified in lobbying FDR. Nonetheless, Eleanor told others she felt strangely numbed at Sara's death and unable to genuinely grieve, although she paid homage to Sara in her public comments. However, Eleanor did understand the deep loss that Sara's death represented for her husband and provided attentive and genuine consolation to him in an intimate fashion that was seldom matched during the later years of their marriage.

Within only a few days Eleanor herself was in need of consolation. Her younger brother Hall, whom she had loved and cared for ever since the death of their father almost a half century earlier, collapsed and went into his brief final decline. He was a confirmed and destructive alcoholic who, like his father before him, had destroyed his liver by consuming huge amounts of liquor and wine over a long period of time. He had a brilliant mind and had Hall been able to focus his life and throw off the effects of alcohol, he might have been an outstanding achiever. As it was, his life was a tragedy and added yet another dismal chapter to Eleanor's personal life.

She had Hall moved from Poughkeepsie to Walter Reed Hospital near Washington, where she kept a grim death watch that was broken only by the need to travel to Hyde Park for Sara Roosevelt's funeral. Eleanor wrote of the extreme pain of sitting by Hall's side and seeing him struggle for breath and life and remembering him as a small child for whom she assumed the role of parent, although herself only a teenager. Her sense of loss and her sorrow over the waste of his life were overwhelming. He died, age fifty-one, on September 25.

War Footing and Race Relations

Despite the severity of her losses and the decline in her position of power and influence by the early 1940s, Eleanor still played an important role in the area of race relations, an interest that continued to grow for Eleanor the rest of her life. The gigantic economic and military mobilization set afoot in the United States during 1940 and 1941 to meet the demands of the approaching war created great new opportunities for African Americans. Jobs were increasingly plentiful in the industrial cities of the North and, despite continued discrimination and segregation, the demand for workers was so great that growing manufacturing plants in places such as Detroit, where car makers were converting auto plants to the production of military aircraft, began hiring large numbers of black workers.

This change, which also involved a dynamic migratory shift in population from South to North, had wide consequences. White workers were thrown into close contact with black workers, and as the pressure grew to increase production it was inevitable that blacks would compete for jobs that traditionally had been reserved for whites. The result was heightened racial tension and confrontation. Not surprisingly, Eleanor was in the middle of the conflicts. She was perhaps more trusted by African-American leadership than any prominent white politician or officeholder, as it was understood that she could be relied on to act as a conduit to the president.

A good example of her role as such came in mid-1941, when African-American leader A. Philip Randolph, head of the railway porters union, launched an aggressive campaign to open more defense jobs to blacks. He and many other black leaders were distressed that despite some overall progress, plant managers all over the country continued to funnel black workers into menial jobs— even educated and trained blacks who could have contributed significantly if allowed to do so. Randolph was determined to force FDR to come to terms with discrimination in the defense plants and decided that only a massive show of support and black solidarity could convince the waffling FDR. Randolph, with the help of other leaders, planned a march on Washington of ten thousand black workers who would demonstrate on behalf of a change in federal policy—an idea that would be echoed many times over during later decades of the civil rights movement.

FDR, aided by his southern appointments secretary Pa Watson, ducked a meeting with Randolph and head of the NAACP Walter White, hoping the controversy would die down without confrontation. However, the president relied on Eleanor to keep his lines of communication and information open. She had traveled widely during the first months of the year and had visited several African-American schools and conferences, trying to absorb the mood of the black community. She passed on to FDR her assessment of the growing concern among blacks over defense industry discrimination; she also told him of the many stories she heard of educated black professionals being wasted as janitors and maintenance workers.

When Randolph turned up the pressure on the president by threatening to expand the protest to a hundred thousand marchers, FDR tried to use Eleanor to get Randolph to back off, but the black leader was determined. Eventually, Eleanor told her husband that the march, which would have been a disaster from the president's point of view, was inevitable unless he acted. He finally acquiesced and signed an executive order that called for an end to discrimination in all work done by federal defense contractors. Randolph called off the protest march and received a telegram from Eleanor, which said in part, "I hope from this first step, we may go on to others."

When African Americans made even the slightest gains, Eleanor became the object of hatred and virulent criticism from white racists, especially in the South. The dislocations of the wartime buildup and eventually the war itself threw the racists' world askew. The need for blacks to work in defense industries and to serve in the armed forces was so great that national policy had to change to accommodate it. In doing so, FDR's government seemed to southern racists to be attacking the very basis of what they understood to be the American way of life. Because Eleanor had long supported the efforts of black Americans to move out of the clutches of segregation and discrimination, she was the most convenient target of the frustrated wrath of racist hatred.

Southern newspapers spewed out invective against Eleanor in an unending stream, blaming her for all the fears and anxieties racists were feeling. According to this perverse reasoning, had Eleanor not treated blacks like full citizens who should be entitled to social, political, and economic rights, the traditional world of the racists would still have been intact. Therefore, they considered

Eleanor to be the most "dangerous woman in America" as they called her, and they kept up a drumbeat of vehement criticism.

Even more distressing was the high volume of hate mail Eleanor received on the topic of race relations. The letters usually were mindless in their denunciation of the First Lady and often crude and obscene. Eleanor seldom let such mail affect her, but it must have been distressing to know she was the object of so much hatred. She was more concerned about a widespread campaign of whispers and rumors. For example, it was taken as truth among certain parts of the South that female black domestic workers were widely organized into "Eleanor Clubs" with the sole purpose of crippling the home life of whites. According to the stories, black maids were intent on reducing their services, demanding shorter hours and more pay, and insisting on being accorded social equality, all in the name of Eleanor Roosevelt. In fact the Eleanor Clubs did not exist, as an FBI investigation showed, although there was a shortage of domestic workers once war industries offered much higher-paying jobs, and Southerners chose to see the shortage as a conspiracy by the First Lady.

One of the most persistent problems of race relations revolved around the deeply ingrained racism in the American military. The Army did enlist black soldiers; however, in almost all cases it kept them strictly segregated and in menial roles (the specialist branches of the Army, such as the Signal Corps and the Air Corps, had no black members at all), and the few blacks who held commissions were restricted to low-level command of black troops only. The worst racist attitudes were in the U.S. Navy, which allowed black sailors only to serve as mess men and denied commissions to all blacks.

Despite the strenuous efforts of African-American leaders and the increasing pressure of national mobilization, the War Department fended off almost all changes to the racial policies in the armed forces. FDR danced around the issue as long as he could, and although he listened when Eleanor told him of dissatisfaction among the black community, he did very little to bring about changes until manpower demands midway in the war finally forced his hand.

From Eleanor's point of view the pressures of war mobilization and wartime itself revealed more starkly than anything since the Civil War the racial inequities in the American social system. She had been interested in changing American perceptions of African Americans before the war, but once the hard edges of racism were clearly and unequivocally revealed from 1940 onward, she grew increasingly concerned with the issue of equality. She often expressed her belief that when American democracy was under such dire and ultimate threat as it was from 1940 until 1945, the contrast between the rhetoric of democracy and the fact of racial discrimination was brought sharply into her consciousness and could not again be tucked away.

Office of Civilian Defense

In early 1939 Eleanor asked to go to Europe as a Red Cross volunteer; however, the German invasion of Poland squelched that plan. In 1941, as the United States appeared to come closer and closer to war, Eleanor desired to find work for herself that was directly related to mobilization and the pre-war effort. In part, she wanted to find some way to ensure that the New Deal social agenda would not be entirely forgotten as the nation geared up for war, and she must have understood the trend that her informal role as activist First Lady would diminish in the context of wartime. The result was what proved to be her only attempt to hold an official office during the Roosevelt administration.

FDR created the Office of Civilian Defense in May 1941 by executive order. It was from the beginning an ill-conceived and poorly thought-out agency, which was to a large measure Eleanor's fault. She had been greatly impressed by accounts of the work of Lady Stella Reading in Britain's Women's Voluntary Services for Civil Defense and thought that an American version might stimulate volunteerism in the United States and keep alive the social justice and welfare aspects of the New Deal, even during wartime. It seemed to her that a civil defense agency could consolidate the gains of the New Deal and focus attention on how a socially just society would be the most potent force to combat fascism and the philosophy of Hitler. Just how the connection was to be made between a practical volunteer civilian defense organization and propagation of social justice by the federal government was unclear. In fact, the entire purpose and operation of the OCD proved to be just as fuzzy.

FDR appointed Fiorello LaGuardia, the colorful reformist mayor of New York City, as the head of the new agency. He was charged with creating structures for the protection of civilians, recruiting volunteers, raising morale, and eliciting the cooperation of existing federal agencies in ensuring that civilian needs would be met during wartime. In retrospect, this was a nearly impossible list of goals, and LaGuardia, who was a remarkable politician in his own sphere but severely limited in administrative skills and broad imagination, was a poor choice to whom to entrust it.

In June LaGuardia asked Eleanor to join him in the OCD and take over the women's volunteer section, but she turned him down, fearing her presence would create too much political pressure and could be an embarrassment to FDR if she became the target of criticism for official actions. (She eventually was proven correct in this fear.) He then moved ahead, concerning himself almost exclusively with matters such as air-raid warning systems, blackouts, and firefighting. LaGuardia had a lifelong obsession with fire trucks and firefighters, so his new job allowed him to indulge himself. However, he almost ignored the social justice aspects of the OCD, which were intended to ensure the New Deal programs were not obliterated. By late summer Eleanor was openly critical of this deficiency, and LaGuardia renewed his offer for her to join the agency.

It probably is significant that Eleanor finally agreed to become assistant director of the OCD on September 29, only days after Hall's death. As she wrote later in *Ladies Home Journal:* "If I feel depressed, I go to work. Work is always an antidote for depression."

When Eleanor showed up for work at OCD headquarters on Dupont Circle, choosing to walk over from the White House for the exercise, she discovered that the agency lacked much in the way of organization. In her typical high-energy fashion she charged ahead to set up a working structure. The notes and memos flew as Eleanor got her teeth into basic office issues such as correspondence, reports, appointments, and the routing of phone calls. All the organizational skills she had perfected during her volunteer and political work in the 1920s came to the fore in setting up OCD's administrative system. Her close friend Elinor Morgenthau (wife of FDR's secretary of the treasury) had agreed to be her assistant, and the two women shared an office.

Eleanor's vision for the OCD differed considerably from LaGuardia's. The mayor concentrated almost all his efforts on setting up specific local civil defense organizations that would be able to deal with the threat of attack in wartime. He had shown almost no interest in the mandate of OCD to foster democracy and social welfare. Eleanor of course saw the OCD in exactly opposite terms and immediately announced to the press her three organizational goals: to train volunteers, create jobs for volunteers that would benefit local communities (things such as nursery schools and housing projects), and prepare civilians for wartime conditions.

For most of her daughter Anna's adult life, Eleanor had a close relationship with her, the closest she had with any of her five children.

(Courtesy of the Franklin Delano Roosevelt Library)

These certainly were worthy objectives, and Eleanor's belief that the nation could be strengthened for war by building up the social infrastructure was theoretically sound. After all, defense workers and soldiers probably would perform their tasks better if they knew their children were being cared for and their families were adequately housed. However, the connection was a difficult one to make in many cases, and several of Eleanor's programs—once subject to critical scrutiny—were hard to justify to anyone not completely in sympathy with her views. There was just too much warm fuzziness in the idea of improving civilian war preparedness by enriching the cultural and social milieu of local communities.

This weak connection between social programs and wartime footing became all too obvious after December 7, when the Japanese navy launched a devastating surprise attack on the U.S. Pacific fleet at Pearl Harbor. Both Eleanor and FDR were in the White House on that Sunday afternoon when the news arrived. FDR was immediately plunged into dealing with the crisis. Eleanor recalled that he was perfectly calm, although seething with bitterness toward the Japanese, whose envoys had been meeting with U.S. officials in Washington even as their bombers and fighters attacked. That evening she spoke over a national radio network on her regular broadcast, saying, "… there is no more uncertainty. We know what we have to face and we know we are ready to face it …." The following day FDR addressed a joint session of Congress, speaking famously of the previous day that would "live in infamy" and declaring that a state of war existed with Japan.

Soon after the president's speech Eleanor and LaGuardia boarded a plane for the West Coast, where they wanted to buck up the local civilian defense workers and assign them to specific duties. They also sought to quell fears and lift morale. We now know that the Japanese were never in a position to mount a serious attack on the West Coast of the United States, and certainly not immediately after making a maximum effort at Pearl Harbor. However, at the time Americans were so shocked by the sneak attack on the fleet that many believed Japanese soldiers would be storming ashore in Southern California within days or hours. Thus, it was an act of considerable courage and inspiration for Eleanor and LaGuardia to step onto a plane bound for Los Angeles. While in the air they received a report that the Japanese were bombing San Francisco, so they ordered their plane diverted to the Bay area. When the story proved false they continued on to Los Angeles.

It is hard to overstate the devastation caused to the collective American psyche by the sneak Japanese attack on Pearl Harbor on December 7, 1941.

The loss of American life and ships was so great and so unexpected by most Americans that many began to look for signs of dark conspiracy to explain the event.

Eventually, a theory developed that blamed FDR. Some of FDR's and Eleanor's domestic critics were so rabid in their hatred (accumulated over the years of the New Deal) that they were ready to believe that FDR had secretly maneuvered the Japanese into making the attack in order to fulfill his desire to take America into the war.

There was no basis for this conspiracy theory, and the truth was that FDR feared having to fight a two-front, two-ocean war, which was just what the Japanese forced the United States to do.

As it turned out, there was not much Eleanor could do except travel from city to city reassuring citizens and trying to calm the mounting panic and hysteria, much of which was directed against the many Japanese Americans and immigrants living on the West Coast. Gripped by fear and paranoia, many of the other citizens of California and Washington turned on their neighbors of Japanese ancestry and demanded that the army or the federal government do something to protect the country from sabotage and infiltration. Despite vicious criticism from the West Coast press, Eleanor evoked her deeply held liberal beliefs and urged Americans to live up to the tenets of democracy that guaranteed civil liberties even in a "time of stress."

Many Americans now tend to see Eleanor's assertion of the rights of Japanese Americans to enjoy full protection of the Constitution as a courageous and admirable response. Indeed, FDR's subsequent decision to intern nearly the entire Japanese-American population of the West Coast is one of the blackest marks against his wartime administration. However, Eleanor's reaction also shows clearly that she did not quite grasp in a practical way the consequences of the entry of the United States into the war. Her instincts were always to look for the long-term social issues at stake in any specific wartime situation and to shortchange the pragmatic needs of the moment. She never really adjusted to wartime conditions and in many ways the war unhinged her.

Since the early 1930s Eleanor had operated in only one gear: full-speed forward. With the coming of the war, she lost a good deal of the context in which she had employed her high energy and moral purpose. She never quite converted to wartime mode; rather she continued boring in on her traditional topics whether or not they were relevant to the wartime situation. When it became difficult for the nation in the short run to pay attention to Eleanor's traditional liberal agenda, she seemed to become isolated. She also became increasingly impatient and frustrated and appeared to lose her previously keen perception. Ultimately, this led to her failure to either understand or properly respond to FDR's physical decline. Although it is difficult to criticize Eleanor for wanting to maintain the great achievements of the New Deal, the fact remains that she was never quite in step with FDR or most of the nation after Pearl Harbor.

This unhappy state of affairs was amply demonstrated in early 1942 when Eleanor's involvement with the OCD came noisily unraveled. Following their West Coast trip Eleanor had grown impatient with LaGuardia's narrow focus and had him replaced with James Landis, dean of the Harvard School of Law. This allowed her a freer hand in focusing much of the work and spending of the OCD on those areas she thought most important. Unfortunately, she was not cautious in allowing some of her friends to take well-paying jobs doing what could easily be interpreted as frivolous activities—things that in peacetime might have passed unremarked upon.

In early February Representative Charles Faddis launched an attack on Eleanor's handling of affairs at the OCD by castigating the agency for paying Eleanor's actor friend Melvyn Douglas (husband of Helen Gahagan Douglas) a salary of eight thousand dollars a year—more than Gen. Douglas MacArthur was making. Worse, Faddis blasted Eleanor for hiring her attractive young friend Mayris Chaney, whom Eleanor had met though Earl Miller. Chaney was a professional ballroom dancer and was being paid four thousand six hundred dollars a year to teach dancing for the OCD. This outraged Faddis and many of his Congressional colleagues, although it is not hard to see why Eleanor, who had taught dance herself at the Rivington Street Settlement House as a young woman, might think it a good use of tax dollars. Faddis was vicious in making the point that Chaney was being paid double the salary of an Air Corps pilot.

After Faddis's attack on the floor of the U.S. House of Representatives brought out the facts about the hiring of Eleanor's friends, the Eleanor haters finally saw the opportunity for a risk-free attack and piled on. Within a few days there was a loud and sustained din from the press and columnists (and from everyday Americans writing letters to the White House) about the iniquity of Eleanor's reign at OCD. The critics not only pounded Eleanor personally; they seemed to sense there was an even larger point in the affair, which was that normal activities and the standard way of doing business for the nation had to be put on hold for the duration of the war. The attacks were viciously personal about Eleanor, but they also were an expression of the war anxiety most Americans were feeling in the first months of 1942. Many people who had long supported Eleanor in her crusades during the 1930s joined the chorus of criticism.

When the House of Representatives voted officially to deny funds to OCD for any activity that included instruction in dance, Eleanor understood that her continued presence would only provide more opportunities for her critics to attack her and, by extension, the president. In February 1942 she resigned, putting the best face possible on the situation. Thus ended the only attempt by an American First Lady to serve as an administrator in the federal government and the only time a president's wife held an official office. The only other instance that comes close was Hilary Rodham Clinton's personal control of her husband's campaign to pass a comprehensive healthcare plan during his first term of office in the 1990s, although Clinton's assignment was purely informal and internal. It is interesting to note that the outcome was much the same: a major and humiliating defeat for the sitting First Lady in each case.

In retrospect it is clear that Eleanor had put herself into an impossible situation. She could pretend to be just another federal employee, but no one could forget for a moment that she was the most famous and powerful woman in the land, who could breakfast with the president whenever she wished before going off to her office. She had vastly more power and influence than anyone else in the government—a fact amply demonstrated when she engineered LaGuardia's dismissal. Any good she contrived to do at the OCD was written off to her extracurricular advantages, and when she made genuine mistakes, such as giving Douglas and Chaney well-paying jobs, she subjected FDR and his wartime administration to political danger just at the time he most needed solidarity of purpose.

Wartime Adjustments

The first weeks and months after the Japanese attack on Pearl Harbor were grim. Most thoughtful American officials had long realized armed conflict with Japan was almost inevitable because of Japanese expansion and imperial ambitions, and the United States' embargo of gas and oil—commodities of which Japan had none herself. However, the sneak attack severely crippled the U.S. Navy and allowed the Japanese to advance almost unopposed across Southeast Asia and the South Pacific. From December 1941 until the battle of Midway in June 1942, American headlines told only of victory after victory by the Japanese. In the North Atlantic, Germany's submarine assault on Britain's oceanic supply lines appeared on the brink of wringing the victory that the Luftwaffe had failed to achieve during the previous year.

The hard first six months of the war created nearly unbearable tension for the average American. For Eleanor the first half of 1942 was torture. Already dealing with her humiliating resignation from the Office of Civilian Defense, she also was in a constant state of worry and agitation over her four sons, all of whom were serving on active military duty. The eldest son, James, had been called up by the Marines the previous fall; FDR Jr. was an officer in the Navy, as was the youngest Roosevelt son, John; Elliott was a captain in the Army Air Corps. Eleanor feared, as did most American mothers, that not all of her sons would survive the war, and she vividly recalled the painful losses suffered by the nation during the previous war. As she wrote: "I was deeply unhappy. I remembered my anxieties about my husband and brother when World War I began; now I had four sons of military age."

Eleanor's usual antidote for anxiety would have been to launch herself into a characteristic frenzy of work, but the disaster with the OCD meant that at least temporarily it was best she stay on the sidelines, out of the way of comment and criticism. Moreover, wartime restrictions limited her ability to travel. FDR of course was consumed day and night with directing the war effort. In most ways he was a superb commander in chief and his great ability to understand and control massive forces would prove vital to ultimate victory, but the effort literally destroyed him by the end of the war.

Although there were notable exceptions, Eleanor spent little time with her husband from 1941 on; thus it was difficult to keep alive their unique political partnership. They discovered they disagreed over several issues, usually stemming from a conflict between Eleanor's tightly held liberal credo and FDR's almost singleminded focus on defeating the Axis Powers. For example, Eleanor was stunned by FDR's sweeping executive order in February that doomed almost all Japanese Americans to internment in what were little better than concentration camps. She had expected some sort of action ever since she experienced firsthand the hysteria that infected white Americans on the West Coast, but she was shocked when FDR essentially suspended the Bill of Rights as it pertained to Japanese Americans.

In early 1941 Eleanor again was in the middle of racial issues, involving herself in a violent situation that had developed in Detroit when black workers were given homes in a new housing development named the Sojourner Truth project. When the first black families attempted to move in they were attacked by a large mob of whites and a race riot ensued. Eleanor demanded government action and eventually the black families were settled in the project under the protection of Michigan National Guard troops. She also continued to agitate for a relaxation of the rigid segregation in the U.S. Navy, and in the spring of 1942 her pressure was responsible in part for FDR's strong stand that forced the Navy to finally accept African-American recruits for general duty beyond that of mess mate. De facto segregation of course continued, but it was a significant step forward to have official naval policy changed.

She also was vocal about women moving out of the home and into the wartime workplace. With many of the nation's male workers in uniform and a huge demand building for industrial workers, especially in the defense plants, it was necessary to reach deeper into the potential pool of women. As historian Doris Kearns Goodwin points out, the first women industry recruits had come from the ranks of low-paid workers who simply moved from being maids or seamstresses to jobs as riveters and drill press operators. In a second round young high school graduates were recruited. Eleanor promoted these efforts and was quoted in a Boston newspaper as saying, "… if I were of a debutante age I would go into a factory—any factory where I could learn a skill and be useful."

By mid-1942, however, these reserves had run dry and a much more controversial movement arose to recruit housewives. When the government and defense contractors began to ask women to leave their homes and children behind and head for the factories, this entailed a major change in what most Americans at the time accepted as the social norm. For once, Eleanor was in tune with the war effort. She of course was the living embodiment of a woman who had chosen to live outside the traditional home; thus she was happy to promote efforts to put married women and mothers into productive jobs.

One of her greatest wartime contributions was to convince the federal government and private industry to not only hire married women and mothers, but also to make specific concessions to their women workers to stimulate production. She lobbied successfully for on-site day care centers (many operating around the clock to help women with night shift jobs), which allowed mothers to put in productive time at a plant with less anxiety about the well-being of their children. This innovation barely survived the end of the war, but it provided the model for what eventually became a common practice in American workplaces. Likewise, many defense plants provided food services for housewives, including complete carry-home meals at subsidized prices.

> American women flooded the workplace during World War II, but their presence in the military was restricted, despite demands from women's organizations that they be allowed to serve. The major branches of the armed forces reluctantly opened ranks to women in 1942–43 when it became apparent that they faced a crucial shortage of manpower.
>
> The WACs of the Army, the WAVEs of the Navy, and the WASPs of the Air Corps (in addition to the Coast Guard SPARs and Marine MCWRs) were kept under careful control and almost always served in clerical or nursing jobs in the United States. Some women served abroad but usually under restricted circumstances. Women officers were seldom allowed to give orders to men.
>
> Regulations prohibited the enlistment of women with children, and African-American servicewomen were strictly segregated.

Eleanor's personal life was shaken in the spring of 1942 when Joseph Lash was drafted into the Army and left for training and assignment. All evidence concludes that at this stage Lash was Eleanor's closest companion. It is extremely doubtful that there was anything more than an emotional and psychological intimacy, but as was usual when Eleanor decided to accept someone into her closely held private world, she did so with an aggressive vigor and commitment that was breathtaking. Lash returned her affection and love, and although his romantic interests were directed at a young married woman named Trude Patterson (whom he eventually married), he had basked in the close association with Eleanor. Now Lash was no longer available for the long talks and intimate visits Eleanor craved.

She also made a significant change in her New York City residences. Sara was now gone, so the Roosevelts sold the dual houses on East Sixty-Fifth Street that had been built soon after their marriage. Eleanor had always hated the houses, which symbolized her lack of independence as a young wife and Sara's domination of

FDR. Eleanor also gave up her Greenwich Village apartment and moved into a new apartment on Washington Square, one that had more room and provided all the space she needed for her work and frequent guests. She had the apartment fitted with an elevator for FDR; however, he visited her at the apartment only once, three years later.

In August 1942, while American troops invaded the Japanese-held island of Guadalcanal, setting off a prolonged but ultimately victorious attempt to take the initiative in the Pacific War, FDR embarked on a long and somewhat leisurely train tour of the Southwest. He invited Eleanor to join him, which she did for part of the trip. FDR loved train trips and boat cruises, which allowed him to get away from his responsibilities and relax at an easy pace. Conversely, Eleanor could barely contain her impatience and boredom with leisurely travel, so accompanying FDR on a slow train tour was a major concession for her.

While on the train and thrown into closer and more prolonged contact with Eleanor than usual, FDR made her a remarkable offer. He wanted to live again as husband and wife and repair the personal separations that had widened during the past decade. He asked her if she would be willing to curtail her travel and work schedule to spend more time with him at the White House. He wanted Eleanor to take over duties as hostess of his daily cocktail hour and to be with him in the evenings when he tried to relax. This was an almost astounding offer—in essence FDR was asking Eleanor to resume much of the relationship that had existed between them before Lucy Mercer and Missy LeHand. Eleanor promised to consider the proposal; however, in the end she apparently could not turn her back on the life she had built for herself, nor could she alter her personality to be the person the president needed to sit at his feet. A few weeks later she let FDR know that the reconciliation he proposed was not to be.

Chapter 9

A Time of Loss

When I went to Washington I felt sure that I would be
able to use the opportunities which came to me to help
Franklin gain the objectives he cared about .... He might
have been happier with a wife who was completely uncriti-
cal. That I was never able to be, and he had to find it in
other people.

—*Eleanor Roosevelt,*
This I Remember

Reluctant to restructure her domestic relationship with FDR
(and with her influence in national affairs on the wane),
Eleanor turned her energies toward helping the war effort by
assuming a role as a sort of public and symbolic mother. For example, she busied herself with issues surrounding the welfare of G.I.s
and their families. She received hundreds of letters from individual
soldiers, wives, and parents, and she kept the armed forces' high
command busy with her requests on their behalf. She also prodded
the Red Cross and the USO to open a serviceman's canteen and
rest area in Washington's Union Station and made regular visits to
area hospitals where wounded soldiers and sailors were beginning
to fill the wards.

Her most visible contributions, however, were the series of trips
she made abroad to visit American servicemen (and women)
and to report to FDR on everyday conditions at the rear of the

fighting fronts. Although she retained some degree of her usual aggressive inquisitiveness during these trips, she was much subdued compared to the tours she had made of the nation during the New Deal. To a large extent she changed her image—at least for some of the public—although she was not entirely happy with her reduced role.

The first of her trips was to Great Britain in October 1942. Thousands of American troops had been sent to Britain as part of the buildup for an invasion of North Africa (scheduled for November) and to shore up Britain's worn-down home island defenses. The Yank presence in Great Britain was already huge, and Eleanor wanted to see for herself what was happening. She also hoped to improve morale among both American service personnel and the beleaguered British.

She had met the half-American British wartime prime minister Winston Churchill several times in the United States when he had come to confer with FDR. In fact the irascible Churchill, who had his own imperious way of conducting wartime business, had turned the White House topsy-turvy while a guest there. Eleanor found him somewhat difficult, and for his part, Churchill apparently was mystified by her position and genuine power, because in his Edwardian worldview, women were mere decorative objects and had no right to hold ideas or opinions, let alone express them forcefully or act on them. As might be imagined, Eleanor's personality and behavior butted hard against Churchill's expectations, and the two of them usually seemed uneasy when thrown together.

Eleanor also had a more deeply seated conflict with Churchill that transcended her violation of his idea of social propriety. Churchill was an unabashed imperialist who believed it was the destiny of the English-speaking nations to rule much of the rest of the world. He confidently expected Great Britain to resume control of her world empire after the war was over (although he was quite willing to include the United States as a limited partner). Conversely, Eleanor saw mostly evil in colonialism and visualized a postwar world united in cooperative action, with the British Empire receding into the background as new nations took their places in a revised world order. Eleanor and Churchill disagreed repeatedly over this basic issue, although they managed to keep the actual clashes to a politely low level.

Nonetheless, Eleanor recognized a greatness in Churchill that seemed to be amplified by his close relationship with her husband. Together, Churchill and FDR were an extraordinarily potent partnership. As she wrote of him later: "I shall never cease to be grateful to Mr. Churchill for his leadership during the war; his speeches were a tonic to us here in the United States as well as to his own people. The affection which he had for my husband, and which was reciprocated, he apparently never lost. It was a fortunate friendship."

After a secrecy-shrouded plane flight across the Atlantic to Ireland and then travel by boat and train, Eleanor arrived in London to be greeted by the king and queen, whom she had hosted three years before at the White House and Val-Kill, and a bevy of dignitaries that included Gen. Dwight D. Eisenhower, who was in command of troops preparing to invade North Africa. She then was taken to Buckingham Palace, which she found enormous and forbidding. As she wrote: "I had been worried by the thought of having to visit Buckingham Palace, but I was determined to live each moment, aware of its special interest. Though certain situations might be unfamiliar and give me a feeling of inadequacy and of not knowing the proper way to behave, still I would do my best and not worry."

Soon, however, she was back in a familiar mode when she toured some of the bombed-out sections of London and then stopped at an American Red Cross club to meet American servicemen. In addition to giving them the expected greetings from home, she listened to the men's complaints, just as she had listened to people across the nation throughout the New Deal. The chief problem, they told her, was socks. They had been issued only thin cotton socks, which caused blisters and were impossible to march in. The next day Eleanor brought up the sock situation with Gen. Eisenhower, who immediately ordered that two and a half million wool socks be taken out of warehouses and distributed to the troops.

Eleanor then launched a whirlwind tour conducted at her accustomed high-energy pace, which left her escorts and hosts fatigued and wilting. She was determined to see as much as possible in the time allotted for her visit. Not only did she inspect U.S. bases, she also toured British factories where women were employed in large numbers. She showed particular interest in the system of child day care facilities, which the British had set up to accommodate working mothers. She also was fortunate to spend some time with her son Elliott, who was based near Cambridge with his Army Air Corps photo reconnaissance unit. He was released from duty to greet her on her first night in London and then joined her for an overnight stay as guests of the Churchills at Chequers, the country estate provided for the prime minister. Eleanor later visited Elliott's base.

From the standpoint of public relations and morale-building, Eleanor's trip to Britain was a huge success. The British press found her charming and reported enthusiastically on her visits and activities. She evoked what appeared to be genuinely spontaneous expressions of enthusiasm and cheering from British crowds wherever she went, which were duly noted in the papers. One paper reported that a knot of Britons stood watch outside the American embassy, hoping to catch a glimpse of her comings and goings. Perhaps even more important, Eleanor's trip also received extensive and favorable coverage in the United States, helping somewhat to repair her image after the OCD failure.

Homefront Travel

In January 1943 FDR traveled without Eleanor to Morocco to meet Churchill in Casablanca, where they laid plans for an invasion of Sicily as a follow-up to finally defeating the Germans in North Africa. It was the first time a sitting U.S. president had traveled outside the country, and the trip was conducted with the greatest secrecy, in sharp contrast to Eleanor's highly publicized trips. Meanwhile, on the homefront Eleanor was able to resume a domestic travel schedule that kept her on the road much of the time during the first weeks of the new year. She toured war industries to investigate the attempt to absorb women into the workforce, and she visited the first recruits for the Women's Army Auxiliary Corps at their training headquarters at Fort Des Moines, Iowa.

However, she made two trips in March to the Midwest that were strictly personal and had nothing to do with inspections or morale-building, other than her own. Joseph Lash had been assigned for Army training at a weather forecasting school at Chanute Field near Champaign-Urbana, Illinois. Eleanor decided she could no longer bear not seeing him so she traveled from Washington to visit Lash for the weekend, arranging for them to stay in adjoining rooms at a local Urbana hotel. Lash got a weekend pass and stayed from Friday night until Sunday at the hotel with Eleanor. Three weeks later, Eleanor again met Lash for a weekend visit; this time at the Blackstone Hotel in Chicago.

The second visit went very sour when the manager of the Blackstone informed Eleanor that the Army Counter-Intelligence Corps had bugged her room and had kept her and Lash under surveillance during their stay in the hotel. The CIC regarded Lash as a potential security threat and a subversive based on his previous activities with the American Youth Congress. They apparently also found the First Lady suspect. When she returned to Washington Eleanor asked Harry Hopkins, who was FDR's chief aide at this stage, to look into the matter, and he confirmed with Army Chief of Staff George Marshall that indeed the CIC had bugged her room and had a dossier on her activities.

FDR was outraged when he learned of the counterintelligence agency's actions and immediately ordered the entire department disbanded. The CIC was, after all, supposed to be catching enemy spies, not harassing the president's wife. Before they dispersed, however, the CIC staff turned its files on Eleanor over to J. Edgar Hoover at the FBI. Hoover added the spicy gossip about Eleanor's weekend stays with Lash to his already bulging files on the First Lady. The FBI had held her under suspicion for several years, primarily because of her activities on behalf of black civil rights and social causes.

Hoover built himself a position of virtually unassailable power in Washington by compiling files filled with sexual surveillance, innuendo, and unsubstantiated allegations on almost all major political figures (which seems highly ironic, as Hoover's personal life and apparent sexual proclivities have proved to be much outside the norm). He hated Eleanor and regarded her as a major threat to the American way of life as he understood it because of her pro-black stance. By the time of her death Eleanor's file at the FBI ran to several thousand pages and included vicious marginalia in Hoover's own handwriting.

Shortly after Eleanor's visits to Illinois Lash and his entire class of student weather forecasters were assigned to duty in the South Pacific and shipped to Guadalcanal. Historians and biographers—Lash himself included—have speculated that FDR might have ordered Lash out of the country to save further embarrassment.

Eleanor toured the Japanese-American Internment Center at Gila River, Arizona, in April 1943.

In April Eleanor joined FDR on a brief trip across the border to meet Mexican president Manuel Aliva Camacho and his wife at Monterrey, and the following day they reviewed the naval training station at Corpus Christi, Texas. Eleanor then split from FDR's itinerary at his request to inspect the Japanese-American internment camp at Gila River, Arizona. She found miserable conditions. The desert dirt and wind made everyday life difficult even in the best months of the year, and during the summer the hundred-plus-degree heat was nearly unbearable.

Worse yet, the camp, which contained twelve thousand people, was essentially one big prison, complete with barbed-wire fences and perimeter guards who had standing orders to shoot any internees who got too close to the fences. Eleanor reported to FDR on her return to Washington that the camps should be closed down and the people returned to their homes—in her opinion the original decision to intern the Japanese-American families was a mistake only compounded by holding people in such conditions. Although he appeared to be convinced to some extent and directed that some Japanese be allowed to depart and others to join the Army for service in Europe, FDR was persuaded by the War Department to keep the majority of the internees where they were.

However distressed Eleanor might have felt over conditions at the Gila River camp, she was much more agitated a few months later when a major race riot erupted in Detroit. African Americans and whites initially clashed on a hot summer day at a public park. Within hours rumors and unrest had spread. Gangs of whites and blacks fought openly in the streets, and by the next day ten people were dead and hundreds were injured. FDR was forced to send in federal troops to quell the rioting and reestablish order.

Eleanor had long been agitating FDR and other federal officials about the inadequate housing of black workers and the building tensions she perceived as hundreds of thousands of black families moved north to industrial cities to take jobs in defense plants. Now that these tensions had burst so dramatically she found herself the target of blame from racists, who loudly proclaimed that the riots were her fault for having promoted racial justice and equality.

Eleanor, who withstood the vicious criticism with her usual public calm, nonetheless was upset when FDR refused to take action or even comment on the causes of the rioting. As he had so many other times since 1933, the president feared the legislative wrath of the southerners in Congress so he withheld comment.

South Pacific

In August 1943 Eleanor undertook her most significant wartime trip: At FDR's urging she traveled to the South Pacific theater of operations to visit the troops and gather impressions for the president. She had considerable trepidation about the journey before she left, fearing criticism would be directed at FDR for sending her on a trip that would divert resources from the war effort. It seemed quite different from her trip to Britain the previous year. As she wrote to Joseph Lash, now stationed on Guadalcanal, "I am so uncertain whether or not I am doing the right thing that I will start with a heavy heart."

The arrangements for the trip were complicated. To deflect criticism that she was assuming an official government role illegitimately, Eleanor asked Norman Davis, the head of the Red Cross, if she could make the trip as a special assignment for his organization. He agreed, and Eleanor had a special Red Cross uniform run up for herself, which she wore throughout the journey as a Red Cross "special delegate." She also decided that she would travel alone, leaving Tommy Thompson behind, and take only a lightweight portable typewriter to allow her to type out her daily newspaper column. She arranged for her usual fees for the column to be donated to the Red Cross and the American Friends Committee, but conservative members of the Red Cross national governing board feared anti-Eleanor donors might stop supporting the organization if the news got out, so they kept her largesse a secret.

She might have approached her long journey with concerns over political fallout but in her heart she surely was more worried over what she could expect to see when she toured the area. Her son James had fought in the South Pacific as part of an elite Marine unit, and his former comrades had been in the heaviest fighting on Guadalcanal. Her fears for her own sons and for all the sons of all American families were heavy in her thoughts. As she wrote later of her emotions:

> I imagine every mother felt as I did when I said good-bye
> to the children during the war. I had a feeling that I might
> be saying good-bye for the last time. It was a sort of pre-
> cursor of what it would be like if your children were
> killed. Life had to go on and you had to do what was
> required of you, but something inside of you quietly died.

No matter how much inner turmoil she felt during her long tour of the South Pacific, Eleanor effectively assumed the role of surrogate mother, bringing to many of the men and women she visited a strong reminder of home and family. She was the most recognizable woman in the United States and an object of both hate and admiration, but for intervals during her trip she transcended her public persona and provided a genuine human connection for thousands of young Americans. The effect was an amplified version of the good she had accomplished by her trips to blighted areas during the Great Depression.

On August 17 Eleanor boarded a military B-24, made a place for herself in the crude, unheated passenger space, and settled in for the long flight to Hawaii. After a brief stopover there she continued on to Christmas Island, a bleak coral atoll in the middle of the ocean, for her first meeting with troops on active duty. Her visit there set the tone for her subsequent South Pacific travels. She overcame her first reaction to the primitive conditions (she found her sleeping quarters overrun with "little red bugs"), and she proceeded to visit and inspect almost every aspect of the base. "I saw everything the men were doing on that island ..." she wrote. She toured the hospital, visited the military installations, and drove forty miles to see the island's rest camp.

Most important, she spent as much time as she could with the ordinary soldiers and sailors, listening to their complaints and requests and noting how they adjusted to duty in such extreme conditions. She reported that for the most part the men reacted well to her visit, often asking her to write to their families when she returned to the United States. Eleanor had been extremely nervous about her reception by the troops. They were told in advance only that a woman was about to visit; she feared that when they discovered it was her instead of a Hollywood starlet they would react badly. In truth, although they probably would have enjoyed a visit from a glamour queen, having the motherly Eleanor speak to them in her direct, simple fashion probably was just as good. Only occasionally on her trip did she meet negativity— usually from pompous officers or diehard Roosevelt haters.

She went from Christmas Island on to the Fijis and from there to the major U.S. base at Noumea, where she met Admiral William "Bull" Halsey, the naval commander for the Pacific theater, who had risen to prominence the previous fall when he defeated the Japanese in the fierce and prolonged naval battles around Guadalcanal, finally forcing the enemy to abandon their attempts to resupply and reinforce their garrison there. By the time Eleanor arrived Halsey already was regarded as a national hero, and she needed his good opinion and cooperation.

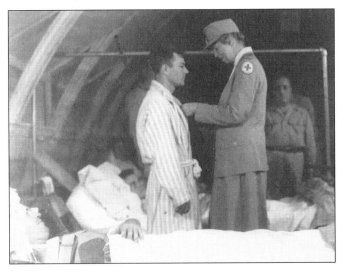

Eleanor visited military hospitals wherever she went during her tour of the South Pacific theater of operations in 1943. Here she pins a medal on a wounded serviceman on the island base at Espiritu Santo.

Although she was interested in seeing as many places as possible on her trip, Eleanor was particularly desperate to visit Guadalcanal, and she presented Halsey with a handwritten letter from FDR, asking the admiral to allow Eleanor to travel to this important symbol of hard-won American victory in the Pacific theater. However, Eleanor's overriding reason to visit Guadalcanal was private: Joseph Lash was serving as an enlisted man on the island. She had not seen Lash since March and could not bear the thought of having been so close without a meeting.

Halsey flat-out denied her request, saying he did not have enough fighters to spare to escort her plane to Guadalcanal, which was still under threat of Japanese air raids. Like many of the high-ranking officers Eleanor encountered on her trip, Halsey assumed she was nothing more than a nuisance to be dealt with or brushed aside. He certainly was not going to make any exceptions for Eleanor just because she was the First Lady and bore a letter from the commander in chief. However, Eleanor turned on her most persuasive manner and convinced Halsey to suspend his decision until she returned to Noumea from her round of other visits.

With that encouragement, Eleanor boarded a plane and flew to New Zealand where she visited hospitals, Army camps, Red Cross installations, and war factories. Part of her purpose in visiting New Zealand and Australia was to see firsthand how women were taking part in war industries. She then moved on to Australia and made a similar round of visits, starting in Canberra and moving on to Melbourne, the north coast, and finally the seaside town of Cairns.

The most affecting moments of her South Pacific tour came in the hospitals in northern Australia. An Australian-American army commanded by Gen. Douglas MacArthur had fought during the previous months a massive and costly series of battles against the Japanese in New Guinea. The hospitals in Australia were full of wounded soldiers, many of them severely hurt and crippled or in the last days of their lives. Eleanor had some of her finest moments when she visited ward after ward of wounded soldiers, stopping to talk to nearly each man, and fighting back the desire to flinch or turn away at some of the more grotesque wounds. Her willpower, energy, and sense of duty drove her on, and the stories of how she revived the spirits of the wounded men were inspiring. Almost all of her escorts—no matter how cynical they were about her presence—came to respect her for the efforts, even though they knew it was a crushingly depressing experience for someone usually so far removed from the grim realities of war.

> *Eleanor's desire to visit Guadalcanal may have been prompted by the presence there of Joseph Lash, her intimate friend, but the island in the South Pacific Solomon chain had great significance with the American public as the scene of a prolonged series of battles between Japan and the United States, marking the first major offensive campaign by the United States in the South Pacific.*
>
> *American Marines had landed unopposed on Guadalcanal in August 1942 in order to seize a vital airfield the Japanese were building on the island. Due to Japanese naval superiority in the nearby waters, the U.S. supply ships withdrew prematurely, virtually stranding the Marines.*
>
> *After the Japanese landed more troops, a long series of battles and raids took place over the following weeks, with vicious fighting and large numbers of casualties on both sides. By February 1943, the United States had full control of the island and surrounding waters.*

Word of her activities apparently had reached Halsey by the time Eleanor returned to Noumea; he relented and gave permission for her to visit Guadalcanal. Once on Guadalcanal she went through all the motions and performed all the expected duties, but her main interest was in seeing Lash. They enjoyed a happy reunion outside her tent on the afternoon of her visit and followed up with two more sessions together. They parted late that night and Eleanor flew back to Noumea the next morning to begin her long trip home.

Halsey was vocal in repenting his original suspicions of Eleanor, and he later wrote an effusive endorsement of her visit, saying "She alone had accomplished more good than any other person, or any group of civilians, who passed through my area."

Troubled Times

Although she obviously had done much good during her tour of the South Pacific theater, when she returned to the United States Eleanor faced criticism in Congress on the grounds that she wasted government funds on a meaningless junket. However unfair the accusations—they came mostly from the president's enemies, and once again Eleanor was a convenient target for displaced political enmity—they stung Eleanor and convinced FDR that she should stay close to the White House at least for several months to let the hubbub die down.

More deeply troubling was the depression into which Eleanor appeared to slip after her return. She thought FDR had shown inadequate interest in her descriptions and reports, and she withdrew into one of her periodic states of loneliness and inner despair, a prolonged and deep Griselda mood. Trude Lash attributed the onset of Eleanor's depression to firsthand exposure to the brutal reality of the war during her trip. As historian Doris Kearns Goodwin points out, so long as Eleanor had toured domestic war plants and armed forces training camps in the United States, she had seen only the potential for actual war. In the dozens of hospital wards she toured in the South Pacific, she saw firsthand with a mother's compassionate eyes the terrible physical devastation of war itself. The broken bodies and broken lives affected her deeply. Compassion for the sick or hurt was one of her strongest impulses, and what she experienced on her tour evoked not only compassion but deep sorrow. She wrote in one of her daily columns after returning that she could not rid her mind of the memory of row upon row of crosses in the American cemetery on Guadalcanal—mute testimony to the thousands of American boys who died so far from home.

A case can be made that for the rest of the war Eleanor never really recovered from the depressing experience of her South Pacific tour. During the eighteen months between her return and FDR's death, she adopted a mode of behavior that can be explained as her usual response to depression. She became almost hyperactive and seemed to seal herself off from reality. Her high energy and single-minded concern for social issues, which had been her greatest strengths as First Lady, took on a neurotic edge, and she failed to respond to pleas from her family and close associates to pay more attention to FDR and his increasingly serious physical decline. Their relationship, unusual as it was, had survived for decades as a source of mutual strength, but during the last year and a half of FDR's life, Eleanor seemed to almost willingly pull away.

One of the first bitter sources of conflict arose when FDR announced that in November he was going to travel to Tehran to meet with Churchill and, for the first time, with Soviet leader Josef Stalin. Eleanor wanted to go along, but FDR adamantly refused to consider the proposition, rejecting his wife's request out of hand and insisting that no woman could make the journey, nor would she be welcome at the conference. Eleanor tried to make the best of the rejection, but when she subsequently learned that Churchill had brought along his daughter, she was outraged.

Anna Roosevelt Boettinger also had asked to go on the trip, in part because of her concern for her husband John, who was serving unhappily in the Mediterranean theater. FDR insisted on leaving Anna at home as well, but the father and daughter quickly repaired their disagreement when FDR return to Washington. When Anna and her children celebrated Christmas with her family at Hyde Park, she and FDR seemed to renew their relationship on a deeper level than had been true for several years. From this grew an almost casual decision that Anna would give up her difficult wartime post with the Seattle newspaper and move into the White House to serve as her father's hostess and personal aide.

FDR desperately needed someone close to him at all times who he could talk to and share ideas with and, most important, who could create that relaxed atmosphere at the end of the day he so craved and needed—especially as the burden of his wartime duties began to erode his customary vigor. Missy was gone, and neither Laura Delano nor Margaret Suckley were capable of replacing her. Moreover, Harry Hopkins, who had been FDR's closest confidant since the beginning of the war, had remarried and moved out of the White House, thereby forfeiting much of his relationship with the president. Eleanor of course had rejected the appeal FDR had made during the fall of the previous year, so he turned to Anna to fill his needs, and she was happy to throw off what had become the burdens of her life on the West Coast and devote herself to her father. Her husband, John, had been transferred to a post in Washington early in 1944, so she settled with her family into the Lincoln suite vacated by Hopkins.

On the surface Eleanor welcomed Anna and her family to the White House; however, she sternly insisted that Anna observe the proprieties and leave official authority for the household in Eleanor's hands. In fact, Eleanor wanted little to do with running the residence or participating in the dozens of official and semi-official social events that filled a week's calendar. By early 1944 Eleanor was so consumed with her travels and filling up her days with incessant work that she became increasingly impatient with even the most important social events, seeing them as a waste of time that could be better spent in writing or dealing with correspondence or any of the other tasks that consumed her energies. Nonetheless, Eleanor was still sensitive to her prerogatives, which some of FDR's female associates had tried in the past to usurp, so the First Lady made it clear that Anna was not to interfere unduly.

Anna's new role was never clearly defined, and she never had an official title or received a salary for her work (in contrast to her brother James when he served his father); however, for the last year of FDR's presidency his daughter was his chief aide and assistant. She not only took over the social role of organizing FDR's relaxation, but she soon became indispensable as his political assistant as well. She worked at FDR's side all day long, taking notes in shorthand she had learned just to better aid her father; then, after seeing her family briefly, she returned to preside at his cocktail hour.

About the same time Anna and her family moved into the White House, Eleanor and Tommy Thompson went on the last of Eleanor's wartime trips, this time to the Caribbean and parts of Central and South America. The United States had thousands of troops stationed in the region to guard against threats to the Panama Canal and to forestall any attempt at invasion, although neither seemed likely by the spring of 1944 when clearly the tides of war had turned against the Axis Powers. However, FDR urged Eleanor to make the tour of southern bases as a way of building the sagging morale of troops stationed there, who justifiably believed the war had passed them by.

The two women made the three-week, thirteen-hundred-mile trip by a series of hops by air, beginning at the American base at Guantánamo, Cuba, and looping through the West Indies and Puerto Rico to the coast of Brazil; then on to Venezuela, the Canal Zone, the Galapagos Islands, and Guatemala; and back to the United States by way of Havana.

There were no large numbers of wounded to visit, but Eleanor took a great deal of time and effort to mix with the enlisted troops. She publicized her trip ahead of time and collected from stateside families the names of soldiers and sailors who they wanted Eleanor to greet. At each stop she arranged for the designated men to report to a central location and then surprised them with a personal visit and greetings from their "mothers, wives, sweethearts, and sisters." After her return to Washington she wrote to hundreds of families at the request of "boys" whom she had met on her trip.

FDR Declines

When she came back from her Caribbean tour Eleanor resumed a heavy schedule of writing, speaking, and travelling. She spent little time at the White House and apparently saw her husband only sporadically. Had she paid closer attention, Eleanor would have seen the signs of serious physical deterioration in FDR. Anna, who was at his side almost all day long, observed problems that she first attributed to several bouts of flu; however, eventually she could not dismiss them as trivial. The president lost weight, his energy level dropped drastically, he had trouble breathing, he could not sleep, and he experienced short periods of mental blackout. He was entirely capable of gathering himself for public appearance and for meetings with the press, but on a day-to-day basis, he was showing signs of failing badly.

FDR's personal physician, Adm. Ross McIntire, seemed to be in a state of denial about the president. At first he maintained that nothing serious could be wrong when Anna consulted him. He finally agreed, however, to a complete examination of the president at Anna's insistence. On March 28, the day Eleanor returned from the Caribbean, FDR went to Bethesda Naval Hospital, where he was examined by the young navy cardiologist Lt. Commander Howard Breunn, who discovered that the president was suffering from high blood pressure, an enlarged heart, and other clearcut symptoms of serious congestive heart failure.

It also was embarrassingly clear that McIntire had ignored all the early signs of the disease and had failed to properly care for the president. After calling in other specialists to consult, Breunn insisted on an immediate course of medication and treatment for FDR, but McIntire brushed most of his suggestions aside and refused to tell the president of his condition. FDR appeared to have little interest in his own diagnosis and failed to ask the doctors what was wrong with him. (One of the specialists, Dr. Frank Lahey of Boston, might have found evidence of a malignant tumor in the president's stomach, but there is no definite proof of this analysis.)

One of Dr. Bruenn's primary recommendations, in addition to a course of digitalis and a change in diet, was that the president take time off and rest completely. This was difficult to do at this crucial juncture of the war—the Allies were in the final stages of preparation for a cross-channel invasion of Europe—but Anna pressed him so he agreed to a vacation at Bernard Baruch's hideaway mansion on the Waccamaw River in South Carolina. The days of rest and the effects of the heart medication improved FDR's condition, and when Anna and Eleanor came to visit him in South Carolina he appeared much healthier than he had been two weeks before.

While relaxing at Baruch's isolated house (the press was kept at a considerable distance and the staff was restricted in number) FDR reopened his longtime relationship with his former mistress Lucy Mercer Rutherford, whose husband had died only the month before. Rutherford, her stepdaughter, and her daughter-in-law drove from her home near Aiken for a luncheon with the president. In fact, she had secretly visited the White House twice in 1941, using the pseudonym of "Mrs. Johnson" to cover her real identity, but during her South Carolina visit she openly used her real name, perhaps because of her husband's death.

Over the next year—the last of FDR's life—he arranged to meet Rutherford repeatedly. To do so he needed the connivance of Anna, who reluctantly agreed to help arrange the meetings. Anna was caught in a terrible struggle between providing her ailing father the comfort he sought in Rutherford's company and remaining true to her mother, with whom she had a strong relationship. Eleanor was kept totally in the dark about the visits, which took place when she was absent from the White House. FDR and Rutherford had other secret meetings at Rutherford's New Jersey estate and at Warm Springs. FDR's staff must have known what was going on, as Rutherford was relatively open about the visits, but none of them revealed the truth to Eleanor or Eleanor's staff.

For example, in March 1945 while Eleanor was on a trip to North Carolina, Rutherford came to the White House for dinner with FDR, Anna, and John. The next day she took a car ride with the president through the Virginia countryside and returned to the White House several more times during the following days. She slipped out of town just before Eleanor returned to Washington to celebrate with FDR their fortieth wedding anniversary, an occasion that doubtlessly would have been filled with bitterness had Eleanor realized what was happening. Anna rationalized her role in facilitating the illicit meetings between Rutherford and her father as providing a necessary form of relaxation for FDR, who was weighed down by the huge responsibilities of his role as leader of the Allies as well as by his declining health.

Eleanor appeared throughout the final year of FDR's life to almost ignore his failing health. In fact, Anna's account of these months shows her mother ratcheting up her insistent hectoring of FDR over political and social issues. The impression Anna gave was that her mother could not be made to understand that FDR was in desperate health and needed more than anything to relax and rest as much as possible. Instead, Eleanor became a source of extreme stress for her husband. Her customary habit of bringing up serious issues for FDR's attention moved from being a normal part of their political relationship to an inconsiderate and even damaging lack of insight and sympathy.

Fourth Term Unserved

No matter how troubled Eleanor's relationship with her husband or how dangerous his medical condition, the worldwide march of events during 1944 seemed to eclipse their personal lives. In June, as the president showed signs of physical improvement, the great invasion of Europe finally took place, and the British and American armies began a long and difficult—but inexorable—march toward victory over Hitler. The next month FDR was nominated by the Democratic Party for a fourth term as president.

The convention was contentious, however, because of FDR's choice of a running mate. He had decided over Eleanor's objections to dump Henry Wallace from the ticket, even though he had petulantly insisted on Wallace in 1940. He instead turned to Harry Truman, a U.S. senator from Missouri, although he toyed with several other possible candidates and was coy about making his choice clear. Eleanor had come full circle in her relationship with Wallace, with whom she had quarreled during the first days of the New Deal when he was secretary of agriculture; she now thought him the man with the best liberal credentials to support FDR's domestic programs. Unfortunately, Wallace had little wide support in the party and Truman was named to the ticket, just as FDR had seemed to want.

Immediately after the convention FDR sailed for Hawaii, where he met Adm. Chester Nimitz and Gen. Douglas MacArthur for a conference on the strategy to be used against the Japanese in the Pacific. The problems were difficult. The United States forces were advancing successfully but at great cost. The fanaticism displayed by the Japanese so far indicated that an invasion of the Japanese home islands and final victory would cost massively. Following his stay in Honolulu, FDR returned to the mainland after briefly visiting troops on the remote Aleutian island of Adak. While the president was out of the country Eleanor kept up her vigorous schedule, visiting North Carolina, for example, to give a speech to a group of Methodist women.

The Republicans nominated New York governor Thomas Dewey as their candidate and launched a vigorous campaign to defeat FDR for a fourth term. They questioned the president's health, and to defuse the issue, FDR decided on a series of campaign speeches designed to show he was still vigorous and capable of leading the country for a fourth term. Of course in reality he was a progressively ill man, but he could rally his strength sufficiently to give rousing speeches in almost his old style. The reaction of crowds to his speeches seemed to invigorate the president, and his campaign gained momentum, aided by the news of MacArthur's invasion of the Philippines. The election itself was closer than the 1940 contest but still a decisive victory. FDR and Truman won almost fifty-four percent of the popular vote and took four hundred thirty-two Electoral College votes to Dewey's ninety-nine.

FDR's final inauguration in January was a subdued affair, far removed from the high drama and spectacle of his first inauguration in 1933, when he had stood on a platform on the Capitol steps and declared the nation had nothing to fear but fear itself. By 1945 he was only a shadow compared to twelve years before, and Eleanor was herself flagging in emotional and psychological strength, much depleted by the taxing war years. FDR's only concessions to the historic nature of his fourth inaugural was to insist that all his thirteen grandchildren attend—they all crowded into the White House the night before, bumping Eleanor from her own bedroom— and he requested that James be given leave to attend so the president could brace himself one more time on his son's arm while taking the oath of office.

The inauguration ceremony itself was a low-key affair, conducted on the South Porch of the White House. FDR made a brief speech to a small crowd gathered in the cold weather. Afterward, two thousand people attended a reception made slightly ridiculous by the irascible Mrs. Nesbitt's insistence on serving only chicken salad and unbuttered rolls to the guests—she claimed anything else was too much bother. Moreover, most of the chicken intended for the occasion had spoiled, so the chicken salad was mostly celery. FDR's frustration with the official housekeeper was doomed to plague him until the end.

A few days after the ceremony FDR left for what proved to be the final grand conference of Allied leaders at Yalta in the Soviet Union. Eleanor had asked to go along, but once again FDR turned her down in favor of Anna. He craved the companionship of his daughter and knew that he probably could not bear the stress of a prolonged trip with Eleanor. The conference itself was difficult, and in the years since often has been interpreted by historians as one of the great failures of FDR's diplomatic career. It usually is claimed that due to his illness and weakened state he was finagled by Stalin into conceding too much to the postwar ambitions of the Soviets, thus making the Cold War inevitable. In any event the trip was taxing, and after his return to Washington the president's strength and health further declined. When he addressed Congress to report on the Yalta conference, for the first time FDR spoke to them sitting down, revealing his diminished condition to the entire nation.

On March 24 Eleanor and FDR rode together by train to Hyde Park, where the president planned a long weekend of rest and quiet. For what proved to be the last time, the Roosevelts were together. Despite FDR's apparent physical weakness—he could no longer drive his specially equipped car around the estate and allowed Eleanor to chauffeur him—he was brimming with ideas for shaping the postwar world, and Eleanor was eager to discuss her ideas with him. After returning to Washington FDR departed for a two-week stay at Warm Springs. Eleanor did not go along but instead returned to her schedule of meetings and appearances in the capital and planned to return briefly to Hyde Park to open the big house for the summer. Anna's youngest child was ill, so she, too, remained behind in Washington but arranged for Lucy Mercer Rutherford to visit Warm Springs during the second week of FDR's stay. His cousins Laura Delano and Margaret Suckley went with the president.

On April 9 Rutherford arrived at the president's house at Warm Springs, accompanied by her painter friend Elizabeth Shoumatoff.

Three days later, on April 12, while chatting with Rutherford and sitting for a portrait for Shoumatoff, FDR slumped forward, holding his head. He muttered that he had a terrible pain and then lost consciousness. When Lt. Commander Bruenn arrived at the house he immediately diagnosed a cerebral hemorrhage. There was nothing the doctor could do, and FDR died shortly before three-thirty in the afternoon.

Chapter 10

The Final Years

I was now on my own.

> —*Eleanor Roosevelt,*
> This I Remember

Eleanor had been alerted earlier in the day by Adm. McIntire that FDR was ill but was not told of the seriousness of his condition, so she went ahead with an afternoon appearance at a fundraiser in Washington. She was at the meeting when Steve Early, the presidential press secretary, telephoned and asked her to come immediately to the White House. As she rode in the car with clenched fists, she later recalled, "In my heart I knew what had happened." Early and McIntire met her in her sitting room and told her that the president was dead.

By the time Anna arrived at the White House, Eleanor was composed and quietly going about planning what should be done. She summoned Vice President Harry Truman and broke the news to him, gently insisting that the new president should call on her for support, as he was "the one in trouble now." After attending Truman's swearing in, Eleanor left for a flight to Warm Springs with Anna and McIntire, reaching FDR's resort just before midnight.

She first asked to see Grace Tully and FDR's two cousins, wanting to hear the story of FDR's last day. Tully and Suckley were circumspect, but Laura Delano blurted out the entire account of Lucy

Mercer Rutherford's visit and how the president was with his mistress when he suffered his fatal stroke. Shocked as she must have been, Eleanor showed little emotion and emerged dry-eyed from spending five minutes alone with her husband's body. She then questioned Laura further and learned of Rutherford's regular visits to the White House and the other meetings with FDR. Delano made it clear that Anna Roosevelt had arranged it all.

> *When FDR died in April 1945, the public mourning that followed was in keeping with the American tradition of political grieving. The pattern was set by the thousands of public funeral ceremonies held for George Washington, who died in 1799, just two years after he left office. Americans often created elaborate private and public memorials—including parades, sermons, pamphlets, and works of art—for their dead leaders.*
>
> *After Abraham Lincoln was assassinated in 1865, Congress held a huge public memorial service in Washington, D.C., before sending his body on a special ceremonial train to Illinois for burial. Wherever the train passed along the way, people held funeral rituals and clamored to see Lincoln's casket.*
>
> *FDR died during a crucial period in America's involvement in World War II, and the period of public mourning allowed Americans to work through their larger feelings about wartime losses.*

In the hours and days that followed, Eleanor put on a grave but composed demeanor, showing little emotion throughout the long train trip with FDR's body back to Washington, where it lay in state, and then to Hyde Park, where he was buried according to his wishes in the rose garden next to the big house. A shock wave of grief had rippled across the country, however, and there was a massive outpouring of emotional response to the loss of the man who had held the country's attention for twelve years, through the depths of the Depression to the edge of victory in World War II.

Nathan Miller wrote about the impact of the president's death in his 1983 biography:

> *For Americans of my generation—I was just short of eighteen—Roosevelt's passing was like a death in the family. We could remember no other President. He*

*dominated our lives as no political leader has been able to
do since. We gathered about the radio to listen to the mel-
lifluous voice of the Fireside Chats, and his face dominated
the newspapers, magazines, and news reels that were part
of every show in the neighborhood movie theater. And during the worst of the Great Depression, most of the people
who patronized my parents' grocery store ... were kept
from starving only by New Deal relief programs.*

While FDR's body had lain in state at the White House, Eleanor
had confronted Anna about her role in Rutherford's visits. The
meeting was one of the worst of Anna's life, and her mother was so
angry and hurt that Anna feared they would never be reconciled.
In time Eleanor was able to absorb the pain of FDR's final betrayal
and Anna's choice to make it possible, but in the immediate aftermath she must have been in torment. Forty years of marriage and
political partnership were now passed, and she would always have
this bitter memory of its ending.

She did not, however, dwell on her losses or descend into one of
her depressions. She turned almost immediately to the questions of
moving out of the White House and dealing with the practical matters of where she would live and how she would support herself. She
organized the packing of all of FDR's and her White House rooms,
pausing to give Bess and Margaret Truman, the new president's wife
and daughter, a tour of the family quarters. (Mrs. Truman, a woman
as unlike Eleanor as is possible to imagine, hated the glare of publicity in Washington and spent much of her time during Truman's
presidency in Independence, Missouri.) After a farewell tea for the
women newspaper reporters who had covered her so faithfully as
First Lady, Eleanor left the White House for her apartment in New
York City.

Eleanor and FDR had talked of giving the mansion at Hyde Park
to the government to serve as a presidential library and memorial;
thus, Eleanor acted at once to speed up the transfer, even though
she and her children could have remained there during their life-
times. She kept her cottage at Val-Kill and purchased a large part
of the adjoining farm. She also retained the cottage overlooking the
Hudson that FDR had built for himself as a retirement hideaway. It

was decided that Elliott would move into the cottage with his family and manage the Hyde Park farm, which he held in partnership with Eleanor. Eleanor also took possession of her original stone cottage at Val-Kill, finally buying out Nancy Cook's and Marion Dickerman's last interest and asking them to move out so she could use the cottage as guest quarters. After sorting the huge accumulation of objects and possessions in the Hyde Park house, much of which had belonged to Sara Delano, Eleanor turned it over to the government, which formally dedicated it as a memorial library a year later.

Having tied up many loose ends quickly and efficiently, Eleanor still had to consider her work. She had been earning large amounts of money since the earliest days in the White House through her writing, lecturing, and radio broadcasts, so there should have been little to fear about income. Her "My Day" column continued after FDR's death to be one of the nation's most popular syndicated newspaper features, and she had new contracts to continue both her *Ladies Home Journal* column and her radio show. In addition, she received about eight thousand dollars a year from the original trust fund left to her by her father and about thirty thousand dollars a year from FDR's estate, so even though her resources were strained when she bought the Hyde Park farm and for the first year after FDR's death until the government assumed full responsibility for the president's former Hyde Park house, Eleanor was never in any serious financial trouble. In fact, she continued for the next seventeen years, right up until her death, to be in demand as a writer and broadcaster.

The United Nations

With FDR's death Eleanor's direct political power disappeared overnight. She still had influence, as was made clear by the way Harry Truman and other important Democrats paid close attention to her, but her ability to directly affect laws and policy had vanished. She had been so long in the White House and had focused so much energy on bringing social matters to FDR's attention or pushing causes through the federal bureaucracy that her next steps were unclear. She was not about to retire—her zest for work had not abated with advancing age—but her accustomed arena was no longer available.

To her surprise, Truman opened the door to an entirely new venue at the end of 1945 when he asked her to accept his appointment as a delegate to the United Nations. The international body had been formed at the end of the war by the nations that had been allied against Germany, Italy, and Japan. It was based almost entirely on FDR's ideas and hopes for the future of the world, and he had discussed it at length with his wife during the war years. She was still intensely interested in international affairs and was devoted to fostering cooperation and world peace; however, she felt completely unprepared for Truman's request. She had no actual experience as a diplomat, and in fact many who had been on the sharp end of her lobbying efforts during the New Deal would have found laughable the concept that she had the patience or the skills to work cooperatively in the slow-speed world of diplomacy, which relied more on compromise than passion.

FDR was buried on April 15, 1945 at Hyde Park. Eleanor is shown to the right, viewing the solemn procession of her husband's casket.

Nonetheless, at the urging of her family, close friends, and associates, she decided to accept Truman's offer. Somewhat surprisingly, her nomination as a delegate swept through a Senate confirmation hearing with only one negative vote, from the Senate's most dedicated racist Theodore Bilbo of Mississippi. On New Year's Eve, 1945, leaving Tommy behind, Eleanor boarded a steamship for Great Britain, where the first working session of the United Nations was scheduled to meet.

As soon as she settled into her stateroom Eleanor began studying the pile of position papers and background reports she found stacked on her table. In her usual fashion, she plunged into the task of learning as much about her new job as possible. It was not so intimidating as she feared at first. Her knowledge of public and world affairs was extensive, and she was completely at home with the complexities of parliamentary maneuvers from her years as a Democratic Party operative and a women's rights activist. Additionally, her high energy and capacity to outwork almost anyone else proved to be major assets. As she showed over and over again during the next seven years of her tenure as a UN delegate, she was completely suited for the role.

At first, however, her colleagues were skeptical. The U.S. delegation was made up of former Secretary of State Edward Stettinius, now the new ambassador to the UN, and Senators Arthur Vandenburg and Tom Connally, two of the fustiest conservatives in the Senate—and previously no fans of Eleanor. All of them looked at her as a rank amateur whose reputation from her days as First Lady—usually pushing causes they opposed—put them on edge. The delegation also included John Foster Dulles, a future Secretary of State, whom Eleanor disliked immediately.

Eleanor understood her position with these men. As she wrote:

During the entire London session of the [General]
Assembly I walked on eggs. I knew that as the only
woman on the delegation I was not very welcome.
Moreover, if I failed to be a useful member, it would not
be considered merely that I as an individual had failed but
that all women had failed, and there would be little chance
for others to serve in the near future.

To her annoyance, Eleanor was told peremptorily by Vandenburg that it had been decided to ask her to accept assignment to Committee Three of the UN, which was slated to deal with humanitarian, educational, and cultural matters. This assignment was suggested, she correctly supposed, to get her out of the way of any important business and keep her tied up on lesser issues. She also was irritated that she had not been included in the delegation deliberations that made committee assignments; however, rather than cause trouble at this delicate stage, Eleanor acquiesced.

As it turned out, one of the most important issues to come before the UN session was assigned to Committee Three, which gave Eleanor a chance to shine in her first outing as a diplomat. The war had displaced hundreds of thousands of refugees, who were still living in camps at the end of hostilities. Many of them had originally come from countries or regions in Eastern Europe that now were under the control of the Soviet Union; for political reasons they did not want to be repatriated to communist regimes, where many feared for their safety.

Although the United States and Great Britain looked favorably on resettling the refugees and avoiding repatriation, the Soviets were adamant. They sent their most potent delegate, Deputy Foreign Minister Andrei Vishinsky, who had been Stalin's foremost prosecutor during the show trials of the 1930s, to make their case that any refugee who resisted returning to his or her homeland must be a traitor and deserved to be sent back for punishment. This basic disagreement showed clearly the split that was rapidly developing between the Western democracies and the Soviets, which within a few years came to the point of full-blown—albeit nonmilitary—conflict. It was the beginning of what came to be known as the Cold War, which lasted from 1946 until the collapse of the Soviet Union in 1991, and Eleanor was thrust into the middle of the dispute. Because no one else in the American delegation knew much about the issue of refugee repatriation, they turned to Eleanor and asked her to speak in rebuttal to Vishinsky.

She rose before the Committee and made one of her typical speeches, delivered without notes, in her high-pitched voice. She refuted the Soviet position point by point and demolished the idea that only traitors would resist being sent back to communist-controlled homelands. She was particularly effective with the many Latin-American delegates by working in references to the principles of Simón Bolívar, the great liberator. The Committee voted to accept the U.S. position and to allow freedom to war refugees.

Her fellow American delegates appreciated her performance, and by the end of the session accepted her as a valuable member of the delegation. She appears to have discarded the aggressive, hectoring tactics that she had employed for so long with FDR; instead, in the years following the war she adopted a much lower-key approach, characterized by much more social sensitivity than she had ever shown during her White House years. Perhaps it was the changed circumstances of her life without her powerful husband or perhaps just the stimulation of working with a wide range of people from other cultures and other places. Whatever the reasons, Eleanor found a very effective mode of behavior within the UN.

For example, during the first session in London in 1946, Eleanor made a point of inviting the sixteen women of the General Assembly—mostly alternates or staff advisors—to regular teas in her hotel apartment, and she used the informal meetings to explore topics that were slated for official consideration. Even the lone woman from the Soviet delegation came. Eleanor understood the value of the occasions:

> The talk was partly social but as we became better
> acquainted we also talked about the problems on which we
> were working in the various committees .... I discovered
> that in such informal sessions we sometimes made more
> progress in reaching an understanding ... than we
> had been able to achieve in the formal work of our
> committees.

After the London session Eleanor returned to New York and was almost immediately pulled deeper into work with the UN. She was asked to serve on a special committee of individually selected delegates that was to set up the structure and program for a new Commission on Human Rights. At the committee's first meeting in New York in April 1946, Eleanor was elected as chair, and over the following weeks she guided the planning. In June the Commission was formally established and given the tasks of writing an international bill of rights for individuals as well as setting up a way to implement it. The decision led to one of Eleanor's greatest opportunities for lasting achievements.

No such thing as international rights had existed previously. One nation did not officially comment on or question the way any other sovereign nation treated its own citizens. The Soviets might use the persecution of blacks in the United States as a powerful source of propaganda, but they had no venue or excuse to formally or officially interfere. Nor had the United States any basis in international agreement to comment on Germany's anti-Semitic laws in the 1930s.

The war and its immediate aftermath had changed the attitudes of many nations, however. The large-scale atrocities committed by both the Germans and the Japanese during the war—the murder of millions of European Jews chief among them—provided the basis for a new concern for individual rights, regardless of national borders. Many people, Eleanor included, saw the establishment of international rights as one step toward maintaining world peace and avoiding the tragedies of World War II. As she wrote in an article for the influential journal *Foreign Affairs:* "Many of us thought the lack of standards for human rights the world over was one of the greatest causes of friction among the nations, and that recognizing human rights might become one of the cornerstones on which peace could eventually be based."

In the following years Eleanor's hopes were not realized as she would have wished, and the growing animosities of the Cold War overtook her belief that the UN might prove to be an effective force in averting international conflict. Nevertheless, her work in establishing the concept and specifics of individual international human rights was extremely significant. At the end of the twentieth century, many of the world's concerns—in places such as Kosovo, for example—revolved around international human rights.

Eleanor was appointed as the U.S. representative to the new Commission on Human Rights, and at its first meeting in January 1947 at the temporary headquarters of the UN on Long Island, she was elected chair. Among the Commission's seventeen other members were several forceful and accomplished thinkers and parliamentary politicians. The Lebanese delegate Charles Malik was a former philosophy professor with a quick mind and great natural skill in diplomatic maneuvering. He eventually became president of the UN General Assembly and played a key role in the work of the Commission on Human Rights, serving as secretary. The Chinese delegate was P. C. Chang, likewise an accomplished diplomat and thinker, and was elected vice chair of the Commission. One of the most colorful and most difficult members was Soviet delegate Alexei Pavlov (nephew of the famous behavioral scientist), who was opposed to much of what Eleanor proposed for the Commission. A Canadian expert in international law, John P. Humphrey, was the senior staff advisor and permanent head of the UN Secretariat's Division of Human Rights.

The following year was filled with high-pressure meetings and long hours of work. Eleanor brought all her organizational skills to bear on the issues to be dealt with. She was uncompromising in scheduling long work sessions for the Commission and held the members' feet to the fire when fatigue and frustration began to set in. Because Eleanor, a woman past her sixtieth birthday, could be seen to put in longer hours and to be more up to date on the necessary reports and papers than any of the younger members, they could scarcely protest. On the other hand, not everything was so intense. Eleanor hosted informal social affairs—often at her New York apartment—that softened the strains on the members and allowed them to discuss issues in a relaxed and productive atmosphere. Throughout, Eleanor exhibited a great store of patience and forbearance that no one knew she had.

The first question to settle was what the Commission actually would try to accomplish. Its charter was threefold: to draw up a bill of rights, to work out a convention that could be ratified by the member UN nations, and to devise a method of implementing the provisions of the Declaration of Rights and the convention. The United States considered this too much to expect and asserted that the Commission should concentrate its efforts first of all on agreeing to a Declaration of Rights that could be forwarded to Committee Three and then on to the General Assembly. Despite objections from some members, this proved to be the only practical conclusion, and the Commission settled on drawing up articles of human rights. (Agreement on a formal convention proved to be the work of decades; it was not reached until 1976.)

From the first formal discussion there developed "fault lines," as they have been called by Mary Ann Glendon, the law professor who has studied closely the history of the Commission. The Western democracies, and especially the United States, were most interested in affirming what they saw as traditional and essential political and civil rights, as most succinctly stated in the Bill of Rights to the American Constitution. The Soviet Union and its republics (several of which had separate votes on the Commission and in the General Assembly) were concerned almost exclusively with economic and social rights. Neither side wanted to give in to the other, and each used its opponent's weak points in the debates; for example, the United States accused the Soviets of using state power to suppress individual rights, and the Soviets pointed at the American oppression of black citizens. The other nations—those that later would come to be known as the Third World—backed one side or another at various times and on various issues, but held out doggedly for recognition of their unique cultures and needs, especially in light of global poverty.

During every session of the Commission stretching for almost a year, these divisions surfaced again and again, and only Eleanor's extreme patience and dogged will to find a solution to each disagreement managed to overcome the obstacles. It was not so much that either side wanted to completely exclude the other's points, but rather it was a question of what rights to emphasize. The precise difficulty was that the Commission had to agree on a specific enumeration of universal human rights in language that would pass muster with the entire General Assembly. At the same time world events brought tremendous pressure on the negotiations. In China the revolutionary communists were making significant inroads against the corrupt Nationalist government; in the Mideast the British faced a conflagration between Zionist Jews and Arab Palestinians. There was a strong sense that the fragile stability of the immediate postwar world was about to collapse. If it did, there would be little hope to agree on international human rights.

Following the June 1947 session in New York, the Commission adjourned until November, when it met again in Geneva in a building formerly occupied by the forlorn League of Nations. The final session was back in New York City in May 1948. Throughout this long period Eleanor devoted much of her energy to the Commission and even toned down the opinions she expressed in her daily column and broadcasts so as not to compromise her position as the chair of the body. Finally, the Commission approved a final draft of the Declaration of Universal Human Rights in June 1948. There were no dissenting votes, but Eleanor was disappointed that the Soviets and their allies abstained from the final ballot.

In the fall the UN General Assembly met in Paris, and the Commission presented its draft of the Declaration to Committee Three for approval and referral. Eleanor had hoped and assumed that the Committee would respect the arduous process that had resulted in the document and not question or reopen the issues with which the Commission had struggled so long and hard, but she was disappointed. The Committee went through all of the provisions and wording yet again, and it took all of her patience and self-control to guide the draft through to approval. In the end the Declaration was passed on to the General Assembly and was voted for full adoption in December. After the vote was taken, the General Assembly rose and gave Eleanor a standing ovation in recognition for her work as chair of the Commission.

New Activities

Even though her work on the Commission had consumed most of her efforts during 1947 and 1948, Eleanor spared some time and energy for other causes. One of them was her support of a new organization of liberals: the Americans for Democratic Action. As the outstanding liberal of her age and the torchbearer of FDR's heritage, Eleanor was seen by many as the fountainhead of liberal opinion and action; however, liberalism was increasingly under attack by 1947 from both ends of the political spectrum. Gaining strength were both the reactionaries to the right, especially those allied with the racists who opposed giving an inch on the issues of civil rights for African Americans, and the communists on the left.

It seemed important to a key group of liberals to make heard their positions as anti-communist progressives. Eleanor was the perfect symbol for this group, as she had impeccable New Deal credentials—after all, she assisted FDR in inventing the New Deal and making it work—and she could be seen in the UN daily resisting the encroachments of the Soviets. The ADA's founders, a group that included Joseph Lash, James Loeb Jr., and Joseph Rauh, also wanted to provide a voice for Democrats who disagreed with President Truman's increasing conservatism. Eleanor had grown increasingly unhappy with Truman's shift to the right, although as an official member of the administration she had to mute her public criticisms.

She also disagreed with much of Truman's foreign policy, whereby under the Truman Doctrine the United States offered arms and aid to nations that pledged to help withstand the spread of communism. Fear of the communists was growing with every month and exploded when the communist revolutionaries in China led by Mao Tse-Dung finally ousted the Nationalists under Generalissimo Chiang Kai-shek, who had been portrayed throughout the war as America's important ally in Asia. Truman's response was to try to buy allies and contain the expansion of communism. Eleanor thought it would have been better and more effective to give almost exclusively economic aid to help eliminate hunger and poverty, which provided the richest conditions for the spread of communist doctrines. Her position was completely consistent with her view about domestic poverty in American during the Great Depression and her efforts to counter leftist doctrines then with benevolent government action. She was of course much happier with Truman in 1948 when the administration instigated the Marshall Plan to provide economic aid to rebuild Western Europe.

On the other hand, Eleanor was not naïve about the dangers presented by the communists. She had seen their political infiltration tactics firsthand during her association with the American Youth Congress in the late 1930s, and she battled their intransigence and subterfuge in the United Nations. Soviet actions such as its blockade of Berlin in mid-1948 convinced her that the Western powers had to remain strong and on the alert. She was irritated when conservatives used the communists as an excuse to clamp down on legitimate humanitarian or liberal activities and feared the effect of the growing tensions in the world and at home—but she was not in any sense a knee-jerk liberal by 1948.

Eleanor posed with a Spanish language copy of the Declaration of Universal Human Rights.

(Courtesy of the Franklin Delano Roosevelt Library)

Eleanor remained relatively aloof during the campaign and election of 1948, one of the most confused—albeit interesting—of the late twentieth century. Truman ran for a full term on his own but southern racist Democrats pulled out of the nominating convention, forming their own splinter party behind South Carolina senator Strom Thurmond. This seemed certain to pull votes away from Truman. Moreover, Henry Wallace, who had served briefly in Truman's administration as a holdover from FDR's cabinet, formed a new third party under the banner of the Progressives and hoped to rally support from left-leaning Democrats. Eleanor's relationship with Wallace had turned around yet again, and she was opposed to his candidacy, especially after it became evident that he tolerated strong support from communists among his backers. The Republicans nominated Thomas Dewey, whom FDR had defeated in 1944, and the former New York governor seemed a shoo-in against the weakened Truman. However, Truman came from behind to beat Dewey in a great political upset, aided at the last minute by a radio broadcast Eleanor made from Paris where she was attending the UN.

During the same year Eleanor faced a potentially embarrassing situation that arose when the latest wife of Earl Miller, Eleanor's one-time bodyguard and companion and still her friend, sued for divorce and named the sixty-four-year-old former First Lady as a correspondent, meaning the woman accused Eleanor of having adulterous sexual relations with Miller. Had the case gone to trial, the publicity could have seriously damaged Eleanor's public career. However, Miller and his wife reached a settlement out of court and the issue never saw the light of day after the records in the case were sealed.

In 1949 Eleanor took on a five-day-a-week afternoon radio show with Anna, who was in financial straits after losing the newspaper she and husband John had bought in Arizona. She was in the midst of getting a divorce from John, who had sunk further and further into what apparently was a clinical depression (he committed suicide a year later). Eleanor allowed her daughter to take all the income from *The Eleanor and Anna Show*, which was carried by two hundred stations at the height of its popularity. However, the show was a commercial failure, and ABC dropped it for lack of a sponsor.

Eleanor also broke into the new mass medium of television, allowing Elliott to put together a deal with NBC-TV for a network talk show, which she hosted on a set that was meant to resemble an afternoon tea party. Again, she gave Anna the income from the show and claimed to have taken it on only for her children's sakes, although biographer and friend Joseph Lash believed she really enjoyed the spotlight. The show's premise was that famous people would stop by to chat with Eleanor. Although the guest list was balanced to include nonpoliticians, potential sponsors apparently found some of the subject matter and Eleanor herself too controversial, and this show also expired for lack of sponsorship. For a brief time, Eleanor also had a forty-five-minute radio show on WNBC, with Elliott acting as the commercial announcer, touting products that "Mother uses."

In 1949 she also finished a second volume of memoirs titled *This I Remember,* but the path to publication was not as smooth as it had been for *This Is My Story.* Bruce Gould, the editor of *Ladies Home Journal* who had first serial rights to the book, did not like the draft manuscript and criticized it strongly—or appeared to as part of a ploy to get a lower price. He was quite nasty to Eleanor about the quality of her work and suggested he could consider the manuscript only if she would agree to work for three months with a collaborator. He also threatened to drop her monthly column, which she had been writing since the early days of the New Deal, if she offered the serial rights to a competitor.

Eleanor was outraged by Gould's rejection and his unpleasant treatment of her, and she also was irritated at her longtime literary agent George Bye for allowing Gould to get away with his high-handed tactics. She had Elliott take over the negotiations, and he offered the manuscript to Otis Wiese of *McCall's* magazine, who bought the serial rights for one hundred fifty thousand dollars and signed Eleanor on for a new monthly column at three thousand dollars a month, considerably more than she had been getting from the *Journal.* Harper & Brothers brought out the hardback version of the book after Eleanor made revisions with the help of an in-house editor. The account of her years in the White House and her memories of FDR sold well and got uniformly laudatory reviews.

At about the same time Eleanor moved out of her Washington Square apartment and into an apartment in the Park Sheraton Hotel. Tommy Thompson of course moved with her but complained that the quarters were cramped compared to their former place. Eleanor continued to spend a great deal of time at Val-Kill, especially in the summer, and she occasionally visited Campobello, although she told friends that the former family resort held too many painful memories for her to ever fully relax there again.

> FDR's "little dog Fala" was a cute Scottish terrier given to the president by his cousin Margaret Suckley, who was a dog breeder. The animal became the most famous dog in the nation when newspapers and newsreels showed him with the president.
>
> During FDR's campaign for a fourth term in 1944, the Republicans accused the president of sending a Navy destroyer to retrieve Fala, who had supposedly been left behind when FDR visited the Aleutian Islands. FDR froze his opponents with a brilliant rebuttal in which he claimed that while he could stand false accusations, Fala was deeply hurt and his frugal Scots nature offended by the allegations of waste.
>
> FDR feared Eleanor would not care for Fala, so the president left the dog to Suckley. However, after FDR's death Suckley gave the animal back to Eleanor, who treasured the pet and was often photographed with the dog.

More Politics

At the turn of the new decade Eleanor was faced, as were all American liberals, with the challenging menace of a powerful new Red Scare. The nation had undergone several previous versions of fright campaigns inspired by fears of communism. Eleanor remembered 1919, when U.S. Attorney General A. Mitchell Palmer's house was blown up just across the street from her own and she had witnessed the suspicions of the Dies Committee in the late 1930s. However, the most vicious and hysterical Red Scare was touched off in the early 1950s by the widespread anxiety caused by the rise of the Soviet Union as an international power and the apparent spread of communism. When ordinary Americans saw the nations of Eastern Europe taken over by communist regimes and former ally China fall to Mao's red revolution, they became susceptible to the belief that communists were infiltrating their own government.

A committee of the U.S. House of Representatives touched off the great scare by investigating supposed communist spies and agents in the State Department. There was truth to some of the accusations, but on the whole, the U.S. government remained in the hands of loyal Americans. The investigators saw communists everywhere, however, especially among the nation's liberals, many of whom had flirted with the communists during the Great Depression.

The investigations then fell under the control of Senator Joseph McCarthy, who proved to be a monstrously unprincipled but effective publicity seeker and demagogue. McCarthy began to make wholesale accusations of disloyalty and seemed to have so much public backing that even the most highly placed politicians and officeholders were afraid to challenge him, no matter how outrageous his behavior. One of McCarthy's basic tactics was to accuse innocent people of guilt by association: If a person had ever had contact with known communists, that person also must be a communist or a "fellow traveler."

Eleanor was particularly outraged by these tactics and protested loudly in public, telling a meeting of the ADA in 1950: "I want to be able to sit down with anyone who may have a new idea and not be afraid of contamination by association. In a democracy you must be able to meet people and argue your point of view—people whom you have not screened beforehand. That must be part of the freedom of people in the United States." She later accepted the honorary chair of the ADA as a way of publicly showing her solidarity with noncommunist liberals who were under pressure.

McCarthy never attacked Eleanor herself, and eventually he overstepped himself during public hearings to investigate the U.S. Army and fell from power, but the senator had wrought havoc in American politics. Part of the fallout that affected Eleanor for years was the way many prominent figures had been too frightened by McCarthy to defend their friends. This was the case with former General Dwight Eisenhower, who had let McCarthy's allies in the U.S. Senate attack his mentor and close friend George Marshall without making a reply. Eleanor could never forgive Eisenhower for his failure to defend Marshall, and she spoke out in public against Eisenhower on this specific topic during Eisenhower's campaign for the presidency in 1952.

Not surprisingly, when Eisenhower beat Democrat Adlai Stevenson, the new president accepted Eleanor's ritual resignation as delegate to the United Nations, and her seven-year career as an official delegate came to an end. Almost immediately, she offered her volunteer services to the American Association for the United Nations as an organizer and international representative, and began to work twice a week at the AAUN headquarters in New York City.

The early 1950s also were marked by important changes in Eleanor's personal life. Her children continued to be sources of concern, as all of them had suffered throughout their lives for their famous parentage.

Anna, who had the closest relationship with Eleanor, remarried in 1951 to physician and medical professor James Halstead and spent several years with him in Iran. James Roosevelt made an unsuccessful run in the California governor's race in 1950 but eventually was elected to Congress as a Representative and served six terms. John was perhaps the most stable of the Roosevelt boys as an adult, following a career in business and investment banking. FDR Jr. also tried politics, running unsuccessfully for governor of New York twice (he eventually served as an undersecretary of commerce in the Kennedy administration). Elliott gave up managing the farm at Hyde Park and eventually moved to Florida, where he became a writer of mystery stories featuring Eleanor as the amateur detective.

According to biographer Joseph Lash (who might not have been an entirely disinterested observer), the Roosevelt children found it difficult to get along among themselves, and during the last decade of Eleanor's life her attempts to have ceremonial family gatherings at holidays—occasions FDR had especially cherished—were marked by increasing squabbles and tension. She finally decreed that she could no longer abide the arguments and fighting and allowed her children and their families to visit her only separately.

In 1953 Malvina "Tommy" Thompson, who had been Eleanor's secretary and nearly constant companion for thirty years, died from a brain hemorrhage. Eleanor later wrote that Tommy "not only made my life easier, but gave me a reason for living." Maureen Corr became Eleanor's new secretary and stayed with her for the rest of Eleanor's life.

By the early 1950s Eleanor's closest companion was Dr. David Gurewitsch, a Swiss-born son of Russian emigrants. He was handsome, elegant, charming, and articulate, and Eleanor was completely attached to him. Although he had been her doctor since 1945, she did not form her intimate attachment to him until 1947 when they were thrown together on a weather-delayed flight to Geneva. Given the chance for relaxed conversation, they discovered a depth of affection and attraction, and for the rest of Eleanor's life, Gurewitsch was seldom far from her company, traveling with her around the world and seeing to her medical needs. As had been the case with Earl Miller, Lorena Hickok, and Joseph Lash before him, Gurewitsch provided that one special relationship that allowed Eleanor to unburden herself completely. She needed no defenses in his presence and could let down the outer wall she showed to the world at large and allow him to see her insecurities and shyness. When the divorced Gurewitsch remarried, Eleanor maintained her affection and spread it to include his new wife Edna. Eventually, Eleanor moved out of the Park Sheraton and into a house on East Seventy-Fourth Street that she shared with David and Edna Gurewitsch.

First Lady of the World

Eleanor spent much of the 1950s traveling the world. As soon as she was freed from her duties at the United Nations she began a series of trips that, when coupled with her previous visibility as a diplomat, earned her the name "First Lady of the World." She usu-ally traveled with Maureen Corr (after Tommy Thompson's death) and often with David Gurewitsch. In 1952 she went to Lebanon, Jordan, and Israel. She had been a strong supporter of the creation of an Israeli state after the partition of Palestine in 1947. In fact she had been so in favor of establishing a Jewish homeland that she had offered to resign her UN post over a difference of opinion on the issue between her and the State Department.

When in 1948 the Israelis declared themselves a nation, President Truman and the United States surprised most of the world by immediately recognizing the new Jewish state. Eleanor's 1952 trip to the nearby Arab countries therefore generated some controversy, and her presence caused a certain amount of tension. She visited Palestinian refugee camps, which captured her empa-thy, but continued to favor Israel and wrote of her pleasure at see-ing it firsthand.

She then traveled to Pakistan, which had been separated from India for only two years, and eventually on to India itself, where she wanted to observe that nation's fledgling attempts to establish a democracy. She was warmly received by Prime Minister Nehru and addressed the national parliament; she also traveled to the Taj Mahal. Her father had visited India as a young man and had told Eleanor when she was a small child that someday he would take her to see the Taj. She apparently was moved by finally paying the visit he never lived to make. On a less pleasant note, she had a seri-ous confrontation with leftist students at the university in Allahabad, who mounted demonstrations against her and American policy toward India, which they regarded as racist.

The following year Eleanor made a five-week tour of Japan. American memories of World War II were still very fresh in 1953, and her trip was highly publicized in the United States. She went under the sponsorship of a Japanese women's organization and spent part of her time observing the place of women in Japanese society. She had an audience with the Emperor and Empress, met with youth groups, and toured Hiroshima. Eleanor had never dis-agreed with the decision to drop the atomic bomb on Japan in

1945 despite her long-held pacifist views, because she saw it as the only way to forestall even worse death and destruction that would have resulted from an invasion of the Japanese home islands, and although moved by the suffering of the citizens of Hiroshima, she made her position clear by mentioning Pearl Harbor. From Japan she continued to Hong Kong, New Delhi, Istanbul, and Athens. She also made an extended visit to Yugoslavia, where she met with ruler Marshal Tito on his Adriatic Island retreat.

Two years later Eleanor—now over seventy years old but not yet much slowed by age—undertook a long tour of Asia, touching again in Japan before traveling on to Bali and Jakarta and then to Thailand and Cambodia, where she toured the monumental ruins at Angor Wat.

Although she had taken only a small part in the 1952 campaign and election, Eleanor was distressed at Eisenhower's victory, which put a Republican in the White House for the first time since Herbert Hoover twenty years before. Additionally, her relations with Eisenhower and his secretary of state John Foster Dulles, with whom she had never gotten along, were frosty to say the least. Thus, in 1956 Eleanor decided to take an active role in support of Adlai Stevenson.

Although Stevenson, the former governor of Illinois, had been the Democratic candidate in 1952, he had a rocky road to re-nomination in 1956. The system was already changing, but in 1956 the national convention still picked the candidate based on per-ceived political strength and backroom deals. Stevenson made a strong run in the primaries (including a win in California where Eleanor campaigned vigorously for him), which were still more publicity showcases than the deciding arenas, but former President Truman backed New York governor Averell Harriman, and Senator Estes Kefauver of Tennessee had many supporters.

Eleanor showed all of her old political vigor at the Chicago con-vention, where the contest came down to Stevenson and Harriman. She took Stevenson on a tour of the state delegates and promoted him heavily to the press. She was asked to address the convention, and in her speech she evoked the heritage of FDR and asked the party to move beyond partisanship and to look to the future when the Democrats could again be a powerful force for change. Their principal target, she said, must be the elimination of poverty in the United States.

After Stevenson's nomination, Eleanor campaigned hard for him, traveling with the candidate and speaking frequently on his behalf all over the country. Despite her desire to see Stevenson elected as a way to restore Democrats to power, she nonetheless found him too sedate and cautious much of the time and repeatedly urged him to be more energetic to counter his passive image. Even though the Democrats put up a strong fight in the face of high odds, Stevenson lost again to Eisenhower, a result that Eleanor attributed to "hero worship" of the former general on the part of the American people.

Eleanor's trip to Japan in 1953 was one of the high points of her world-hopping travels during the last decade of her life.

(Courtesy of the Franklin Delano Roosevelt Library)

In the year following the election she made an important and highly publicized trip to the Soviet Union. Her "My Day" column had been dropped by several conservative newspapers after Eleanor's active campaigning for Adlai Stevenson, and as a result it had been picked up for the first time by *The New York Post,* whose liberal publisher Dorothy Schiff asked Eleanor to write a series of articles on the Soviet Union. This was at the height of the Cold War, when many Americans believed the Soviets might launch a nuclear attack at any moment, so interest ran high in her firsthand reports of what life in the Soviet Union was really like.

David Gurewitsch acted as her interpreter for the trip, which included more regimented visits than Eleanor would have liked. She did manage a side trip to Tashkent, which she enjoyed as the most exotic site she was allowed to visit. The highlight of the trip, however, was a personal interview with Soviet leader Nikita Khrushchev at his vacation *dacha* on the outskirts of Yalta. She had a spirited exchange with the Soviet premier, but neither made much headway in convincing the other. (Two years later Khrushchev returned the favor by visiting Eleanor at Val-Kill.)

Although at this time some of her friends thought they noticed a slowing down, Eleanor's normal schedule during the late 1950s would have exhausted most people half her age. When not on an international trip, she traveled widely in the United States—a week or two weeks out of every month—and she gave around a hundred fifty lectures every year. In addition, she continued to write her newspaper column and to appear regularly on television and radio. Maureen Corr usually was at her side, ready to take dictation for a column or article and to organize the responses to Eleanor's still-voluminous mail.

Eleanor also continued to work at the American Association for the United Nations, helping to organize new chapters and promote grassroots support for the UN, and she rounded out her memoirs with the publication of *On My Own* in 1958. In the same year Eleanor again traveled to the Soviet Union, although the trip was more politically low key than her previous visit. She also visited Morocco with David Gurewitsch and Elliott and his family, and followed up in 1959 with another tour of the Mideast, stopping in Israel and then visiting Anna and her husband in Iran.

Eleanor's final political campaign was in 1960, when she again backed Stevenson for the Democratic nomination. She distrusted John Kennedy, who appeared to be making the strongest run at the nomination, because of his cautious behavior in ducking the Senate vote to censure Joseph McCarthy and then waffling in a later public statement. Eleanor's influence was apparently waning to some degree, however, and Stevenson was swept aside by a tide of support for Kennedy, despite Eleanor's strenuous efforts to rally the convention behind a draft Stevenson movement.

She invited Kennedy to Val-Kill after the convention, and the two of them concluded a well-publicized truce. Eleanor wrote to Stevenson supporters, making it clear that she had reconciled herself to Kennedy's candidacy as the Democratic standard bearer: "My final judgment now is that here is a man who wants to leave a record (perhaps for ambitious personal reasons as people say) but I rather think because he really is interested in helping the people of his own country and mankind in general."

Eleanor was not a strong supporter of John Kennedy, but she reconciled herself to him when he became president.

(Courtesy of the Franklin Delano Roosevelt Library)

Eleanor was happy with Kennedy's narrow victory over Richard Nixon and pleased to have a Democratic administration once again in Washington. When Stevenson was appointed as ambassador to the UN he asked Eleanor to again serve as a delegate; for a while she was restored to official status in the General Assembly, although as her energies finally began to flag she attended sessions only part-time. Kennedy also appointed Eleanor as the ceremonial head of his Commission on the Status of Women, but she actually played only a small role in the Commission's work.

Final Days

In 1960 Eleanor's health began to deteriorate seriously. Her fabled energy, which had carried her at a breakneck pace through an extraordinary public career, began to fade. She felt frequent fatigue and often was unable to attend to her paperwork and meetings without interruptions for rest or naps. Maureen Corr noticed that Eleanor even nodded off in the middle of work sessions. David Gurewitsch ordered tests that revealed she had severe anemia. By the fall of 1961 her condition worsened; she received two blood transfusions in an attempt to restore her depleted red blood cells. Although she experienced allergic reactions to the transfusions, Gurewitsch and her other doctors prescribed more throughout the following months. They also prescribed the drug prednisone, hoping to stimulate her bone marrow to produce more red and white blood cells. Unfortunately, the prednisone increased Eleanor's susceptibility to infection and aggravated her reactions to the transfusions, and she had to be hospitalized in mid-1962.

Given her rapidly declining condition, which by then included a persistent cough, her doctors began to suspect she might have tuberculosis; however, tests and x-rays were inconclusive so they continued to treat her for anemia. By September it was clear that Eleanor was very seriously ill. She was extremely weak and in pain much of the time. She could barely tolerate the repeated treatments in the hospital and clearly had reached the end of her physical resources. Her doctors then began to suspect—correctly as it turned out—that Eleanor had a rare, extreme form of the disease known as military tuberculosis, which had spread bacteria through her bloodstream and infected her lungs, vital organs, and bone marrow.

She passed her seventy-eighth birthday in the hospital, but on October 18 insisted on returning to her own apartment. She knew she was dying and hated the injections, transfusions, and her invalid state. She implored Gurewitsch to make no heroic efforts to keep her alive. However, as her doctor and intimate friend he found it hard to comply. During her last days he and her children were at odds over her treatment. In early November Eleanor suffered what appeared to be a stroke and slipped into a coma. She died on November 7, 1962.

Eleanor was buried next to FDR at Hyde Park, the grave marked only by a plain monument, leaving behind an immense political and social legacy. Much of how American government and society came to be shaped by the end of the twentieth century was due to her vision and efforts, and she remains a symbol of achievement for anyone who has compassion for fellow human beings.

Appendix

Further Reading and Sources of Information

Books by Eleanor Roosevelt

The Autobiography of Eleanor Roosevelt. New York: Harper, 1961. (an abridged, one-volume compilation of *This Is My Story, This I Remember, On My Own,* and *The Search for Understanding*)

Eleanor Roosevelt's "My Day": Her Acclaimed Columns. 3 vols. New York: Pharos Books, 1989–1991.

If You Ask Me. New York: Appleton-Century, 1946.

India and the Awakening East. New York: Harper, 1953.

It Seems to Me. New York: Norton, 1954.

It's Up to the Women. New York: Stokes, 1993.

Mother and Daughter: The Letters of Eleanor and Anna Roosevelt. Edited by Bernard Asbell. New York: Coward, McCann and Geoghegan, 1982.

On My Own. New York: Harper, 1958.

This I Remember. New York: Harper, 1949.

This Is My Story. New York: Harper, 1937.

The White House Press Conferences of Eleanor Roosevelt. New York: Garland, 1983.

You Learn by Living. New York: Harper, 1960.

About Eleanor Roosevelt

Atwell, Mary Welek. "Notes and Comments: Eleanor Roosevelt and the Cold War Consensus," *Diplomatic History* 3 (1979): 99–113.

Beasley, Maurine H. *Eleanor Roosevelt and the Media: A Public Quest for Self-Fulfillment*. Urbana: University of Illinois Press, 1987.

Beezer, Bruce. "Arthurdale: An Experiment in Community Education," *West Virginia History* 36 (1974): 17–36.

Berger, Jason. *A New Deal for the World: Eleanor Roosevelt and American Foreign Policy*. New York: Columbia University Press, 1981.

Black, Allida M. *Casting Her Own Shadow: Eleanor Roosevelt and the Shaping of Postwar Liberalism*. New York: Columbia University Press, 1996.

———. "Championing a Champion: Eleanor Roosevelt and the Marian Anderson 'Freedom Concert,'" *Presidential Studies Quarterly* 20 (1990): 719–736.

———, ed. *Courage in a Dangerous World: The Political Writings of Eleanor Roosevelt*. New York: Columbia University Press, 1999.

———. "Struggling with Icons: Memorializing Franklin and Eleanor Roosevelt," *Public Historian* 21 (1999): 63–72.

Black, Ruby. *Eleanor Roosevelt: A Biography*. New York: Duell, Sloan and Pearce, 1940.

Cook, Blanche Wiesen. *Eleanor Roosevelt*. 2 vols. New York: Viking, 1992 and 1999.

Davis, Kenneth S. *Invincible Summer: An Intimate Portrait of the Roosevelts, Based on the Recollections of Marion Dickerman.* New York: Athenaeum, 1974.

Douglas, Helen Gahagan. *The Eleanor Roosevelt We Remember.* New York: Hill and Wang, 1963.

Edens, John A. *Eleanor Roosevelt: A Comprehensive Bibliography.* Westport, CT: Greenwood, 1994.

Glendon, Mary Ann. *A World Made New: Eleanor Roosevelt and the International Declaration of Human Rights.* New York: Random House, 2001.

Goodwin, Doris Kearns. *No Ordinary Time. Franklin and Eleanor Roosevelt: The Home Front in World War II.* New York: Simon & Schuster, 1994.

Graham, Hugh Davis. "The Paradox of Eleanor Roosevelt: Alcoholism's Child," *Virginia Quarterly Review* 63 (1987): 210–230.

Gurewitsch, A. David. *Eleanor Roosevelt: Her Day, a Personal Album.* New York: Interchange Foundation, 1973.

Hareven, Tamara K. *Eleanor Roosevelt: An American Conscience.* Chicago: Quadrangle, 1968.

Harrity, Richard, and Ralph G. Martin. *Eleanor Roosevelt: Her Life in Pictures.* New York: Duell, Sloan and Pearce.

Hershan, Stella K. *The Candles She Lit: The Legacy of Eleanor Roosevelt.* New York: Praeger, 1993.

——. *A Woman of Quality.* New York: Crown, 1970.

Hickok, Lorena. *One Third of a Nation: Lorena Hickok Reports on the Great Depression.* Edited by Richard Lowett and Maurine Beasley. Urbana: University of Illinois Press, 1982.

——. *Reluctant First Lady.* New York: Dodd, Mead, 1962.

Hoff-Wilson, Joan, and Marjorie Lightman, eds. *Without Precedent: The Life and Career of Eleanor Roosevelt.* Bloomington: Indiana University Press, 1984.

Johnson, M. Glen. "The Contributions of Eleanor and Franklin Roosevelt to the Development of International Protection for Human Rights," *Human Rights Quarterly* 9 (1987): 19–48.

Kearney, James R. *Anna Eleanor Roosevelt: The Evolution of a Reformer.* Boston: Houghton Mifflin, 1968.

Kornbluh, Joyce L. *A New Deal for Workers' Education: The Workers' Service Program, 1933–1942.* Urbana: University of Illinois Press, 1987.

Lachman, Seymour P. "The Cardinal, the Congressmen, and the First Lady," *Journal of Church and State* 7 (1965): 35–66.

Lash, Joseph P. *Eleanor and Franklin: The Story of Their Relationship, Based on Eleanor Roosevelt's Private Papers.* New York: Norton, 1971.

——. *Eleanor Roosevelt: A Friend's Memoir.* Garden City: Doubleday, 1964.

——. *Eleanor: The Years Alone.* New York: Norton, 1972.

——. *"Life Was Meant to Be Lived": A Centenary Portrait of Eleanor Roosevelt.* London: Norton, 1985.

——. *Love, Eleanor: Eleanor Roosevelt and Her Friends.* New York: Doubleday, 1982.

——. *A World of Love: Eleanor Roosevelt and Her Friends, 1943–1962.* Garden City: Doubleday, 1984.

MacLeish, Archibald. *The Eleanor Roosevelt Story.* Boston: Houghton Mifflin, 1965.

McElvaine, Robert S., ed. *Down and Out in the Great Depression: Letters from the "Forgotten Man."* Chapel Hill: University of North Carolina Press, 1983.

Mower, A. Glenn Jr. *The United States, the United Nations, and Human Rights: The Eleanor Roosevelt and Jimmy Carter Eras.* Westport, CT: Greenwood, 1979.

Pfeffer, Paula F. "Eleanor Roosevelt and the National and World Woman's Parties," *Historian* 59 (1996): 39–57.

Roosevelt, Elliott, and James Brough. *Mother R.: Eleanor Roosevelt's Untold Story.* New York: Putnam's, 1977.

——. *A Rendezvous with Destiny: The Roosevelts of the White House.* New York: Putnam's, 1975.

——. *An Untold Story: The Roosevelts of Hyde Park.* New York: Putnam's, 1973.

Roosevelt, James, with Bill Libby. "My Parents: A Differing View." Chicago: *Playboy,* 1976.

Scharf, Lois. *Eleanor Roosevelt: First Lady of American Liberalism.* Boston: Twayne, 1987.

Seeber, Frances M. "Eleanor Roosevelt and Women in the New Deal: A Network of Friends," *Presidential Studies Quarterly* 20 (1999): 707–717.

Steinberg, Alfred. *Eleanor Roosevelt.* New York: Putnam's, 1959.

——. *Mrs. R.: The Life of Eleanor Roosevelt.* New York: Putnam's, 1958.

Ward, Geoffrey C. *Before the Trumpet: Young Franklin Roosevelt, 1882–1905.* New York: Harper & Row, 1989.

——. *A First-Class Temperament: The Emergence of Franklin Roosevelt.* New York: Harper & Row, 1989.

——. "Eleanor Roosevelt Drew Her Strength from a Sanctuary Called Val-Kill," *Smithsonian* 15 (1984): 62–73.

Weaver, Robert C. "Eleanor and L.B.J. and Black America," *Crisis* 79 (1972): 186–193.

Winfield, Betty Houchin. "The Legacy of Eleanor Roosevelt," *Presidential Studies Quarterly* 20 (1990): 699–706.

Youngs, William T. *Eleanor Roosevelt: A Personal and Public Life.* 2nd ed. New York: Longman, 2000.

About FDR

Davis, Kenneth Sydney. *FDR, Into the Storm, 1937–1940: A History.* New York: Random House, 1993.

Freidel, Frank Burt. *Franklin D. Roosevelt: A Rendezvous with Destiny.* Boston: Little, Brown, 1990.

Morgan, Ted. *FDR: A Biography.* New York: Simon & Schuster, 1985.

Ward, Geoffrey C. *A First-Class Temperament: The Emergence of Franklin Roosevelt.* New York: Harper & Row, 1989.

Web Sites

Eleanor Roosevelt Institute at Val-Kill www.ervk.org/

Arthurdale New Deal Museum
www.arthurdaleheritage.org/museum/newdeal.html

UN Declaration of Human Rights
www.udhr50.org/history/Biographies/bioer.htm

FDR Presidential Library and Museum
www.fdrlibrary.marist.edu/index.html

PBS "American Experience"
www.pbs.org/wgbh/amex/eleanor/

Historic Sites

Arthurdale Heritage, Inc., New Deal Museum
A museum on the site of the homestead community of Arthurdale and the Arthurdale School in Arthurdale, West Virginia.

Hours: June through September, Monday through Friday 10 to 1, Saturday 12 to 5, and Sunday 2 to 5.

Eleanor Roosevelt National Historic Site

Run by the National Parks Service. Tours of Val-Kill, walking tours of the gardens, and hiking trails.

519 Albany Post Rd.
Hyde Park, NY 12538
914-229-9115

The Eleanor Roosevelt Center at Val-Kill

A research center, nonprofit organization, and historic site at Eleanor Roosevelt's stone cottage, Val-Kill.

PO Box 255
Hyde Park, NY 12538
914-229-5302
E-mail: Ervalkill@aol.com

Franklin Delano Roosevelt Presidential Library and Museum

Home of the Franklin and Eleanor Roosevelt Institute, museum exhibits, and research archives.

4070 Albany Post Rd.
Hyde Park, NY 12538
1-800-FDR-VISIT (1-800-337-8474)
E-mail: library@roosevelt.nara.gov
Museum hours: 9 to 5 every day

Index

Q – R

Sarah J. Purcell

Sarah J. Purcell teaches American history at Grinnell College in Iowa, where she also earned her B.A. degree. She received both her A.M. and Ph.D. degrees from Brown University in Providence, Rhode Island. She is the author of the forthcoming *Sealed with Blood: National Identity and Public Memory of the Revolutionary War* and collaborated previously with her father on *Encyclopedia of Battles in North America, 1517 to 1916*, an award-winning military history reference book. She has also published several articles and presented papers at many historical conferences in the United States and abroad. She is currently at work on an historical survey of the Early American Republic and, with her collaborator, on a biographical reference book on international women travelers and explorers.

L. Edward Purcell

L. Edward Purcell, Sarah's father, is an independent historian and writer with 20 books to his credit as author, co-author, or editor, including *Vice Presidents; Who Was Who in the American Revolution; Years of Struggle: The Farm Diary of Elmer Powers, 1931–1936; Immigration: A Social History; Almanac of World War I;* and *Encyclopedia of Battles in North America, 1517 to 1916* (in collaboration with his daughter). He is a history graduate of Simpson College and the University of Iowa and for several years was Editor in Chief of the State Historical Society of Iowa. He previously taught history at several colleges and universities and now operates his own book publishing services company in Lexington, Kentucky.